# THEY DARED RETURN

# THEY DARED RETURN

## RETURN

### THE TRUE STORY OF JEWISH SPIES
### BEHIND THE LINES IN NAZI GERMANY

## PATRICK K. O'DONNELL

DA CAPO PRESS
A MEMBER OF THE PERSEUS BOOKS GROUP

Designed by Timm Bryson
Set in 11 point Arno by The Perseus Books Group

First Da Capo Press edition 2009
Library of Congress Cataloging-in-Publication Data

O'Donnell, Patrick K., 1969–
  They dared return : the untold story of Jewish spies behind the line in
Nazi Germany / Patrick K. O'Donnell.
    p. cm.
  Includes bibliographical references and index.
  ISBN 978-0-306-81800-4 (alk. paper)
  1. Espionage, American—Germany—History—20th century. 2. Anti-
Nazi movement—Germany—History. 3. World War,
1939-1945—Participation, Jewish. 4. Jews—United States—Biography.
5. Jewish refugees—United States—Biography. 6. Spies—United
States—Biography. 7. World War, 1939–1945—Secret service—United
States. 8. United States. Office of Strategic Services. I. Title.
  D810.S7O37 2009
  940.54'86730923924—dc22
                          2009022802


Published by Da Capo Press
A Member of the Perseus Books Group
www.dacapopress.com

Da Capo Press books are available at special discounts for bulk purchases
in the U.S. by corporations, institutions, and other organizations. For more
information, please contact the Special Markets Department at the Perseus
Books Group, 2300 Chestnut Street, Suite 200, Philadelphia, PA 19103, or
call (800) 810-4145, ext. 5000, or e-mail
special.markets@perseusbooks.com.

10 9 8 7 6 5 4 3 2 1

TO . . .

*Lily Bear, my "cute-o-saurus"—*
*the greatest daughter in the world*

*My Parents*

*Fred Mayer, Hans Wynberg, and the other*
*members of the German-Austria Section,*
*whose intrepid heroism inspires the next*
*Greatest Generation of modern warriors*

*David Stapleton, who knows it takes more than cold steel to win wars*

# CONTENTS

*Illustrations appear after page 124.*

# ACKNOWLEDGMENTS

My journey into World War II history began thirty-five years ago when I was four years old. After picking up a World War II pictorial history book by accident and scanning a few combat photos, I was completely drawn in. This journey of discovery has included interviewing twenty-five hundred World War II veterans, traveling to Western Europe's most important battlefields, and even experiencing combat, as an embedded historian with today's American warriors, to find out if this generation is the next "Greatest Generation." They truly are, as my book *We Were One: Shoulder to Shoulder with the Marines Who Took Fallujah* (2006) demonstrates. *They Dared Return* is my sixth book on a subject that I cannot seem to escape. I'm fascinated by history and feel strongly about honoring the veterans by telling their stories. Each passing year more of our World War II veterans' stories slip away, lost to future generations, never to be told. Helping tell these stories is not just my job, it's my passion! It's a part of me, something I have willingly risked everything for, including my life.

Serendipitously, the stories always seem to find me, and this is certainly the case with Frederick Mayer, whom I met eight years ago. After interviewing hundreds of World War II veterans, I found Mayer and his story captivating. This book is about Fred's mission: Operation Greenup. It also touches upon members of "the Jewish five," five best friends, including

Operation Greenup's Mayer and Hans Wynberg. All were former refugees
from Nazi Germany, who dared to return behind the lines. The other members of the Five: Bernd Steinitz (Dillon Mission) and George Gerbner and
Alfred Rosenthal (Dania Mission) are touched upon in this volume when
they intersect with Greenup, but they deserve separate treatment. Nevertheless, I included their original mission reports as an addendum to shed
light on their extraordinary stories. Their daring was fueled by patriotism
and a willingness to make a difference against an enemy that killed many of
their family members. But this book is not just about the "five"; it also includes the untold story of a hero who turned his back on the German army
for his own private reasons: Hermann Matull. But Frederick Mayer is the
focal point of this volume, and a special breed of man he is. At eighty-nine
years young, he still chops wood every day, mows the lawn, and serves food
to the poor every week. He is humble and shies away from telling this story.
He's an extraordinary person—someone who has taught me a great deal
about life.

But the story is the story. In an unbiased manner, I tried to tell it by presenting the reader with exactly what happened, from all the key stake-
holder's points of view, including Austrian civilians, members of the
German security service, and, of course, the daring and heroic OSS agents
who went behind enemy lines to bring down Hitler's Third Reich.

I would like to thank first and foremost the OSS veterans for sharing
their stories, especially Frederick Mayer and his best friend to this day,
Hans Wynberg, a retired professor emeritus of chemistry at the University
of Groningen. Wynberg is an equally extraordinary individual, who spent
countless hours on the phone with me and sent long e-mails recalling his
time behind the lines. I am also grateful to Bernd Steinitz and George Gerbner, who provided invaluable information about the other missions of the
Jewish five. Finally, I want to acknowledge those brave veterans mentioned
in this book who have died—admirable men, such as Dyno Lowenstein
and Walter Haass, whose hidden contributions made the missions possible.

I would also like to thank my agent and friend, Andrew Zack, and the best publicist any author could ever have, Lissa Warren. I am grateful to Chris Butsavage for his keen suggestions and editorial comments, and to historian Dr. Troy Sacquety for his thorough and critical feedback for this book and on my previous book, *The Brenner Assignment: The Untold Story of the Most Daring Spy Mission of World War II* (2008). My friends Madison Parker and Casey Trahan, for their keen eyes. And also Ben Ibach for his excellent and numerous ideas that enhanced the narrative. Special thanks to Morgan Wilson. The OSS Society's current president, Charles Pinck, who has advocated and encouraged my work and books, deserves my heartfelt gratitude. Most importantly, I would like to thank my editor and friend, Robert Pigeon. Bob's peerless editorial skills, judgment, and ideas greatly enhanced this narrative and made this book a reality.

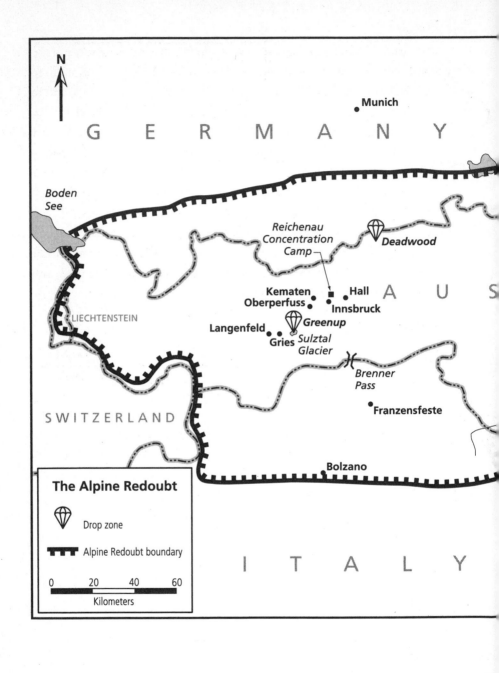

N

GERMANY

• Munich

Boden
See

Reichenau
Concentration
Camp

⌖ Deadwood

Kematen
Oberperfuss•

• Hall

AUS

Innsbruck

LIECHTENSTEIN

Langenfeld

⌖ Greenup

Gries•

Sulztal
Glacier

Brenner
Pass

•Franzensfeste

SWITZERLAND

ITALY

Bolzano•

**The Alpine Redoubt**

⌖   Drop zone

▀▀▀   Alpine Redoubt boundary

0        20        40        60
Kilometers

Salzburg

T R I A

CARINTHIA

Dillon

Treffenboden

Klagenfurt

Drava River

Deutschlandsberg   Frauental

Dania

Vured   Maribor

S L O V E N I A

Y U G O S L A V I A

GERMANY

SWITZERLAND

LIECHTENSTEIN

Innsbruck

Mauthausen
Concentration
Camp

AUSTRIA

FRANCE

Bolzano

YUGOSLAVIA

MONACO

Trieste

Ligurian
Sea

CORSICA

I T A L Y

Adriatic
Sea

Rome

SARDINIA

Aversa

Naples

Bari

Tyrrhenian
Sea

TUNISIA

SICILY

0          100
Miles

N

# PROLOGUE

April 1945, Gestapo Headquarters, Innsbruck, Austria

"Jude!" the tall one barked, glaring into the man's swollen eyes.

"Ach Quatsch!" (Nonsense!), another Gestapo officer stated. It was inconceivable that a Jew would dare return to the heart of the Third Reich as an Allied agent.

In the dank room, the Gestapo officers slapped and punched the spy in the face. His cover wasn't holding water, and so the tall one stripped him from head to toe. Despite the agent's bullish strength, the SS men brutally manhandled him, shoving him to the floor. Cuffing his hands in front of him and pulling his arms over his bent knees, they forced him into a constricting fetal position, then shoved the barrel of a long rifle into the tiny gap behind his knees and his cuffed hands. With a man on each side of the rifle, they lifted his naked, rolled-up body and suspended the human ball between two tables, like a piece of meat on a skewer. Uncoiling a rawhide whip, the tall one put his full weight behind each swing, mercilessly thrashing the agent's body like a side of beef.

"Wo ist der funker?" (Where is the radio operator?)

"Wo ist der funker?"

A crimson pool spread beneath the agent's body. In spite of the torment, he refused to crack, reiterating that he was merely a foreign worker (like thousands employed in the Reich's factories).

When the whipping didn't work, the Gestapo men decided to waterboard their prisoner. They brought out two pitchers of water, and tipping their captive's face to the ceiling, they poured the cold liquid down his mouth and nose. The water splashed into his mouth, forced open by rough hands. He felt like he was drowning, while the liquid painfully dripped into his perforated eardrum. The Nazis were methodical. One man poured while the second refilled the other pitcher. The torture assembly line kept running for six hours.

Suddenly, the door to the dank room swung open, revealing a tall man dressed in the full regalia of a high-ranking Nazi officer. His looming presence filled the room, throwing a shadow over the men in their work. Surprised, they turned and the session stopped—for the moment.

1
—

# "GET ME OUT OF THE INFANTRY!"

The desert sun beat down on Frederick Mayer as he hugged the ground and carefully maneuvered into position. Fred's adrenaline surged as he moved closer to the enemy headquarters. He heard the din of battle in the background, as the staccato drumbeat of a machine gun pierced the afternoon air. As first scout of the Eighty-first Infantry Division, Mayer was at the tip of the spear and led an elite reconnaissance unit, the Wildcat Rangers,* forward on the battlefield. In the immediate background, Mayer heard the chatter of voices and the whirl of radio broadcasts relaying and barking orders. He was deep behind the lines, and, remarkably, the enemy headquarters he spied was not that well guarded. On his belly, .45 in hand, he slithered forward. In the blink of an eye, Mayer stealthily snuck past the guards and into the compound.

Mayer had been operating alone behind enemy lines for the past day. As a scout, Fred relied on his instincts, his ability to improvise, and his plain

---

* The Wildcat Rangers were organic to the Eighty-first Infantry Division and not officially part of the six U.S. Army Ranger battalions formed during World War II.

old chutzpah. Earlier in the day he had told his comrades that it was "silly to capture just a couple soldiers. Let's bag the headquarters."

With that, Mayer maneuvered into position and charged forward toward the headquarters building. Mayer burst into a room containing the headquarters, and several officers, including a brigadier general, looked at the 5'7", broad-shouldered, olive-skinned scout in disbelief. Reality seemed suspended for a brief moment. Stunned, the U.S. Army general stammered, "You can't do that! You are breaking the rules!"

Fred responded, "War is not fair. The rules of war are to win."

Cornered, the general had no choice but to concede defeat, and he sheepishly raised his hands in the air.

For Mayer this was a bittersweet moment: The 120-degree desert heat nearly melted away his glorious feeling of capturing the blue army's general during the Eighty-first Division's training exercise on a stifling July 1943 day in Gila Bend, Arizona.

Brig. Gen. Marcus Bell, assistant division commander of the Eighty-first, was impressed by the young Jewish corporal from Brooklyn. The next day he summoned Mayer to his command tent located at Camp Horn, Arizona.

Since mid-February, Mayer had participated in the special reconnaissance unit within the Eighty-first Division. As a Wildcat Ranger, he learned advanced infantry skills, such as infiltration, demolition, raiding, sniping, and hand-to-hand combat techniques. The youthful corporal excelled at the training and became the unit's lead scout, a position reserved for only the most daring of men.

After the maneuvers, Bell told Mayer he was "wasting his time here with the Rangers" and asked if he wanted another challenge to do "something more interesting." With a large grin, pearly white teeth, and wavy black hair, Fred responded, "Get me out of the infantry."

Within a few weeks, a letter arrived requesting that Frederick Mayer report to the headquarters of the Office of Strategic Services (OSS) in Washington, D.C. The letter would change his destiny. A Jewish refugee from

Germany, an enemy alien whose family had barely escaped the camps, Frederick Mayer was now a naturalized American citizen holding a paper in his hand telling him to report to the Congressional Country Club in Bethesda, Maryland, where the OSS had established a training base.

Frederick Mayer was born in 1921 in the city of Freiberg, Germany. He embarked on his military training at an early age as his father inundated him with stories of the horrors that occurred in the French fortress town of Verdun, where one million souls lost their lives. Mayer's father, a lieutenant in the Kaiser's army, had been decorated with the coveted Iron Cross Second Class for gallantry at Verdun. He had been a war hero and often regaled his son with tales of his wartime exploits, making quite an impression on the boy. Mayer later recalled, "This was my military training." A businessman after the war, Mayer's father provided for his family in the postwar chaos of the hyperinflated Weimar Republic.

Bull-like, with a stocky frame, Mayer was a great athlete. Until Hitler gained power, he had been a member of the ski and athletic clubs in high school. Known for his inquisitive mind and his ability to tear things apart, then reassemble them, Mayer soon sought an apprenticeship as a diesel mechanic with the Ford Motor Company. Charismatic, with an everpresent smile revealing his inner confidence, Frederick Mayer's view of life was to "do your best at everything everyday, control what you can, and what you can't, don't worry about." His optimism expressed a joie de vivre, and he had few enemies—until the rise of the Nazi Party.

The Mayers were Jewish. During the early 1930s, a wave of virulent anti-Semitism accompanied the Nazis' rise to power. Despite his father's heroic service to his country during World War I, Mayer's family was not immune to the anti-Jewish sentiment. Fred remembers firsthand being called a "Jew bastard." Yet he always stood up for himself and promptly flattened the perpetrator, knocking him to the ground. The Nazis soon turned anti-Semitism into a state religion. Mayer's father was a patriot and believed,

like many other patriotic Jewish veterans, that their service would trump
the radical racial views of the Nazi Party. In 1938, Mayer's father still clung
to the false hope that his service in the Kaiser's army would insulate the
family from harm. He took the view that as he had been "a German officer,
nothing [would] happen to [him and his family]." Mayer's mother was
more pragmatic, stating bluntly, "We are Jews, and we are leaving."

After a two-year struggle with bureaucrats on both sides of the Atlantic,
the Mayers finally obtained a visa through contacts in the United States.
Arriving with only the clothes on their backs, the family immigrated to New
York, where Mayer's father and the entire family sought work in Brooklyn.
A jack-of-all-trades, young Mayer held more than twenty different jobs.
While he was working in one of these positions, he recalled, his boss made
an anti-Semitic remark, and as he had done in Germany several times, he
took matters into his own hands and laid out his boss, quitting on the spot.

Hitler's December 8, 1941, declaration of war against the United States
following the Japanese bombing of Pearl Harbor was a call to arms—and
Mayer answered the call. That morning, he promptly showed up at his local
recruiting center in Brooklyn. Mayer felt that "the United States [had] provided [his family] a haven. I felt a need to give something back." The morning Mayer reported to the draft board, he was summarily dismissed for
being an "enemy alien."

Discouraged, yet undaunted, Mayer's opportunity to serve his adopted
country came unexpectedly, weeks later, when his brother was summoned
before the draft board. His brother was a college student at the time, and
Mayer wanted him to finish, so he went before the draft board in his
brother's place and volunteered his own services. Seeing Mayer's determi-
nation, the board acquiesced.

The twenty-year-old Jew was then shipped to Fort Rucker, Alabama,
where he received several months of basic training. Graduating boot camp,
Private Mayer received orders to report to the Eighty-first Division. For
the most part, Mayer kept his nose clean, except for an AWOL incident
while on maneuvers in Tennessee, after which he found himself digging

ditches into red Tennessee clay. After the Tennessee maneuvers, Fred's division was shipped to Camp Horn in Gila Bend, Arizona, for desert training. Ironically, the training would prove almost useless when the division was shipped off to the Pacific. It was while en route to the California port town of San Luis Obispo for amphibious warfare training that Mayer received the letter that would change his life.

# 2

COUNTRY CLUB

Fred Mayer carefully opened the manila envelope with a return address stamped Washington, D.C. Inside his orders indicated that he was to report immediately to the nation's capital. He hopped on a train and, after several days of travel, arrived in Washington. Exhausted from the long ride, Mayer nevertheless swiftly hailed down a cab outside the imposing marble facade of Union Station and asked the driver to take him to the Congressional Country Club. Remarkably, considering Mayer's orders were secret, the driver knew exactly where to go and even hinted at a knowledge of the location of the secret training ground.

A few miles later, the quaint neighborhoods of northwest D.C. had given way to rolling farmland and the summer homes of Washington's elite, when the cab arrived at a posh golf club and stately Georgian-style building fronted by large white columns. The building was flanked by olive drab pyramidal tents, and the grounds were a beehive of activity, with uniformed operatives milling about. Bomb detonations and the high-pitched crack of pistol fire sounded in the background.

Orders in hand, Mayer reported to Capt. Howard Chappell, command-ing officer of the German Operational Group (OGs). A former parachute instructor at Fort Benning, Georgia, Chappell was a mountain of a man. A muscular 6'2", sun-bronzed and blond-haired, with an ornery temperament and commanding presence, Captain Chappell was obviously in charge. Mayer thought to himself, Chappell could pass for a Nazi officer.

After brief introductions, Chappell rounded up Mayer and all the other new "OGs," as they were called. A more eclectic group of desperados could not be found: former Luftwaffe pilots, Jewish escapees from German death camps, Polish deserters, world-class athletes, and even a former convict. Sixty years later, one recruit mused, "The whole bunch were the craziest people I have ever met in my entire life." Fred felt at home; he fit perfectly into the ragtag outfit.

Chappell informed them why they were all gathered at the upscale coun-try club: to penetrate enemy lines and strike at the heart of Nazi Germany. On these grounds and fairways, Chappell would try to forge what would ul-timately be a precursor to the U.S. Army's Special Forces. The gathered men were the roots of a tree that would eventually grow many branches: America's Special Operations units.

Without a model to guide them, Chappell and his group made it up as they went along. The OG units divided into teams according to the coun-tries in which they would operate. The basic unit of organization consisted of four officers and thirty enlisted men, further segmented into two sec-tions of sixteen men. Each section required a variety of operatives with dif-ferent functional skills: radio operator, medic, demolitionist, weapons specialist, and team leader. But all OG operatives had two things in com-mon: "aggressiveness of spirit and willingness to close with the enemy."

The OGs were part of a much larger organization called the Office of Strategic Services. The OSS, born in the summer of 1941, had initially been

called the Office of the Coordinator of Information (COI) and was America's first central intelligence organization.

America had long had an aversion to spying. A foreign navy intelligence
officer once complained that, for Americans, "espionage is by its very nature not to be considered as 'honorable' or 'clean' or 'fair' or 'decent.' . . .
The United States has always prided itself on the fact that no spies were
used and its intelligence officers overseas have always kept their hands immaculately clean." When deciphered Japanese messages once landed on
Herbert Hoover's desk in 1929, Secretary of State Henry Stimson infa-
mously remarked, "Gentleman do not read each other's mail." Appalled by
its use of what he perceived to be underhanded techniques, Stimson shut
down the "Black Chamber," a cryptographic service cracking Japanese
codes.

Before the OSS was created, multiple government departments gathered information in reports sent arbitrarily up the chain of command in the
hope that the most crucial information would find its way to the White
House. No clearinghouse existed to ensure the information was shared,
funneled, or packaged for White House review and direction.

When first formed, the fledgling COI came under assault by the government agencies then responsible for gathering intelligence, who viewed
its head officer, William Donovan, as an intruder in their territory. The very
agencies the COI was attempting to coordinate—the Federal Bureau of
Investigation (FBI), the Office of Naval Intelligence (ONI), Army Intelligence (G-2) and the State Department—formed a loose anti-COI alliance.
The four departments took steps to curb the new agency's scope and influence. For example, the military put code-breaking off limits, and the ONI
and FBI excluded the COI from operating in the Western Hemisphere.

COI nevertheless expanded its intelligence scope into research, analysis,
and propaganda, collaborating closely with the British intelligence services.
British hand-holding and tutelage was present from the very beginning. Co-
incidentally, a young lieutenant commander in British intelligence, Ian
Fleming, future author of the James Bond books, helped lay the founda-

tion for the nascent American intelligence services. Still, American special operations and secret intelligence lagged behind other branches of the OSS because it took so long to train effective operatives and saboteurs.

The advent of war didn't help establish COI's position in the eyes of the other American intelligence-gathering agencies, including the newly formed Joint Chiefs of Staff, who trusted their own intelligence organizations and distrusted Donovan. In order to solve this problem of perception and, at the same time, gain the support of the military and access to greater resources, Donovan proposed bringing COI under the command of the Joint Chiefs.

On June 13, 1942, President Franklin D. Roosevelt officially endorsed the idea. COI's name was changed to the Office of Strategic Services, and the organization was placed under the authority of the Joint Chiefs.

To lead the new agency, the president could not have chosen a more dynamic or qualified figure than Wall Street lawyer William J. Donovan. One of America's most highly decorated heroes of World War I and a former assistant attorney general of the United States, he was a larger-than-life figure. Commanding a battalion of the 165th Infantry Regiment, better known as the "Fighting Sixty-ninth," Donovan won the Medal of Honor, a Distinguished Service Cross, and two Purple Hearts, earning himself the nickname "Wild Bill."

After the war, Donovan traveled extensively, resuming his legal practice and serving as assistant attorney general under President Calvin Coolidge. In the late 1920s, he served as personal political advisor to President Herbert Hoover. His position of influence and power allowed him to build relationships at all levels of American society and throughout the world.

In 1940, Donovan traveled overseas as an official emissary of President Roosevelt to report on Britain's staying power in the war. Hoping to win American support, Prime Minister Winston Churchill granted Donovan unprecedented access to Britain's greatest intelligence secrets. Churchill eventually recommended that FDR appoint Donovan as America's intelligence chief.

Many of the techniques and strategies America has used to fight every clandestine war since World War II developed out of Wild Bill Donovan's vision. After his appointment as chief of the OSS, Donovan formulated an integrated "combined arms" approach of shadow-war techniques: "persuasion, penetration, and intimidation . . . are the modern counterparts of sapping and mining [used] in the siege warfare of former days." Propaganda represented the "arrow of initial penetration." Espionage, sabotage, and guerilla operations would then soften up an area before conventional forces invaded. His integration of shadow-war techniques was a groundbreaking approach to covert warfare. Unlike today's Central Intelligence Agency, which is largely "stove-piped" and focused on intelligence gathering and analysis, the OSS was truly an integrated organization which covered everything from anthropology to nutrition.*

Donovan considered the Germans his main competition, saying they were "big league professionals in shadow warfare, while America lagged behind as the bush league club." The only way to catch up with Germany, he told Roosevelt, was to "play a bush league game, stealing the ball and killing the umpire."

Making the best of his vast network of personal contacts, Donovan possessed a flair for picking the right people for the right job. In several cases he drew upon the social elite in America; many OSS staffers had prominent military, political, and business relationships in Europe, especially Germany. As one senior OSS staffer put it, "We looked for people with existing connections into Germany." In the organization's early months, acceptance into the OSS was largely through invitation and recommendation. Wild Bill threw together the OSS practically overnight from scratch. Or-

---

* This groundbreaking approach to shadow warfare has led some counterinsurgency/ counterterrorism experts, including David Kilvillen and Max Boot, to argue that an OSS-like organization is precisely what America needs to combat its current enemies. The author suggested a similar approach in a *Washington Times* op-ed piece (May 2004).

ganized into many departments Donovan's OSS quickly grew into a complex organizational chart of alphabet soup–like acronyms. Major departments of OSS under Wild Bill included:

- Research & Analysis (R&A) for intelligence analysis
- Research & Development (R&D) for weapons and equipment development
- Morale Operations (MO) for subversive, disguised, "black" propaganda
- Maritime Units (MU) for transporting agents and supplies to resistance groups and to conduct naval sabotage and reconnaissance
- X-2 for counterespionage
- Secret Intelligence (SI) to put agents in the field to gather intelligence covertly
- Special Operations (SO) for sabotage, subversion, fifth-column movements, and guerilla warfare
- Operational Groups (OG) also for sabotage and guerilla warfare, made up of highly trained foreign-language-speaking commando teams

To fill these departments, he tapped his high-society connections: Ivy League schools, law firms, and major corporations. Some may have dubbed the OSS "Oh So Social" for its blue-blooded foundation, but in truth, the OSS recruited anybody with useful skills. Safecrackers freshly sprung from prisons purloined documents from embassy safes and delivered them to Ivy League professors for analysis. Debutantes worked alongside army paratroopers. One study noted, "The OSS undertook and carried out more different types of enterprises, calling for more varied skills than any other single organization of its size in the history of our country."

For work in the field, the OSS needed not only the best and the brightest intelligence analysts but also out-of-the-box thinkers and risk takers. The OSS was filled with iconic and dynamic figures who would continue to capture the spotlight long after the war had ended: film giant John Ford; chef extraordinaire Julia Child; future Supreme Court justice Arthur Goldberg; Teddy Roosevelt's son Kermit; and even Chicago White Sox catcher Moe Berg.

Fred Mayer and the other OGs found themselves in this environment, and their personalities fit the OSS's mission like a glove. Mayer's personal attitude of "If you don't risk, you don't win" epitomized the spirit and vision of Donovan's OSS.


Back at the Country Club, Chappell whipped his men into shape. They mastered map reading, demolitions, and other basic skills needed for operations behind the lines.

Within Mayer's thirty-man group, a clique formed among five Jewish refugees, including Mayer, who had all escaped the clutches of Nazi Germany. They all spoke German, and they all wanted vengeance for their families' suffering at the hands of the Nazis. They all also shared a sense of duty to serve their adopted country.

Brilliant and "somewhat of a know-it-all," George Gerbner was a Jewish refugee from Hungary; the twenty-four-year-old spoke four languages and later became an Ivy League professor. OSS records described him as "intelligent, resourceful, in splendid physical condition and known for his good judgment." Alfred Rosenthal, a German refugee nicknamed "Rosie," was a nineteen-year-old graduate of the U.S. Army intelligence school who spoke German and Italian; he was "quiet and conscientious." Bernd Steinitz was a stocky world-class athlete with a gregarious and charming demeanor who barely escaped Nazi Germany in 1939; his entire family would later languish in the camps. Hans Wynberg was a natural-born radio operator: He had a mathematical mind and an ear for music, which, for him, made the dashes and dots of Morse code sing.

Within the Jewish clique, the men forged deep relationships that would last a lifetime. Rosie and Gerbner became good friends, and Mayer and

Wynberg formed a legendary friendship. They met in radio school, which for Mayer merely entailed some additional training in case his team's radio operator went down on a mission. For Wynberg, radio school was training in his specialty. "Hans latched on to me and saw me as kind of an older brother," Mayer later recalled. An OSS report described Mayer as "aggressive, husky, resourceful, and a natural leader who has a remarkable ability to improvise in special situations." The same report described Wynberg as "intelligent, cautious and completely loyal to Fred." Mayer was the yin to Wynberg's yang.

Hans Wynberg, the lanky, blond-haired, 6'2" Jewish operative, was born on November 28, 1922, in Amsterdam, Holland. In 1939, Wynberg's father decided to send Hans and his twin brother, Louis, both in their fourth year of high school, to the United States. His younger brother, mother, father, and most of his relatives remained trapped in Holland. His father put $3,600 in a bank account, and the two boys lived with a diamond cutter, a business contact of their father's, in New York City. Hans enrolled in Brooklyn Technical High School and excelled in his studies, particularly chemistry. When money got short, he obtained a job as a research assistant at the pharmaceutical giant Pfizer, where he assisted the doctor who was one of the primary scientists involved with discovering penicillin. Hans was present during purification tests for the drug. While working for Pfizer, the Dutch army called him up for service, but the Nazis soon overran Holland, nullifying the request. During the sweltering month of August 1943, Wynberg joined the U.S. Army and reported to boot camp. Meanwhile back in Europe, communication from the Wynberg family ceased. Hans did not know it at the time, but the SS had rounded up his mother, father, and younger brother and placed them in Auschwitz, the infamous extermination camp.

Wynberg's life changed at boot camp when an officer approached him and said, "We understand you speak German, Dutch and English. Would you like to help your country?"

Wynberg replied, "Sure," and two days later he was on a train to Washington, D.C.

While at the country club, the men learned the basics of hand-to-hand combat. Mayer recalled that he was "good at it, [especially] the jujitsu." The men learned their craft from a fifty-something, gray-haired combat instructor from Shanghai, British Major Ewart Fairbairn, who developed one of the deadliest systems of street fighting known to man, called "gutter fighting." Gutter fighting evolved from hundreds of street fights he was involved in as the assistant municipal police chief in one of the most dangerous cities on earth at the time, Shanghai, China. Fairbairn summed it up like this: "There is no fair play, no fair rules except to kill or be killed." The major emphasized knife and close-combat fighting: "Gutter fighting is for fools; you should always have a pistol or a knife. However, if you are caught unarmed, the tactics shown here will greatly increase your chances of coming out alive." Fairbairn's gutter-fighting tactics involved such things as a karate chop called the "axe hand." A single blow to the Adam's apple with the bony edge of a hand could kill a man, he told the men. Mayer and the other OGs also learned knife fighting and the art of weapon improvisation, such as how to roll a simple newspaper into a stiletto that could pierce the soft tissue underneath an enemy sentry's chin.

The men also met another notable character during their training, John Hamilton, known for his rugged good looks, red hair, and bushy eyebrows. In reality he was the famous movie actor Sterling Hayden. Hamilton taught various commando tactics on the fairways of the Congressional Country Club. Once, when demonstrating countermoves against bayonet thrusts, he flipped young Bernd Steinitz over his back with the flick of a wrist, dislocating the trainee's shoulder, and sarcastically quipped, "Suppose I gotta ease up a bit."

After learning hand-to-hand combat, demolitions, and other infiltration tactics at the Congressional Country Club, the men were sent to Fort Belvoir, where they learned to drive tanks and other military vehicles. Although some of the recruits looked like "drunken fools driving [the tanks] and accidentally drove one of the vehicles into a ditch," Mayer was a natural. He later described his tank-driving skills: "I was a damn good tank driver."

Following their brief stint with vehicle training, the thirty-plus-man German Operational Group hit the rails and traveled to Chappell's old haunt, Fort Benning, where they were integrated into the airborne training program. The men underwent the rigorous U.S. Army parachute-qualification program, during with they learned to pack their own chutes. The training was tough; it was meant to wash out most of the recruits and to test whether they had the physical and mental acumen to be paratroopers, which even today is a mark of warrior status in the U.S. Army. The men had to complete rigorous physical conditioning and five qualifying jumps to earn the coveted silver jump wings identifying them as paratroopers. To maintain their cover as normal soldiers, the OSS issued them regular M-42 paratrooper jumpsuits. Discipline was strict at Fort Benning and included several daily rituals, as Hans Wynberg recalls:

> We had to wash our uniforms every night and put them on in the morning (dried or not, but at Fort Benning that spring it was warm enough for the clothes to dry). Boots had to be polished including the soles. . . . We also had to refold our own chutes after we had jumped. The 16 risers [the ropes] were of course usually entangled because as you hit the ground and were tugged along by the partly inflated chute for a few yards, before being able to gather the chute together. This exercise (refolding the chute) has given me a lifelong expertise in untying knots!

To his dismay, one of the instructors punished Wynberg for merely looking up into the air:

> Punishment was frequent but fairly mild [twenty push-ups] for minor infractions. Since other teams were of course also training at Fort

Benning, planes were overhead all the time and paratroopers were jumping out on neighboring fields. But, there was a strict rule that we were not allowed to look at the men who were jumping. This was done in order to prevent us from counting. Every jump consisted of a "stick,"* meaning twelve men who would jump, and if we did watch and count, it might occur that we counted eleven men instead of twelve, thereby realizing that one parachute had not opened! So watching the jumps was a strict no-no.

I was caught one time watching the jumpers and my punishment was running around our training field, while having my arms out and rotating my arms while shouting: "I am a bad soldier." I watched the planes. All this doing double time.

During the early days of U.S. airborne training, chutes sometimes didn't open, and training was hazardous; the school had a high washout rate, giving paratroopers elite status. Equipment failure was an ominous threat, and incorrect parachute rigging meant death. During one of the parachute jumps, Mayer recalled being blown off course: "A crosswind caught us and we ended up in the Chattahoochee."

Despite nearly drowning in the muddy waters of the Chattahoochee, Mayer and most of the other men in the group successfully made their five qualifying jumps. For the members of the German Operational Group, this marked an important milestone. Since they had the mental toughness and physical prowess to graduate from one of the army's toughest training programs, they received the coveted silver wings representing their qualifications as paratroopers. With their newly minted, shiny parachute wings and smart jump boots, the men headed back to the country club.

---

* Paratrooper "sticks" varied in size.

# 3

## THE WAIT

After one too many run-ins with cabbies who knew the commandoes' "secret training ground," the always security-conscious, bordering-on-paranoid Captain Chappell persuaded Donovan to move America's secret warriors to California's Catalina Island. Located twenty miles off the Southern California shoreline, Catalina was an ideal location for amphibious warfare training. Known for its lush green hills and red-roofed vacation homes, the island was a resort. However, Chappell's men were headed for the other side of the island, a compound of dilapidated wooden buildings that had served as a boys' summer camp before the war. Life was soon to get a whole lot more spartan for the German OGs.

At Catalina, the men embarked upon survival training. Dumped into the remote, unpopulated section of the island, they split into six-man teams, and Chappell instructed them to live off the land for five days on their own. They slept under the stars, officers and enlisted men alike, in only their sleeping bags. During an initial training exercise, the teams were ordered to "capture" an airport. In charge of one of the teams, Mayer later recalled that his team "took the airport. [We] came in from the back. There were

only a few guards [protecting the airport], and we took them too." Mayer
always approached things unconventionally. Instead of mounting frontal
attacks, he preferred taking the unexpected route and liked to employ the
element of surprise. After Mayer's group seized the airport, the men received a rare pass to travel to the resort side of the island.

Later, Hans Wynberg reflected upon the experience:

> The one time we got a few hours leave was a brief visit to the only
> port of Catalina Island, namely, Avalon. It was the first time in months
> that we had received a pass. All of us were of course far from home.
> At that time I was sergeant and in charge of the entire "company" of
> thirty men. As we returned to our camp from the outing in Avalon, it
> was clear that several men had had a lot (or too much) to drink. At
> that time [spring of 1944] I was twenty-one years old and had *never*
> drank any alcohol!
>
> After we returned to our base camp and turned in, I was awoken
> by the shout of [the unit's executive officer]: "Sergeant Wynberg, get
> that man." As I got up I saw Private Willy (that was his name. He was
> a former inmate of a prison, and he was called "Chicago Willy")
> standing next to his sleeping bag with a (forty-five) pistol in his hand
> (we were all armed at all times), wildly swinging the pistol around
> and shouting, "The Japs are coming. The Japs are coming." While the
> other officers were ducking behind their sleeping bags, I got up and
> calmly walked over to Private Willy and calmly asked him to "give me
> his pistol," which he did after I assured him, "It is alright, Willy. There
> are no Japs. Believe me."

Wynberg always put his men first. Despite the fact that this was survival
school, he requested extra rations from the executive officer of the unit. As
he recalled, "A few days later the men complained that we had way too little to eat, which was true. We were doing lots of marching and climbing
amidst the hills of Catalina Island and living on C rations."

Wynberg went to the executive officer to demand extra rations from the unit's leadership. "Lieutenant, the men are hungry and want more to eat."

The lieutenant replied, "Wynberg, not another word. I do not want to hear such things."

"But, lieutenant, the men are hungry."

"Wynberg, I said 'not another word.'"

Later Wynberg once again pestered the lieutenant, whereupon he was "demoted to private for disobeying an order."

Hungry and armed with Fairbairn-Sykes fighting knives and .45s, the men soon took matters into their own hands. Survival training be damned, they put their weapons to good use and blasted a lone steer. Industrialist Philip K. Wrigley, son of the founder of the famed chewing gum company and the owner of the entire island, kept a herd of dairy cows near the woods. The men "snuck up on the cattle, much like Indians hunting buffalo." At a prearranged signal they "picked out a calf at the edge of the herd and shot it." One man, Tiny Waggoner, an experienced butcher who had "worked in a New York butcher shop before the war," took it from there. He "did a masterful job converting part of our bounty into delicious steaks." Healthy and practically unscathed, these full-bellied German OGs rolled back into camp. Chappell interpreted the men's resourcefulness as a positive trait and did not chastise them excessively. Instead, he filled out an IOU for Mr. Wrigley's dead calf.

After they had successfully completed survival training at Catalina Island, Chappell felt his OGs were ready for the real deal.

During the balmy, early summer days of 1944, Fred and the other OGs finally got their call to action: They received orders to embark on a troop ship for Europe. The Jewish members were particularly excited to get into the fight and potentially make a difference in a war that threatened to destroy their race and, on a more personal level, their families. The team boarded a Liberty troopship bound for an unknown destination.

The ship was packed with regular infantrymen as well as Chappell's group of thirty of America's special operations troops. Everyone on board took part in a guessing game as to their final destination. Only Chappell knew they were steaming into North Africa. The rest of the OGs logically thought they were headed for England.

The Liberty ship maintained formation in a convoy to avoid the torpedoes of the enemy wolf packs. The journey was uneventful. Mostly the men played cards, shot craps, and were bored out of their minds.

After weeks at sea, a foreign port finally came into view through a thick fog. Excitement rippled through the OGs as they approached land. A tugboat came out to guide the ship to its mooring near the wharf, and the men prepared to disembark.

Once ashore, the operators found themselves in Oran, an Algerian port of two hundred thousand. Three-quarters of the population were of European descent. Founded by Moorish traders in 903 BC, the Barbary Coast town had been sacked countless times by a wide assortment of European and Middle Eastern navies, armies, and pirates. The ambience of the city's pirate legacy still lingered as the commandoes stepped ashore. The rugged city fit Chappell and his motley crew like a glove. Oran had been captured by the Allies in 1942 and became an improvised depot for men and supplies on their way to the Italian front. It suddenly became obvious to the OGs that "no one in Oran knew we were coming, and no one knew what to do with us," recalled Wynberg. Soon they learned why: They were in the *wrong* city.

The OGs filed ashore with the rest of the troops. Chappell's first stop was to see the commanding officer of the replacement depot, or "repo depot," to which the OG had been assigned. A replacement depot was essentially a holding tank for men who were to be shipped off to existing units to replace combat casualties. Chappell entered the white stone building serving as headquarters for the repo depot. After requesting a meeting with the commanding officer, Chappell was ushered into the general's office, located prominently in a cluster of stone buildings set aside as repo depot HQ.

With signature bravado, he extended a calloused hand.

"Sir, my name is Captain Howard Chappell of the OSS." The general looked at him, sneering.

"Who the hell are you?"

"OSS. Office of Strategic Services."

"We don't know anything about OSS," responded the general, who then announced, "You are to report as replacements for other units."

At this point in the war, very few people had any idea what the OSS was because it was still a secret organization whose existence was disclosed only on a need-to-know basis. OSS headquarters was equally disorganized and had neither formed an office in Oran by the time Chappell arrived nor sent instructions to anyone in the city. One of America's most highly trained operations units was marooned in a bureaucratic nightmare. No one knew who they were, and it was beginning to look as if this crack unit would soon be used as replacement cannon fodder for other chewed-up units. In fact, the commanding general initially decided to send Chappell's OGs to England to be used as replacements for airborne units. Chappell refused the general's orders, while he made repeated requests to other high-ranking officers. But his requests fell on deaf ears.

With no radio, telephone, or other means to communicate with OSS headquarters, Chappell took matters into his own hands. "After almost getting court-martialed in Oran, I learned that the OSS had a secret base in Algiers," he recalled. By hook and by crook, Chappell obtained train tickets for all of his OGs from Oran to Algiers. Wynberg recalled the memorable train ride:

> The train trip to Algiers was slow since the trains stopped in at least half a dozen villages in between. When the train stopped, it was immediately surrounded by dozens of yelling and gesticulating Arabs, youngsters as well as grown-ups. We soon realized that they were aiming at buying our bedsheets [as clothing]. Without hesitation I joined my fellow comrades in arms in making money by opening the

windows at the next stop and, with my bedsheets in hand, offered
them to an Arab boy who was waving a pack of paper money notes.
As the train pulled away the boy grabbed the sheets and pushed the
notes in my hand. As I sat down to count my money I realized that the
top of the bunch of notes was indeed a low-value piece of paper
money while the rest was merely blank paper.

After a few hours' journey, the train rolled into Algiers and the OGs disembarked and set up camp twenty miles outside of town.

But in Algiers, the men once again had to contend with being at the
wrong place at the wrong time. As the days in bureaucratic limbo rolled by,
boredom set in, and the men began to wonder if they would ever be able to
utilize the months of intense training they had received. Quite frankly,
Mayer's team began to have serious doubts about whether they would see
any action at all. There were numerous rumors that the OGs would deploy
behind the lines on a mission, but every time the men got their hopes up,
the rumors proved false. Regardless, Chappell continued pushing his men
and finding ways to keep them busy. Wynberg recalled one experience that
broke the monotony:

> In Algiers we had of course nothing to do, so our officers had to think
> of keeping us busy. Our captain, a bit of a cowboy, ordered us, Fred-
> die, Alfred, George, Bernie, and I, together with five others, to march
> to the airport and back and do this without rations, only our canteens
> with water. After a few hours of marching we decided that we would
> go into a village and into an eating place in this village. We were
> greeted with enthusiasm by the Algerian owner, whose daughter
> waited on us and served us delicious eggs and pancakes. We left the
> cafe and pitched tents about two miles outside the village. As I woke
> up early the next morning I saw a group of about two dozen Arabs
> marching towards our camp. I woke the rest of the fellows, and as the
> group arrived it became clear after much shouting and gesticulation

that the father of our waitress had the impression that if you talked to his daughter, the way Alfred had (he knew enough French to have talked with the daughter/waitress the previous evening), it meant marriage! It took at least an hour of shouting (and some money) to convince the father that Alfred was not going to marry his daughter.

Algiers was a cosmopolitan city that contained a sizable Jewish population. Several of the five were able to find a Sephardic Jewish synagogue and attended services. Wynberg later reflected on his time in Algiers and the extracurricular activities of one particular member of the five:

> Having nothing to do in Algiers meant we did get evenings or even weekends off and were allowed to go into Algiers (we had pitched camp about twenty miles outside the city). Although I visited the Kasbah just once, George Gerbner, the fellow from Budapest, not only went to town every night but befriended one of the many pretty French girls left behind while their mates were fighting with De Gaulle's Free French.

They had been trapped in North Africa for months, barely escaping the clutches of the repo depot numerous times. But like traveling vagabonds, the OGs were eventually on the move again, this time by ship. Captain Chappell had finally been able to contact OSS headquarters in Italy and arranged for the group to travel to Europe. Nevertheless, as Wynberg recalled, they were kept in the dark and told that their travels were top secret. One member of the team, however, had other things on his mind:

> After two months in Algiers we received orders to embark on a British troopship which was in the harbor and which, with 500 British soldiers aboard, would take us to Naples. In complete secrecy we broke camp that morning at 5 a.m., got into our trucks, and headed for the harbor of Algiers; [we were repeatedly told] that we were [traveling]

under great secrecy. . . . We got aboard the ship, being greeted by the British soldiers and sailors, and as I wandered to find a place to sit for the trip to Italy, I noticed that the ship was tilting towards the shore where it was anchored. I went to the railing of the ship as five hundred British soldiers and sailors were cheering and staring at a pretty French girl standing on the waterfront waving her arms and shouting, "George, George [Gerbner]. Don't leave me. Take me along."

# 4

## A ROLL OF THE DICE

Fred Mayer cupped his hands together, shaking the dice as he wound up and tossed them against the side of the tent. Gerbner, Rosenthal, and Steinitz craned their necks to watch with anticipation for the result of the roll. They were betting "blood money," literally: They had donated their blood to the local Red Cross. For $10, Mayer crapped out. He was a lucky man, but his luck had never held with dice.

"I lost my blood," recalled Mayer.

Frustration was mounting. For the past several months, Howard Chappell's German Operational Group had been homeless and missionless. After Chappell had successfully spirited the group away from North Africa into Italy, their original destination, Mayer's operations team found itself, once again, without a mission. But Mayer kept his frustration to himself. For several more weeks, the OGs pondered their fate. Boredom is one of the toughest challenges any soldier faces: Each person has his own threshold for it, and the anticipation of combat makes most men want to get the fight over with in order to confront their destiny. Besides that, however, and beyond the sense of purpose and duty that had brought them here,

Mayer and four others had a larger axe to grind. They were Jewish, and this was their war—more so than for most of America's other GIs.

Mayer's frustration boiled over after his unlucky dice roll, and he turned to the others in the group. "We are going to sit here until doomsday unless we do something about it," he said sharply to the other OGs.

With emotion apparent, the men stared at Mayer, nodding in agreement. Then, he boldly suggested how they should take action: "We're going to go to Allied Intelligence in Caserta and try to change our fate," he told the others. Wynberg would later recall, "We essentially mutinied."

Because the men had not informed Chappell of their intention to try their luck elsewhere and had left without even speaking to him, they were essentially AWOL. Procuring a jeep, the five set off for Caserta, where they had a vague idea that Allied Forces Intelligence was headquartered. Roaming the streets of Caserta, the men found an MP and asked where they could find the headquarters. They were directed toward a villa, which served as a headquarters for the battalion stationed there. Stumbling and bumbling around, the men somehow found their way into LTC Howard Chapin's office. Before the war, Chapin was an advertising executive for General Foods; now, he sent intelligence agents into central Europe, including Austria and Germany. Chapin's special German-Austrian Section was a branch within OSS's SI, or Secret Intelligence, division. Differing from the commando-like OGs, SI was devoted to the craft of intelligence and the art of espionage. Hundreds of OSS secret intelligence agents around the world had infiltrated the Third Reich, from the carefully planted valet of the Gestapo chief in Paris to the former circus acrobat surreptitiously serving as a German nurse. With the assistance of their British counterparts, the OSS was learning and mastering the rules of human intelligence gathering and spy craft that are still being used today.

At Chapin's SI desk, the men found the sympathetic ear they sought. When the five walked into the office, Chapin nodded and asked them to take a seat. They took turns telling Chapin their unique stories as to why they were there.

Mayer spoke first and directly. As he recalls, "I told him I was Jewish and that I wanted to jump behind the lines to help end the war."

Chapin nodded, listening to the men's stories and understanding their intensely personal reasons for joining the OSS. The small group had put their guts on the table and convinced Chapin they were willing to lay down their lives for a cause greater than themselves. Getting caught, each of the five Jews knew, likely meant a death sentence, not only because they were enemy spies but also because they were Jewish. Each of them wanted to return to Germany; they dared to return.

Chapin was receptive to their stories and, after he had heard them, stated flatly, "You will hear from me."

In an orderly fashion, the men filed out of the room and awaited their fate.


Chapin recognized the men's potential and ordered the Jewish five to Bari the next day. Upon arrival, they were escorted into the offices of Lt. Alfred C. Ulmer Jr., a sales and advertising executive before the war, known for his quick wit and boyish demeanor. Ulmer, like Chapin, had a background in advertising at a Fortune 500 company. Pulled from the ranks of the U.S. Navy, the twenty-eight-year-old Floridian ran the day-to-day operations at OSS's German-Austrian Section in Bari. The section's task involved inserting agents into the heart of Hitler's Third Reich—perhaps the most difficult of OSS's spy missions. Thus far, their results were mixed.

Ulmer first inquired about the prospective agents' backgrounds. He asked each man if he would kill: Mayer responded yes without hesitation, but Hans Wynberg allegedly said no. Ulmer quickly got to the larger point and matter-of-factly asked the men, "Do you appreciate what can happen to you?"

Mayer stared directly into Ulmer's eyes: "This is more our war than yours."

Yet Ulmer had reason to be concerned.

On October 7, 1942, Hitler had spoken to the German people as well as the German armed forces, proclaiming, "All terror and sabotage troops of the British and their accomplices, who do not act like soldiers but like 'bandits,' are to be treated as such by the German troops. They must be slaughtered ruthlessly in combat wherever they turn up. From now on, all enemies on so-called commando missions in Europe or Africa challenged by German troops, even if they are to all appearances soldiers in uniform or demolition troops, whether armed or unarmed, in battle or in flight, are to be slaughtered to the last man." The speech laid the groundwork for addenda A and B of Directive 46, more widely known as the infamous "Commando Order," which provided for the immediate execution of all captured enemy commandos and spies, whether they were caught in uniform or not.

The Allied efforts at irregular warfare were having an impact on the German war machine. As German chief of staff Gen. Alfred Jodl later recalled, "The order arose from Hitler's excitement about two kinds of intensified warfare which made their appearance about the same time in the autumn of 1942. One was the fatal efficacy of excellently equipped sabotage detachments, which landed by sea or were dropped from the air. The other, special agents running wild in the fighting methods of enemies [Russian partisans] who acted singularly or in small groups."

Hitler's order was also retaliation for a British commando raid on the island of Sark, located in the English Channel, in which British commandos bound and executed members of the German garrison there. Following the raid, the Germans discovered British documents ordering commandos to execute German prisoners.

Since the failed July 20, 1944, plot to kill Hitler, the Gestapo and the SS were given wider authority to roll up enemies of the state. A reign of terror enveloped the southern Alpine districts of Styria, Carinthia, and the Tyrol. The Security Services, now under SS command, wove the strategic junctions and key cities within the *Alpenland* districts into a security network.

The SS and Sicherheitsdienst (SD) arrested and executed thousands of men, women, and children. Also caught up in the net were Allied agents who were sometimes conveniently executed under the auspices of Directive 46. The Jewish five were headed straight into a hornet's nest.

Prior to the arrival of Mayer and the others, nearly all of the missions the German-Austrian Section had sent into the Reich had been doomed. The first mission, Dupont, in which the team was dropped by parachute into Austria near Vienna in October 1944, was an unmitigated disaster. Jack Taylor, a former dentist from California turned OSS agent, led three deserter-volunteers* (DVs), behind the lines. Their parachute drop was successful; however, their radio fell into a lake. Without communications, Dupont fell into a black hole, and Ulmer had feared the worst. Taylor nevertheless found several safe houses, and the team continued gathering intelligence. They compiled complete data on the "Southeast Wall,"† including the exact location of fortified hills, anti-tank ditches, pillboxes, artillery sites, machine gun emplacements, etc. . . . They also located some excellent targets for Allied bombing raids, including a locomotive factory and a secret airfield. Taylor shifted his team to a different safe house every night. On October 25, they found a farmer in Schützen who kept the agents in a hay loft. That evening, the entire mission was blown by a deserter-volunteer who had fallen in love and "bought his girl a diamond ring." The big-ticket purchase aroused the suspicions of the local Gestapo, who quickly arrested the love-struck team member.

The Gestapo then raided the farmer's home, and Taylor was taken into custody, along with three Austrians, and tortured. Heroically, Taylor refused to be doubled or to transmit a false message back to OSS headquarters on the Gestapo's radio. As a result, the Austrian deserter-volunteers and Taylor were all sent to Mauthausen, among the most notorious of

---

* Deserter-volunteers were captured German army soldiers who had "deserted" the Nazi cause and "volunteered" to help the OSS in their covert operations behind German lines.

† The Southeast Wall was located in the lower Danube in the Styria. It was built with the manpower of Jewish prisoners and slave laborers under the auspices of the Todt Organization.

Hitler's concentration camps. There, Taylor toiled everyday, carrying unbelievably heavy loads of rock up steep grades, guarded by brutal German
and Ukrainian SS guards with whips, who, for sport, frequently tossed inmates too weak to work off the cliff at the top of the quarry. The American
agent Taylor was later scheduled to be executed and would have been, had
it not been for a Czech clerk who burned his execution orders. Mauthausen
was one of the last concentration camps to be liberated by the Allies or the
Soviets. His liberators found Taylor withered away from a lean 165 to a
skeletal 115 pounds. The three Austrians also miraculously survived Mauthausen and were freed by the Allies.

Another mission sent from Italy by the OSS's Labor Desk was a three-
man team known as Orchid. Orchid was dropped by parachute behind the
lines into a region controlled by Tito's partisans. The official operation report describes the start of operation:

> On October 25, the men, with a band of Yugoslavian partisan guides,
> crossed the Reich border and the "New German Boundary" estab-
> lished by the Nazis after the initial occupation of Yugoslavia in
> 1941—a line long since ignored by both the Germans and the Yu-
> goslavs. Only the ruins of barbed wire, gatehouses, and bunkers re-
> mained, which testified to the efficiency of the partisans fighting in
> the area.... In all, there were close to sixty or seventy men in their col-
> umn; 20 or 30 carried rifles, three carried machine guns and the rest
> of the partisans acted as porters. Leaving the main roads, the column
> found a mountain trail through the woods and at all times kept on
> the alert for ambush attacks.

Orchid's sojourn into the borders of the Reich was extremely circuitous
because of the rapidly changing positions of the German army in Yugoslavia. The sole surviving member of Orchid described the journey as

> routine and perhaps prosaic, yet the actual movement was provided
> with a high degree of excitement, based on both genuine peril and

false alarms. The very capable Partisan couriers and patrols, [a team member] pointed out, erred if at all on the side of extreme caution. On many occasions, the party was given advance reports that a given railroad or highway would prove a major stumbling block in their progress, because of the movement of German guards, only to find that the crossings were easily accomplished. Conversely, the fluidity of the guerilla warfare and the presence of large numbers of German units moving through the countryside made for unexpected en-counters with or narrow escapes from the enemy. In one village the party walked through the streets to find themselves hailed as "liber-ators," since the Wehrmacht detachment had been evacuated only a few hours before. On another occasion a farm in which the party spent the night was in German hands only an hour or two after their departure.

The mission enjoyed some initial success when it provided headquarters with intelligence on bombing targets. However, friction mounted when the partisans "refused to move any further north without a large supply drop from the OSS." They "politely declined permission for the team to move north of the Drava River without them."

The partisans had good reason to be cautious. A band of five thousand men, heavily armed with artillery, had crossed the Reich border in the fall of 1943 in an attempt to cut off the Agram-Laibach (Ljubljana) railway, a vital German artery carrying supplies from the Reich to the Balkans. The Luftwaffe, in coordination with Wehrmacht and SS police armored units, engaged the partisans in battle for seven days. Eventually, reinforcements from the Ninth SS Panzer Division and the Sixteenth SS Panzer Grenadier Division with Stuka dive-bomber support completely annihilated the par-tisan battle group.

During the standoff between Orchid and the partisans, Orchid myste-riously went off the air, and the other members of the team were never heard from again. It was presumed that German forces had wiped out the partisan unit with whom they were operating. Although the OSS agents

were all killed, the official report does credit the value of the intelligence
they gathered:

> The intelligence forwarded by the team contained some items of ex-
> treme value to the Air Forces: information about bomb damage, lo-
> cation of certain Nazi factories in Carinthia, and details of railroad
> traffic—and traffic dislocation—on a number of lines in southern
> Austria and northern Yugoslavia.

In another of Ulmer's missions, code-named Dillon, the operatives, including deserter-volunteers, were dropped near Klagenfurt in December
1944. The team immediately transmitted useful intelligence, but in February 1945, the Gestapo captured one of the deserter-volunteers. He
promptly ratted out his teammates and volunteered to lead the Germans
to their hideout. A dramatic shootout ensued between the SS and Dillon
team leader Lt. Miles Pavlovich:

> Hans [one of the deserted-volunteers] agreed to lead the police to
> Lt. Pavlovich's hideout. Tied by a ten meter rope to his captors, he
> conducted them to the home of Martha Frais and knocked on the
> door with a signal customarily used by the team. Victor, hearing the
> knock, roused Martha, who opened the door. Standing in the door-
> way was a police officer, who fired a shot into Lt. Pavlovich's stomach,
> as the latter reached for his own pistol. He then withdrew from the
> doorway. A moment later shots were fired through the window, and
> two grenades tossed through the window exploded in the room.
> Martha Frais became hysterical and begged Lt. Pavlovich to kill her
> to prevent vengeance upon her by the Nazis. Lt. Pavlovich fired a shot
> through her brain, and almost immediately afterwards a shot through
> the head killed Lt. Pavlovich instantly.
>     The police made no effort to enter the house until morning. Vic-
> tor sat in the room with the two bodies waiting for daybreak and pos-

sible escape, but at 0700 a crowd of police and SS men, led by a young boy, entered the house. One of the SS recognized Victor and addressed him by his correct name. They searched him for weapons, without doing him any bodily harm, and then led him to the police station where Prester [see below] and Hans and twenty of their local contacts had already been incarcerated.

The other members of the team, including Julio Prester, an American merchant marine of Yugoslav descent from New Jersey, were then doubled by the Gestapo and put back on the air. Prester repeatedly sent the distress signal back to OSS headquarters, but he altered letters in his messages to alert the OSS to his capture. It was all to no avail because another member of the team would eventually be sent into the waiting arms of a gun-toting Gestapo reception committee anyway. Failure to recognize the coded messages sent back to OSS headquarters by captured agents was a recurring problem. Headquarters all too often missed the nuances indicating an OSS agent was under Gestapo control.*

Inside Ulmer's office, the five friends were greeted by two fellow Jewish refugees, Dyno Lowenstein and Walter Haass. Both had escaped the horrors of the Reich before the onset of war and were now working for the OSS. Rosenthal, Gerbner, Steinitz, Wynberg, and Mayer realized they were among friends with the same goal and purpose: to strike back at the Nazi regime.

The thirty-year-old Lowenstein had been born in Germany and was known for his keen intelligence. As noted in a report, "He was resolute and had a thorough knowledge of the European underground and the German order of battle." Soft-spoken yet decisive, he had recently graduated from the army's intelligence program at Camp Ritchie, located in the bucolic

---

* Refer to Appendix B for the original Dillon Report written in 1945.

Blue Ridge foothills of western Maryland. Highly analytical, with a hint of nobility, Lowenstein had graduated from Paris's elite La Sorbonne University, where he was employed by the League of Nations for statistical research. After escaping from Germany, he spent two months in Prague, then eventually fled Nazi-occupied France in 1941. He spoke German, French, and English with only a slight accent. One colleague described Lowenstein as tailor-made for covert operational work: "[His] analytic mind, keen intelligence, complete dependability and discretion and a highly activist temperament, in my opinion, makes him ideal for field work."

Twenty-three-year-old OSS spy Walter Haass, known for his chiseled face, wavy dark-blond hair, and penetrating blue-green eyes, radiated self-confidence. His father had run a textile workers' union in Aachen—a reflection of Haass's blue-collar roots. The Haass family fled Germany in 1933 and took up residence on the Belgian-German frontier, where Haass was employed as a "border secretary." In this capacity, he "performed extremely valuable work in maintaining underground contacts [with German and Belgian Jews]." During jump training, Haass sprained both ankles, and the OSS put him in a job utilizing his brain rather than his brawn. Known to be highly intelligent, he could also fly an airplane. In 1940, Haass immigrated to America and joined the U.S. Army, and in 1943 he became a naturalized citizen, shortly before the OSS plucked him for intelligence work.

After the introduction to the unit, Ulmer divided the five into teams and gave each team a room in an old Italian mansion known as the Villa Suppa. Located in a rural area outside Bari, the castle-like estate housed the German-Austrian Section. The walled mansion, with its tree-lined courtyard and manicured lawns, sat on the outskirts of the Adriatic port town in a secluded area. The OSS also utilized a nearby villa called Villa Pasquali. The two villas were the central training grounds for OSS's secret intelligence agents in Italy, but they also functioned more surreptitiously as a training ground for deserter-volunteers.

Throughout 1944, Allied intelligence agencies had difficulty finding and recruiting plausible agents who could infiltrate the most notorious police state in history. With Allied armies now at the very borders of Hitler's Germany, it became imperative to find agents who could blend in completely and avoid capture by the Gestapo. Unlike in France and Italy, where the civilian population was largely sympathetic to the Allied cause, the agents would have to move about among a hostile German population, making finding safe houses and food incredibly challenging. Rather than rely solely on American agents with flawless knowledge of German language and culture, the OSS turned to the primary source readily available to them— German prisoners of war. The British had reached the same conclusion, believing that using POWs represented the "only possible chance to penetrate Germany and Austria."

Various American OSS stations, such as the Labor Desk in London, had been dispatching German POW teams into the Reich, but the legality of the operations was a thorny issue. According to the Geneva Conventions, using enemy prisoners as agents was to step on slippery legal ground. Nevertheless, their need for bodies forced the OSS to trump the Geneva Conventions; in this case, the ends justified the means, and they discarded the rules.

OSS agents such as Lowenstein and Haass methodically checked local POW cages to find suitable DVs for missions. Handfuls of men with anti-Nazi leanings were plucked from the cages and thoroughly screened. If they passed, they were given the option to volunteer for a mission back into Germany. Many of their families were under watch because they had deserted the German army. If recaptured, their fate, as well as their families', would almost certainly be death.

Now, Mayer and his team, in one of the most ironic couplings of the war, would be paired with these former Nazi soldiers in a mission to wreak havoc on their fatherland.

Lowenstein and Haass escorted the men to their own separate rooms within the Villa Suppa. Lowenstein instructed the men to craft their own missions based on their personal expertise and knowledge of German politics, geography, and culture.

Best friends since their training days at the Congressional Country Club, Ulmer quartered Gerbner and Rosenthal together. Shortly after the pair settled in, Lowenstein introduced them to their new teammate, Paul Kröck. With a round baby face and doe eyes, he was etched with physical and emotional battle scars from five years of war. A five-year veteran of the Wehrmacht and highly decorated with an Iron Cross Second Class, Kröck had fought in most of Germany's legendary campaigns in Poland, France, and Russia. An old man among boys, he deserted from the German army in 1944 and shortly afterward fought with Italian partisans in northern Italy against the very force on which he served.

Prior to the war, he taught skiing with the Reichsbund für Leibesübungen (German-Nazi Sports Organization) and tested rifles (he was a crack shot). Kröck became an asset to the OSS for his intelligence, his strong democratic political convictions, and, most importantly, his local knowledge of the Austrian city of Graz.

Steinitz was quartered with another deserter-volunteer, while Freddie and Wynberg shared a room at the villa. For operational security, the men were separated and only saw each other in the gardens and courtyard; nevertheless, many of the DVs bonded with the Jewish OSS members. In a lame attempt at further operational security and compartmentalization, the men were given English-sounding code names. Hans Wynberg became Hugh Wynn, Frederick Mayer stayed Frederick Mayer, since it was German enough, and Paul Kröck was given the inauspicious code name of George Mitchell. Rosenthal, Gerbner, and Steinitz also received code names. Later, they were given additional cover stories for their particular missions behind the lines, but behind the walls of the villa, the agents were to address each other with these anglicized names.

After the men settled into their new quarters, Lowenstein gave Mayer and Wynberg a crash course in spy craft. The OSS augmented their OG training and held classes on setting up human intelligence rings and gathering and disseminating operational intelligence. They also taught classes on how to identify German units and operate undetected behind the lines. Mayer recalls, "Dyno was a damned good teacher."

Hans remembered the "training" given to them by Lowenstein:

> When we got up in the morning and before we sat down for breakfast he made the [very small group] of OSS members stand up and take out our .45 caliber pistols. Then he would take out his pistol, removed the clip and bullets, told us to do the same and, pointing the gun at some fictitious German he would squeeze the trigger, telling us that that was the only exercise we need, pull the trigger when you see a German.

For all its sprawling grandeur, the Villa Suppa was in the sticks and lacked creature comforts like electricity and entertainment. Hating the isolation, Mayer, true to his character, took matters into his own hands and found a way to get wheels. One evening, Hans and Freddie crept into the motor pool of a nearby army unit and "procured" a half-track. Freddie recalled, "One of the first things Hans and I did was to steal a half track, we would use the vehicle all over the place and then park it in the back of the villa."

On one of their excursions into town, the men wandered into the Bari opera house and sat in one of the front-row seats. Enjoying the show, they propped their jump boots on the seats in front of them. The local paper captured the moment, carrying a picture of them and acidly deploring the culture of American soldiers.

Lowenstein looked the other way regarding the half-track since it demonstrated Mayer's initiative. Freddie's risk taking and creativity epitomized OSS philosophy. After using it heavily for several months, they surreptitiously returned the vehicle to the motor pool with a paper sign on its windshield: "Thank you and Merry Christmas."

The villa included the Counterfeit and Documentation Department, where the German-Austrian Section created the proper documents to match an agent's cover story. Every detail when inserting an agent behind the lines had to be absolutely perfect, especially the documents. Original, genuine documents were the best; however, in many cases, the department had to fabricate documents to fit an agent's cover story. The devil was in the details: The document creators had to obtain proper paper and ink, they had to age the photos, and they had to insert the appropriate stamps. The wrong watermark or stamp could easily lead to an agent's being arrested and killed. At the villa, the desk employed several expert counterfeiters and forgers.

Using his charm and wit, Freddie convinced the chief document forger inside the villa to make counterfeit quartermaster documents, which authorized him to procure a movie projector and a generator. With electricity and a projector, the men could now watch movies in the villa.

The men also got some rest and relaxation when Lowenstein issued them leave passes. Hans recalls how he spent his leave:

> Luke (my brother) had participated in the Normandy landings and his outfit (with the First Army) remained in Normandy for a while. I had found out where he was located, got a week pass and took off from Bari. I got a ride with some GIs (I was in soldier's uniform as a Sergeant) to Foggia, the big U.S. Air Corps base, and after talking with some of the plane crews they gave me a ride in a bomber to their base in Southern France (I believe it was Montpellier). There was an OSS outfit at that place, and I joined a group which would take me to Paris. We were driven in an fine American car, a Packard!! A chauffeur, next to him an OSS agent, separated by a glass partition and in the back I sat in the middle and on either side of me there were two operators (spies) dressed as Catholic priests. It had snowed heavily and the roads were covered with snow and ice. The chauffeur drove too fast I thought and I was very tense. At 80 km per hour, about fifty miles outside Montpellier, the car was unable to make a sharp curve and headed straight for a tree. I was alert enough to be able to duck underneath the front seat. We crashed. I was stunned but alive.
>
> Two dead and two heavily injured (one man went through the glass partition). After one day in the hospital whereupon I went to

Paris, where I was able to get a jeep and driver (and in this open jeep I arrived in Normandy almost entirely frozen!). However, I saw my brother, but after one day I received an urgent message to return ASAP. I still have a photo of my brother and I, in Normandy!

Lowenstein also sent the two friends on several mock missions to hone their spy craft. One mission involved their posing as German agents wearing Allied uniforms and infiltrating Brindisi Harbor, which was under British control at the time. Given the task of purloining maps of the harbor's defenses, the men got to work quickly. They infiltrated the harbor compound wearing no insignia on their uniforms. Hans Wynberg recalled the incident: "With very strong German accents and no papers, we looked for maps that showed the location of all Allied minefields in the Brindisi and Bari harbors. We found them and offered the sergeant in charge of the maps a bottle of scotch, which he accepted. We walked away from the ports. This was security at its finest in October 1944."

After successfully completing the mock exercise, Mayer and Wynberg's stock rose in Lowenstein's book. German-language proficiency, however, became the central issue as Lowenstein and the others debated whether Mayer's German could pass behind the lines. Lowenstein devised another test: Insert Mayer into a POW cage with captured Germans for three days and see if he could pass as a German soldier. Lowenstein's test was about to begin.

5
---

# INTO THE CAGE

Aversa, Italy, January 1945: A compliment of MPs pushed through the front gate of the stockade and escorted a lone German soldier, Fred Mayer, into the camp. The gray wool uniform Mayer donned kept him warm as they walked among men who had once been the pride of the German war machine: The khaki uniforms of the vaunted Afrikakorps, black tanker jackets of the Panzer battalions, and camouflage tunics of the SS were all included among the motley gaggle of vanquished fighters of the Third Reich. Allied POW Camp 209, nestled in the hills of the Campania region, about nine miles from Naples, now housed thousands of German prisoners. Ironically, Fred Mayer, a Jew dressed as a German officer, now swam in a sea of the Reich's former finest, while family members of the Jewish five suffered unbelievable horrors in camps inside the Reich.

Dressed in MP uniforms, several OSS men escorted Frederick Mayer through the main gate of POW Camp 209. The two MPs turned around after dropping Mayer off in the courtyard, where he mingled with the rest of the prisoners. It was all part of Lowenstein's plan to "get me up-to-date on my German," Mayer later recalled.

In the camp, Mayer was bivouacked in a small tent with two cots. Upon his first day of arrival, a stern-looking German first sergeant laid down the law.

"If you see a British or Amis [American] officer, it is still 'Heil Hitler' around here, got it?"

For the first sergeant and many of the men in the camp, the war was far from over. Still proud and unbroken, the Germans continued to display an ardent Nazi fervor. The first sergeant escorted Mayer into a small tent that, in a twist of fate, would change the course of Fred Mayer's life. Occupying the tent with him was Lt. Franz Weber, and Mayer immediately felt his presence.

Confidant and cool, Franz Weber was no ordinary soldier. He had been born and raised near Innsbruck, the very town slated by Lowenstein for Mayer's future operation. Tall, brown-haired and blue-eyed, the twenty-four-year-old also spoke English and Italian. A veteran of the Wehrmacht's Polish, Russian, and Yugoslavian campaigns, he had served as a company commander and as commandant of Titel, Yugoslavia.

As an officer, Weber always put his men first, exhibiting the German chain of command viewed as a leadership style that bordered on treason. He allowed his men to listen to foreign radio broadcasts, which led to his demotion to platoon leader. Before Mayer, his only interaction with Jews occurred in April 1941 while he was traveling through Poland. He noticed many weak and starving people. When Weber asked a fellow officer about them, the officer rebuffed him sternly and told him that they were merely Jews being transferred to a "camp." While not a Nazi, Weber was certainly a patriot. Following the failed assassination attempt of the Führer in July 1944, the traditional German military salute was replaced with "Heil Hitler!" For Weber, saluting Hitler went too far. He considered himself a soldier first and never a Nazi Party member. Now the trappings of the party seemed to permeate all aspects of military life. In the summer of 1944, he found a way out of the system he despised and sought a way to strike back at it.

For the next three days, Mayer blended into the camp and went about the mundane tasks associated with POW life, sharpening his colloquial

German along the way. More importantly, however, he initiated a close bond with Franz Weber. Slowly, Weber revealed tidbits about his former life. He discussed the Russian front and how "terrible" the fighting had been there. Then, surprisingly, Weber began to tell Mayer how he had come to be a POW and revealed how he had deserted from the German army. He also mentioned that he was from a town called Oberperfuss, located near Innsbruck, Austria. Hesitantly, he stared at Mayer and said, "I am glad that the war is over for the two of us."

Not knowing it at the time, Fred Mayer had happened upon the very man who would facilitate his return into the Third Reich.

On his third day, Mayer was removed from the camp. The entire time he had been a sheep in a wolf's clothing, a Jew impersonating a German soldier. Had his fellow inmates determined his true identity, he could have been killed.

Back at Villa Suppa, Mayer briefed Lowenstein about his stay at the POW camp. He also mentioned his fateful encounter with Weber. He looked Lowenstein square in the eye and said flatly, "I trust him."

Lowenstein heartily agreed that Weber was a potential asset and suggested the Wehrmacht deserter be brought back to Villa Suppa for further vetting. Weber was then escorted to the villa, where he was brought into a room where Mayer was seated. When Weber first spotted Mayer in the room, his jaw hit the floor in surprise. Mayer pressed the German officer further about his background. Weber told him that he had studied law, fought on the Russian front, and was glad to be in Italy as a POW. He then revealed that he came from a family of farmers.

Mayer suddenly asked Franz a direct question. "Are you willing to parachute behind enemy lines with us?"

"Yes," Weber replied without a moment's hesitation.

Wynberg was then introduced to the tall German and soon agreed with Mayer that he was trustworthy. Mayer presented his findings to Lowenstein and Ulmer.

Mayer told them that he trusted Weber and was willing to "risk my life going in with him."

With Weber on board, Lowenstein began to outline the mission's broader goals, while Mayer bore the responsibility for planning most of the operational details. Ulmer tasked the mission with reporting intelligence in the Innsbruck area. An Alpine fortress, or redoubt, where Hitler supposedly planned to make his last stand, was rumored to be hidden in the crags of southern Austria. The importance of the area in Hitler's plan prompted the OSS to send Mayer's team into this region. The team's mission, soon to be code-named Greenup, involved gathering intelligence in the Innsbruck area on everything from the rumored *Alpenfestung* to German jet production. Another key goal involved obtaining intelligence on the rail and road traffic coming in and out of the Brenner Pass, a key mountain pass and thoroughfare linking Austria to Italy. The OSS wanted to know everything about the fortress and all activity in the area.

Rolling up his sleeves, Mayer began crafting the small but important details of Operation Greenup with Lowenstein. Villa Suppa became the operation's proving ground, while the team began to plan the mission and strengthen its bond with Franz Weber and another newly recruited deserter-volunteer named Hermann Matull.

# 6

---

# THE HUSTLER

Three months earlier, on October 1, 1944, Haass and Lowenstein had confidently strode through the POW camp's alleys of canvas tents. They were familiar guests at Allied POW Camp 326, located outside of Naples, but on this day they had a specific mission: to interrogate a German POW highly recommended by one Captain Kolish from the Fifth Army POW cage. They sought candidates from that special breed of men: traitors to the Nazi cause who would turn their backs on their country and return as Allied agents. Lowenstein's German-Austrian Section was cultivating its own pool of deserter-volunteer candidates. Several teams had already recruited DVs, who, when teamed with Americans, proved their worth. They knew best the lay of the land for any mission inside the Reich. On the first day of October, Lowenstein and Haas were in camp to vet their most unique deserter-volunteer, a trained radio operator who also had the necessary survival and radio skills to operate behind the lines alone, without an American handler.

Twenty-six years old, 5'8", with slicked-back dark hair, the handsome, yet edgy, Hermann Matull could have doubled for Lee Harvey Oswald.

Matull made Lowenstein think, hustler. While they didn't know it at the time, the clever, cunning, and brilliant Matull was the perfect spy. And Lowenstein and Haass had proven a way of screening deserter-volunteers and discovering the prime candidates.

Over the previous few months, the OSS duo developed a shtick for vetting DV candidates. They posed as counterintelligence officers trying to find German spies or moles within the camp. They questioned prisoners, testing their loyalty to Hitler and the Nazi Party. If a prisoner was genuinely anti-Nazi, the officers' supposition or accusation that he was a spy provided an opening for a confession of his anti-Nazi beliefs. This was the first step in separating the hardest-core Nazis from those who might actually collaborate with the Allies. Their technique: Lowenstein acted stately and charming, while Haass appeared menacing, tough, and powerful. With mannerisms that mirrored European nobility, Lowenstein carried a cigarette in an upturned hand, while his speech remained graceful and inviting. Lowenstein offered carrots and rewards for cooperation. Lurking in the background, Walter Haass's brutal glare threatened the stick and intimidated the candidates: a classic good cop, bad cop routine. This first set of wickets helped size up potential DVs' motivations and characters. The two would confront a potential candidate and state, point-blank, "You're a German spy." The typical candidate would then express his anti-Nazi sympathies.

Matull had been pulled from the rest of the prisoners and was seated in an interrogation room. Lowenstein did the talking while Haass lurked in the shadows. "Do you know what your people did to my people?" Lowenstein gazed into Matull's beady eyes searching for a reaction. The twenty-six-year-old deserter began to tell his story.

Born in Hamburg, Germany, on December 21, 1918, to middle-class parents with Communist sympathies, Matull joined the Communist Youth Organization at an early age. For three years, he traveled the world on German ships as an assistant radio operator. He remained a rabid anti-Nazi and reluctantly reported for duty as a radio operator when the German navy drafted him in 1937. "Being a sailor and having been abroad, he [did] not like a system of dictatorship." As a sailor, Matull formed strong connections with leftist circles who were "known to help underground people in difficulties with the police." With the onset of the war, the Hamburg native remained an outsider, a rebel. "In December of 1940," he later recalled, "I was accused of a self-inflicted wound, a bullet accidentally shot me in the leg." Accused of cowardice, Matull was shuttled to various German hospitals. The authorities acquitted the young radio operator for "lack of proof"; nevertheless, they administered twenty-one days of punishment for the injury and the appearance of an attempt to evade duty. After he recovered from his wounds, the navy shipped Matull to North Africa, where they assigned him to a ground unit in the Afrikakorps. In the North African desert, Matull's rebellious side rose up again, and he was sentenced to two years for "lowering the morale of troops." Luckily for the young radio operator, the sentence was reduced to six months in prison and, more precariously, three months in a frontline unit tasked with seeking out land mines. To avoid this virtual death sentence, Matull turned to a familiar tactic and soon found himself in the infirmary, having "accidentally" been shot in the hand.

From Tunisia, the wounded German was flown back to Munich where he convalesced in a military hospital for several months. Matull, not eager to return to the horrors of the front, learned to milk his injury for all it was worth. "When released from the hospital, he lived on false papers for three months in Germany, one month in Hamburg, and two months in southern Germany," where he became a black marketeer. Ostensibly, he was now living underground in his own country, where he was able to fade into the woodwork. Ably avoiding detection by the Gestapo and the police, Matull flourished as a black marketeer, while the police were trying to find him as a deserter. If caught and exposed, he would either be shot or placed in another penal unit where he would have an equally short lifespan. He repeatedly dodged the police, until finally, cleverly, he forged his own travel orders and reported back to a hospital in Munich. From there, he was sent to a replacement unit where he obtained a new *Soldbuch* ("pay book") with his real name but a false military history. The Wehrmacht assigned Matull, fake papers in hand, to "probationary battalion Z.B.V. #7," gloriously staffed by "former inmates of prisons [and] concentration camps." Here, he smooth-talked a noncommissioned officer into "[giving] him furlough papers twice a month" to travel back to Hamburg to treat his "wound." Through a stroke of genius, Matull built an extraordinary cover story to support the dummy furlough papers. He also found an Italian doctor who provided him with an ointment that when "applied on his arm [would] make it swell considerably for about a month."

As the oily deserter rambled on, Lowenstein and Haass grew both skeptical of and impressed by Matull's survival skills and ability to move around the Reich undetected. In the story of his past life, and even in the ointment, the interrogators saw the seeds of a plan, one that would include getting Hermann Matull back behind the lines. He was intelligent, confident, streetwise, oily—the ultimate survivor and, therefore, the ultimate agent. Matull passed the vetting process and returned to Bari with Haass and Lowenstein to begin training as an agent. Back at Bari, Lowenstein told Ulmer, "He's a hustler. If he wants to do a mission, let him hustle for the OSS."

The winds of autumn 1944 did not blow favorably for the Germans. The Allies had landed in Normandy and had broken out of the Normandy beaches deep into Holland while pursuing the Germans all the way to the Rhine in the failed Operation Market Garden. In a further setback for the Germans, the Allies had landed in southern France in Operation Dragoon, while they continued their torturous advance up the highly defensible, rocky spine of the Italian peninsula. In the East, Soviet armies were advancing on the very borders of Germany as the Nazis suffered unbelievably heavy losses. The Allies were worried about the Germans "turtling" and sending units into the Alps for a final last-ditch stand. The OSS needed to infiltrate the Alps, the heart of the Reich, in order to understand the area where Hitler was planning to make this final bloody and desperate stand.

# 7

ALPENFESTUNG

Gauleiter Franz Hofer looked down at the typewritten secret report in his hands. The rotund leader of the Nazi Party for the Tyrol-Vorarlberg region knew he had struck gold. Always the opportunist, the forty-three-year-old Nazi was affable, yet pragmatic and power hungry. He immediately recognized the importance of the intelligence in the report and the opportunity it presented for him to enhance his power.

Hofer acquired the report from the Innsbruck security services (the Sicherheitsdienst, or SD), whose electronic eavesdropping had intercepted radio transmissions from the American State Department legation in Berne. The transmissions indicated that the Americans had figured out the Germans were creating a series of fortifications and moving troops into Hofer's Alpine region for a final, last-ditch stand. The State Department had estimated that Nazi Germany would collapse in mid-1945; however, they calculated that if the Germans fortified Austria, especially the region near Innsbruck, the war could be prolonged another six to eight months. Hofer seized upon the idea of creating what the American's feared, an Alpine fortress, and coined the term *Alpenfestung*, or "Alpine Redoubt." In the fall of 1944, he sent a proposal to Martin Bormann, Hitler's secretary, for approval. As a fellow Austrian, as well as one of his Führer's earliest and most ardent supporters, Hofer, through Bormann, had Hitler's ear. The Americans' fears were realized as Hitler soon gave the order to construct what would become the legendary, almost mystical place where Nazi warriors could gather to make one last stand, the Alpine Reboubt.

Hofer had a storied past. An early leader of the nascent Austrian Nazi Party, he put his life on the line for his beliefs. In 1933, serving as Gauleiter, or Nazi Party leader, in the Tyrol-Vorarlberg region, he was imprisoned by the Austrian government for his activities. Four SA men dramatically broke into the prison to free the thirty-one-year-old Hofer and shot their way out. Wounded amid the gunfire, Hofer and the Nazis escaped to Germany, and from a stretcher he addressed the Nazi Party rally at Nuremburg only two weeks after the prison break. The moment is captured on celluloid in Leni Riefenstahl's 1934 classic propaganda film *Triumph of the Will*. After his appearance at Nuremburg, Hofer convalesced in Germany for four years, slowly recovering from his gunshot wounds. Following the German annexation of Austria, he was again appointed Gauleiter of the Tyrol-Vorarlberg region. During the war, Hofer's power in the region grew to enormous proportions, and on September 1, 1940, he was appointed governor of Tyrol-Vorarlberg. Following Italy's capitulation in the summer of 1943, Hofer was chosen to be the Supreme Commissar in the Operation Zone of the Alpine foothills, which included his own *Reichsgau* of Tyrol-Vorarlberg, as well as the neighboring Italian provinces of Belluno, Bolzano-Bozen, and Trento.

Using Innsbruck's natural defenses, Hofer proposed bolstering the city with troops and underground fortifications. As the more immediate crisis of the war diverted resources, Hofer's plan ultimately amounted to nothing more than a scrap of paper. Nevertheless, the Allies picked up intelligence on the proposal, and Joseph Goebbels cleverly exploited their worst fears. He quickly created a special department within the Ministry of Propaganda to use words rather than brick, mortar, troops, and ammunition to convince the allies that tens of thousands of well-equipped SS troops with the latest in German arms were prepared to make the Reich's final stand. But Hofer continued to push his idea toward reality, even in the final days of the war. He flew to Hitler's bunker in Berlin and convinced the Führer to approve an actual preparation plan. For his efforts, he was appointed Reich Defense Commissar of the *Alpenfestung*.

The power-hungry, fanatical Nazi seized upon the opportunity to transform his region into something resembling the Third Reich's Bastille. A consummate politician, Hofer pulled all the diplomatic strings to promote his *Alpenfestung*, a name he had coined. He firmly believed what the American believed: An Alpine Redoubt, complete with fortifications, food stocks, underground factories, and tens of thousands of troops could prolong the war for months and perhaps even force the western Allies to the bargaining table. But Hitler still had reservations: The very idea of defensive warfare and withdrawal was anathema to him. Bormann, in fact, refused to share the plans with Hitler during the ongoing Ardennes offensive for fear of being labeled a defeatist. Nevertheless, planning for the Redoubt tentatively went forward, although not much was ever set in stone.

Despite the fact that the Alpine Redoubt never developed far beyond the planning stage, the Minister for Public Enlightenment and Propaganda, Joseph Goebbels, had brilliantly begun to build up its mythical quality. Although coming in the final months of the war, the Redoubt myth was one of Germany's finest deception coups. Goebbels achieved what concrete and man-hours didn't. He leaked information that elite Nazi units were entering the area, and underground fortresses were being created. German security services leaked more information to the Swiss press, which published detailed maps of Alpine fortresses. And the American press took on the story with earnestness. Western newspapers began to refer to the impregnability of the Alpine region, which included Hitler's retreat at Berchtesgaden. The Germans, the press speculated, had already demonstrated their mastery of mountain warfare in Italy. The *New York Times* ran an article with the ominous headline "Last Fortress of the Nazis":

SS formations are likely to retreat swiftly southward to a region already selected as the last theater of operations in Europe. . . . It will stretch from Lake Constance to the eastern approaches of Graz and Styria with an approximate length of 280 miles and width of 100 miles, a total land area slightly greater than that of Switzerland. . . . It would be relatively easy to defend this fortress "for a very long time" . . . behind the formidable barrier of a giant chain of eastern Alps. . . . The few gaps in the valleys can be sealed with more fortifications and pillboxes dug in the rocks. . . . [There is] little doubt that the Todt Organization is already being used to the limit for that purpose. . . . We can assume that the Nazi command has started hoarding arms, munitions, oil, food, and textiles in a series of depots deep within the alpine quadrangle.

German propaganda added additional nuggets of information to instill fear, stating that V-2 rockets were hidden in Alpine underground facilities.

The OSS also weighed in on the subject. On January 22, Allen Dulles of the OSS station in Berne stated, "The information we get here locally seems to tend more and more towards a withdrawal toward the Austrian Alps with the idea of making a last stand there." Several weeks later he added, "When organized German resistance collapses, there will probably be more than one Reduit [sic] or fortress of Nazi resistance."

Dulles's Swiss sources further confirmed, "Substantial amounts of foodstuffs being collected here and . . . some underground factories are being prepared to supply arms for mountain warfare." Food was considered "the main economic deficiency (of the Redoubt)." OSS nutritionists calculated the amount and type of dietary foodstuffs needed to support the German units in the Redoubt.

The British were fooled as well. Decoded German orders seemed to indicate that all substitute training units were being diverted toward the Redoubt. The OSS later tempered some of these reports to indicate that they were not fully aware of the extent of the preparations; nevertheless,

Gen. Dwight Eisenhower's battle plans were ultimately altered based on Hofer's dream and Goebbels's myth. Ultimately, the Allies changed their objective from Berlin to the Danube Valley, closer to the Alps. Allied commanders agreed: Hitler would be given "no opportunity" to establish the "Redoubt."

In the northern Italian and Tyrol region, OSS intelligence-gathering missions, in particular Mayer's Operation Greenup, now took on epic significance. At the same time, Hofer and the growing security forces under his control tightened their iron grip on security within the redoubt region. The Greenup team was about to be dropped into one of the most heavily fortified areas of Germany.

The man Hofer charged with implementing security measures in the region, the local Gestapo chief, was a career officer known as Friedrich Busch. He was deputy chief of the SD in Innsbruck in charge of counterespionage. Busch's right hand man, who carried out a local reign of terror and was ostensibly known for his own checkered past, was Chief Detective Superintendent (*Kriminalrat*) Walter Güttner. Short, wiry, slovenly, and slothful, Güttner, typically garbed in a single-breasted brown suit, was hardly Robocop. Known as Innsbruck's "bloodhound" and charged with both crushing any Austrian resistance and preventing any Allied infiltrations, he was, in fact, on probation. In his own words, he recalled, "[I spent] seven months in jail for an extended furlough which I took to Bad Schaller, as well as several minor incidents which probably caused me to lose the respect of the SS and Gestapo." He may have lost the respect of a few, but he was feared by many.

Güttner was a bit of a bumbler, but his sadism more than compensated for that shortcoming—as it did for his counterpart further to the south in Bolzano, Maj. August Schiffer. Known to his own men as "the evil genius," forty-two-year-old Schiffer ascended to the height of his power, at least in his own mind, after being on the job as Gestapo chief for six months. In the autumn of 1944, during the first days of his command, the broad-shouldered major lined up his entire staff and stated emphatically, "This headquarters did not accomplish anything to defeat the enemy, and that must be changed!"

Schiffer ran a tight ship and ruled with an iron fist. He killed at the drop of a hat, which earned him the fear and respect of his subordinates. "In several instances where Schiffer's instructions were not executed properly, he threatened his men at the point of a gun to carry out his orders immediately. . . . Without hesitation . . . [he] would have liquidated us," recalled one of his henchman sheepishly.

The Gestapo major mastered the craft of counterinsurgency and utilized human intelligence, informants, and all the other tools of the trade to roll up enemy spies, including several OSS agents, many of whom he personally participated in executing. Furthermore, Schiffer, without any hesitation, sadistically employed torture to elicit the truth from the tight-lipped agents he captured.

The two men, Güttner and Schiffer, working in concert with the other German security forces in the area were making Hofer's Alpine Redoubt "far more tightly controlled than any other part of Europe [including the rest of Germany previously attacked by OSS]." While the plan itself languished, these two Germans instituted some of the terrifying elements of Hofer's scheme.

The severity of their reign and their control of intelligence in the area were made manifest when it was discovered that the Germans had "parachuted [fake Allied agents] into Austria [with the knowledge of Franz Hofer] complete with agent equipment to seek safe houses and friendly contacts in the area." Locals discovered offering help and support "were liquidated. As a result, Austrians were too terrified to offer much assistance to real Allied agents." Even the British intelligence services used only a limited numbers of agents in the area and "never cooperated extensively with the OSS." Fred Mayer, Hans Wynberg, and Franz Weber were about to embark on an impossible operation. The fact that they were Jewish made it a suicide mission.

# 8

OPERATION GREENUP

Mayer pushed the yoke of the *Johnny B* forward, and the nose of the B-24 plunged downward. Breaking all the rules and hardly a qualified pilot, Mayer was having a little bit of fun. As the plane, piloted by Lt. John Billings of the 885th, flew toward Bari's harbor, it also passed over some familiar territory. Mayer, Wynberg, and Franz, as well as the crew of the B-24, could see OSS headquarters below—the Villas Pasquali and Suppa. Utilizing some glider training he'd had as a boy in Germany as well as the training he'd received at Fort Belvoir, where agents were given rudimentary instruction that might enable them to escape, if they had to, in a German plane, Fred gleefully buzzed the villas. Not only was he having a little fun, but he was also venting his frustration. Recently, the Greenup mission had been scrubbed a second time, and he was wondering if he would ever be able to get behind the lines.

Nothing about Greenup was routine. The mission was planned to begin with a flight over potentially flak-filled skies deep into enemy territory. But most challengingly, the plane would have to fly through the canyonlike crags of the Alps and arrive exactly at a pinpoint drop zone where the men would parachute onto a glacier. The slightest deviation to the left or right could have them careening over the side of a sheer cliff or getting their chutes entangled in the rocky fingers of the Alps. Before the use of complex GPS navigational systems, the flight crew had to "drop a pickle in a barrel" from several thousand feet up without electronic navigational aids. Fortunately for Mayer and Greenup, fate provided them with the perfect crew.

"If they're crazy enough to jump, we're crazy enough to fly 'em," quipped Lieutenant Billings.

Already known for flying scores of sorties behind the lines to deliver Allied agents into the Reich, an American covert squadron, the 885th, had agreed to take on the job of dropping Greenup. Utilizing eight modified B-24s and a few B-17s spray-painted a modal flat black and dark green, the unit had carried out numerous covert missions before. One mission involved flying a C-47 deep into Poland to retrieve a gyroscopic guidance mechanism from a crash-landed V-2 rocket recovered by the Polish underground. The squadron also earned the Presidential Unit Citation for action over southern France, where its planes delivered, under heavy flak, over a dozen Allied agents and several tons of arms and ammunition to the resistance before the invasion. Initially, Ulmer had contacted the Royal Air Force, which refused the mission outright, considering it too hazardous.

February 22 marked the second time Greenup had to be scrubbed; the first attempt to drop the team had occurred two days earlier. On the twenty-second, the clouds were too heavy to reveal the frozen lakes and fresh snow, and an unlucky avalanche had hidden the ice-covered bodies of water even more. The targets were impossible to spot from several thousand feet, and the mission again had to be aborted.

Over the past month and a half, Lowenstein and Haass worked overtime with Mayer to get everything ready. Before the mission got off the ground and into the air, the first step was to develop OSS's documentation and cover stories for each of the Greenup team members. Much of the material had to be fabricated and forged by the German-Austrian Section's

Counterfeit and Documentation Department. Frederick Mayer retained his original name since it was considered Germanic enough. To mask his identity as a deserter-volunteer, Franz Weber received two sets of identity papers: One set identified him as Oberleutnant Erich Schmitzer of the Hochgebirgsjäger Battalion Four and the other as an Italian railroad worker by the name of Niccolò Palmezano. Hans Wynberg became Hugh Wynn.

Everything had to be perfect—the documents, the weather, the drop zone, the crew, and even the equipment. Lowenstein and Haass raided the supply room to equip Operation Greenup and took the following items out of storage: fourteen boxes of rations, skis, one British-type hand generator, a Eureka homing beacon (complete with gelatin batteries fully charged), and various weapons. Three containers, each with colored parachutes, held the bulk of the men's equipment. Mayer and Weber each carried leg bags that held their personal items, rucksacks, clothing, food supplies, and even sixty small flashlight batteries for a radio.

The radio was the lifeline of any clandestine mission, allowing the agents to transmit their valuable intelligence back to base and make requests for additional supplies. It was imperative that the messages be coded. Ulmer had prepared a signal scheme for Greenup, which represented the coded radio plan for the mission. It was placed on microfilm, and Mayer and Wynberg were each given a copy. One scheme for alerting the team to be on the lookout for new supply drops used Austrian BBC radio broadcasts. Airing at 7:00 p.m. and 9:45 p.m. GMT, the broadcasts would "usually notify [them] of a drop scheduled for late that night or the following day." The Austrian BBC coded message for Greenup was "Achtung Alice Moll. Florence Nightingale geht Krankenhäuser."

For security reasons, German and Austrian cities in the mission's radius were given pseudonyms: Innsbruck was Brooklyn; Munich, Jersey; Garmisch, Flatbush; Obersalzberg, Bay Ridge; and Switzerland, the Bronx.

For several weeks, Mayer, Lowenstein, and even John Billings and his crew had pored over countless maps and aerial photographs trying to find the perfect drop zone. It was one of the few times during the war when crew and agents bonded; security concerns normally prohibited the agents and crew from getting to know each other, and on a practical level, most missions dropped the agents on the first pass.* Since they were dropping into the Redoubt, they needed to find an area remote enough to escape detection yet near their intended center of operations, Innsbruck. Additionally, they had to walk off the side of an Alpine glacier in chest-deep snow. Freezing to death or falling off the side of a sheer precipice were real possibilities. After days of careful study, the men identified a set of lakes near the Sulztaler Glacier, which rose nearly two miles into the sky at ninety-five hundred feet above sea level.

On February 23, the Greenup team loaded up once again in the *Johnny B*, and after an uneventful flight to the Redoubt, the men crisscrossed the region for two and a half hours. Wrestling with the latch that secured the bottom hatch over the "Joe hole," the men pried it open. It was dark; they couldn't see a thing. Heavy turbulence began jolting the plane back and forth as the men huddled and shivered in the back with the *Johnny B*'s tail gunner. A violent downdraft forced the plane into a freefall, shedding thousands of feet of altitude within seconds. Billings pushed every button and pulled back on all the levers as he fought to keep the plane from crashing into the valley below. Slowly, painfully, the plane began to nose upward.

"Damnit, turn, turn!" the pilot barked as the plane began to stall.

The propeller blasts swirled snow off the nearby trees below. Billings and his copilot stared blankly at the solid rock wall in front of them as they slowly regained just enough altitude to avoid an imminent crash.

The men were now headed toward the heavily fortified Brenner Pass, a hornet's nest of all kinds of flak guns. Mayer wanted to proceed to the drop zone, but John Billings vetoed the idea and decided to return to base. Operation Greenup would have to wait.

––––––––––––––

* On the final mission, Mayer slipped Billings his mailing address, and the two have been lifelong friends.

# 9

___

# OPERATION DEADWOOD

Sometime during the first two weeks of January 1945, a canvas pouch arrived at Lt. Al Ulmer's office in the Villa Suppa. Ulmer regularly received similar pouches carrying secret documents, photos, gadgets—the lifeblood of a spy headquarters—but today's pouch carried something highly unusual. Ulmer gingerly reached in and pulled out a jar labeled "Irritant Ointment" above the word "POISON" stamped in black letters. Ulmer handled the vile cautiously—the last thing he needed was the acidic goo on his bare skin. Known as chrysarobin, the ointment was a witch's brew of iodine, aquaphor, white wax, and a touch of carbonic. Ulmer hoped that the tiny jar held the key to the mystery of Hermann Matull's return to the Reich. It was, after all, Matull's own idea, a scheme he had perfected to evade the Gestapo during his stint as a black marketeer.

Recently snatched from the POW cage by Lowenstein and Haass and incongruously code-named John Mason, Hermann Matull proved himself the German-Austria Section's "most promising candidate." He'd aced a variety of deserter-volunteer spy exercises and recently completed jump training, having shown himself proficient. Matull's jump instructor said this about the Oswald-like deserter, "Mason [a.k.a. Matull] has a high degree of intelligence and was always able to quickly grasp the idea involved in every step of instruction. He was also able to apply his knowledge to the successful completion of all of the training exercises." On the downside, Matull had a loose tongue and a tendency toward showboating: "Easily aroused, and in order to prove his points [he] would often relate revealing experiences from his past." For the OSS, Matull's behavior raised a red flag.

Besides the loose tongue, the twenty-six-year-old spy wannabe had some additional baggage, and during the training, several of his ailments surfaced. He had bad kidneys; when exposed to cold weather for weeks at a time, the organs pained him, and he would pass blood. Fortunately, his wounded hand did not hinder his ability to parachute out of a perfectly good airplane. In fact, his hand, scarred and swollen from his self-inflicted wound of months earlier, was the Trojan horse that Lowenstein and Ulmer hoped would guide their man into Germany.

Ulmer, Lowenstein, and Haass spent the next several weeks working out Matull's mission and cover story. They borrowed freely from his personal history, freshening up tactics he had invented himself and pulled off successfully while surreptitiously operating in Germany's black market. Lowenstein proposed that Matull jump "blind" behind the lines without a reception committee. Inauspiciously dubbing the mission Operation Deadwood, the OSS furnished Matull with papers identifying him with the German Fourth or First Parachute Division, where he would be transferred into a signal battalion within the unit. His wound provided the necessary cover for him to travel from the front lines back into Germany for treatment. As the mission planning progressed, Lowenstein explained to Haass and Ulmer, "It depends on the swelling of the arm, whether Mason [Matull] has to be on emergency furlough or can be an individual transferred from a field hospital to a home hospital. If he gets an emergency furlough, I would suggest his paper reflect that his home was 'totally bombed out with loss of next of kin.'"

The pieces of the puzzle began to come together. Matull would travel into Germany on furlough using his wound as his cover. Essentially the plan called for him to jump blind into northern Italy or perhaps Austria itself. With his chrysarobin-slathered hand and false papers, he would carry packages from soldiers at the front addressed to their families, thereby disguising Deadwood's suitcase-sized mission radio; a couple of packages contained sugar and other confectionaries. While Matull assured the OSS that no one would open the packages, he nevertheless wanted a couple of real ones to ensure believability. Matull would make his way toward Hamburg. Once in the city, he would reestablish his contacts within Hamburg's black market. The entire mission would be cloaked in the secrecy and contacts of the market, already ostensibly a covert operation functioning effectively under the noses of the Gestapo. The black market could hide him in safe houses, create false papers, and even gather intelligence. Matull stressed the power of the market: "The dollar is worth a hundred marks and opens every door."

Once in Hamburg, Matull's first task involved contacting his trusted friend Charley. A crusty, sixty-two-year-old character "completely unfit" for military service, he now acted as a superintendent in one of the city's skyscrapers. The OSS knew about Charley. "[His] intentions were not completely altruistic; he was also motivated by money. He hoped to open a restaurant when the Allies occupied Germany after the war. . . . We told Mason [Matull] we would do what we could for any families who would help him."

Matull's web of contacts stretched beyond Charley to include the owner of a "great butchery store, who was at the same time a meat control official. He was working for the black market in a very clever way using his official capacity as a cover." Matull also maintained contact with a secretary at "a big lawyer's firm in Hamburg," as well as with several noncommissioned officers in the German navy with whom Matull had gone through service schools and who were permanently stationed at German manufacturing plants in Hamburg. They would be able to furnish information on "German shipbuilding and Navy experiments."

Once behind the lines, the spy had several specific missions. OSS wanted him to gather intelligence on train schedules from Munich as well as other military intelligence. Lowenstein elaborated on the plan: "In Hamburg he would contact Charley and send him down to Munich to accept the job as waiter in a restaurant in which he was working previously. Charley would provide for quarters for Mason to follow him. . . . With the help of the black market Mason will be able to travel to almost any town that we would want him to go."

Even before the planning for Operation Deadwood was complete, the operative continued to raise red flags. Labeled a guttersnipe by some and a hustler by Lowenstein, Matull struck Ulmer's boss at higher headquarters as a security risk. He would be going back behind the lines alone, unlike other deserter-volunteers who typically accompanied American agents on a team. OSS would have to give Matull the keys to the security castle: a radio and codes printed on "one-time pads." If Matull willingly turned these over to the Gestapo and worked with them as a double agent, there was risk to the organization.

With the rough outline of a plan in place, Lowenstein and Ulmer moved to the next phase of the mission. The chrysarobin had to be tested, and Matull became the guinea pig. But before the actual experiment took place, in mid-January Ulmer inserted into the Deadwood mission file a CYA (Cover Your Ass) memo:

SUBJECT: scar on Mason's left-hand:

There's a scar on the back of Mason's left hand between the base of the first and second fingers. The scar was caused by a bullet and has left a permanent swelling.

SIGNED ACU.

To test the ointment and outline the poison's side effects, Ulmer consulted Walter T. Carpenter, a major and surgeon attached to OSS headquarters in Italy, who described the toxic goo.

Chrysarobin is an anti-parasitic but also a powerful irritant to the skin. Therapeutically it must be used with caution. It is especially indicated in chronic dermatitis in which the production of an acute inflammatory reaction is sometimes desired. The same reaction could be used to simulate an infection. The skin would also be discolored in parts—brownish. The salve can be supplied. It probably will not cause too acute an inflammation and the inflammation would be local. Chrysarobin is most uncommon and would not be recognized as such. Iodine can cause a burn when applied locally and tightly bandaged. . . . Do not use American gauze. With this memorandum is some of the ointment. This is an extremely strong percentage and should be used with caution.

Ulmer had additional questions for the spy doctor: "How frequently can preparation be reapplied without permanent or serious injury to the member?"

Carpenter responded, "It should be only dermal in character and the worst effect should be scarring."

"How long does the inflammatory reaction last?"

"The duration of the inflammatory reaction depends on the amount applied and the force of application. Frankly, it must be experimented with, as each subject's reaction is different," revealed Carpenter.

Despite OSS headquarters's initial reservations about Matull's trustworthiness, the mission went forward. And a day or so after Ulmer wrote the memos to Carpenter, Matull shuffled into Ulmer's quarters, where he became a guinea pig for the chrysarobin. They expected the antiparasitic ointment to irritate and discolor the skin, making it brownish.

German gauze was even brought in from the supply room to add a realistic effect. The iodine could cause a burn and the desired inflammatory reaction. Matull looked down as the good doctor uncorked the salve and spread it on his scarred hand and forearm. He briefly winced as the German gauze was wrapped carefully around his arm. For several hours, the arm was allowed to marinate in the goo. Dr. Carpenter removed the gauze, and the experiment was a dud: Only a minor rash existed, not the major rash necessary to pass Matull off as a seriously wounded German soldier. Carpenter went back to the drawing board and became an alchemist, mixing various chemicals into a witch's brew. The doctor memorialized the ingredients in a file: "Menthol 0.5, Phenol 3.0, Salicylic Acid 1.5, Petroleum 9330: Will burn skin—poison."

The experiment was conducted once again on Matull, and again it failed. But eventually the salve worked, and Deadwood became operational. Meanwhile, despite previous bad weather and scrubbed missions, Operation Greenup was ready to move forward at full throttle.

# 10

---

# THE JUMP

The *Johnny B* torpedoed through the substratosphere at a cool clip of a 150 miles an hour. The bomber's supercharged, quad twelve hundred horse-power engines roared as the plane plummeted down the mountain range, rushing by snow-capped peaks. John Billings, as he had done many times in the past, skirted disaster as the plane blew powdery snow off the gray crags, while treacherous updrafts from the valley floor threatened to smash the bomber against the canyonlike walls.

Their trajectory took them deep behind German lines in the Austrian Alps, near Innsbruck. Inhaling pure oxygen deeply from their masks, the pilots pushed the yoke forward as the flat black bomber nosed downwards. Using lakes and other landmarks as signposts, the plane approached the drop zone. At 11:45 p.m. the bomber arrived near the glacier, but clouds covered the area, and they were unable to dip into the valley. The pilot turned to the secondary drop zone, six miles south of the original.

"Two minutes to drop zone."

The crisp voice of the copilot rang in the men's ears. Seated in the back of the darkened cigar-shaped interior, the three agents stood by the portal that once housed the B-24s belly turret. After removing a thin plywood cover, all three men would jump through the "Joe hole." Fred gazed down through the aperture, spotting the shadowy outlines of the glacier, their drop zone. His eyes then moved back to his fellow agents, crammed in the rear next to cylindrical containers holding the military hardware needed to complete the mission. The team had equipped itself for any hazards the men might face. The containers held rations and gear, skis and a hand generator. They had even thought to bring some creature comforts: four cartons of cigarettes, a box of cigars, two pounds of tobacco, and packages of condoms. Greenup was prepared for any contingency. Pushing up through the hole, the wind hit Mayer's face. The bomber's engines drowned out jumpmaster Walter Haass's voice as he tried to mouth something to the three men. They moved closer to the hole, seating themselves on the smooth edges with their legs dangling into the frosty darkness. Their hearts raced as they peered through the portal into the inky blackness. Before them lay the greatest adventure of their lives.

Initially, the turbulence was too severe to drop through, so the pilot pulled back on the throttle and lowered the plane's speed to 125 knots. He threaded the plane through the treacherous peaks as the moonlight reflected off the lakes and the gradual slope of the glacier that once again emerged three miles to the south of the plane. The plane cruised at eleven thousand feet, but the icy tundra of the Alps cut the air only one thousand feet below them. His British canvas leg bag tethered to his left ankle by a coiled hemp rope, Mayer looked at Haass. The bag contained the mission's lifeblood: the radio, gold coins, and rations. At around eleven o'clock, Haass tapped Mayer on the shoulder; it was the signal he awaited, and Mayer used his arms as leverage to thrust his body through the hole. He disappeared into the blackness below. Weber looked over to Wynberg and hesitated in the hole for "two or three seconds." Wynberg, stood up behind him and pushed the veteran of the eastern front into the hole. Finally, Wynberg took a step forward and dropped upright directly through the portal.

Mayer looked up as the white silk canopy of his *X*-type parachute mushroomed above him. The canvas harness on his chest snugly gripped his midsection, comforting him in his descent. The resistance of the white silk gently carried him down toward the glacier. Pulling the risers, he softly maneuvered himself toward the icy shelf. Had the crew not been so precise, the team could easily have fallen off the side of the steep precipice. Mayer looked down as the terrain closed in quickly below him. "As I looked around, the jump was beautiful, floating down over those Alpine peaks," recalled Mayer. In seconds his feet and legs plunged into the deep powder, which absorbed the impact of his landing. Ice and rocky crags could break limbs like dry timber. For Mayer, the flakes also served another purpose: "It was so cold in the plane that I was happy to get out, and the snow felt warm."

Hans and Franz landed within one hundred yards of each other. Mayer looked up to see the plane gain altitude, circling around the sheer peaks for another run. Without hesitation, he plunged his fingers into his leg bag and pulled out his homing beacon, flashing the ground signal for "all okay" to the B-24. The pilot guided the belly of the plane toward the glare of the green light. The penetrating glow of Fred's beacon also acted as a natural rallying point for the other team members who had landed nearby.

Scrambling in the back of the fuselage, Walter Haass and the two waist gunners manhandled the bulky supply canisters out of the Joe hole. Haass watched as the chutes deployed and landed on the tablelike glacier. Down below, Mayer kept the green light trained on the plane, even as it was gaining altitude and making its way back toward Italy.

Greenup had pulled off the drop without a hitch.

Mayer thought to himself, Hopefully we were unobserved. The team specifically chose the ninety-five-hundred-foot-high Sulztaler Glacier as its drop zone in the hope that not even a wandering hunter would spot them. Now, the men's first order of business was to get their bearings. It was freezing that night, and the snow was up to their waists, in some cases up to their chests, making a movement forward seem more like crawling than walking. Finding their way would be tough going.

Realizing they probably hadn't been observed, the men went about the difficult business of gathering the drop containers and parachutes. Fumbling through chest-deep snow for four hours, they groped around in the darkness, uncovering all but one container of equipment—the one in which they had packed two pairs of skis. Ideally, they would have found all three sets and could have made their way cross-country down the glacier; instead, they were forced to assemble a crude sled. They hastily buried the parachutes and containers to avoid detection by the Germans.

At around 6 a.m., the pink fingers of first light crept over the top of the glacier. The men resumed their painful odyssey off the side of the mountain. At the bottom of the glacier, they noticed a small valley, which they moved into. It took hours to trundle even a mile. "Ten steps in snow up to our hips, the air that high up was hard to breathe, so we had to rest because we became exhausted quickly," recalled Wynberg. It was still freezing that morning; the sun was bright, and the snow magnified it. The white powder around them created a beautiful holiday-like vista. Instead of vacationing, however, the men struggled to fight the harsh elements as they "virtually had to crawl the whole distance" of two and a half kilometers. Weber, an excellent skier who had skied the area before the war, led the way. After ten hours of painful crawling and trudging through the waist-deep powder, Weber spied a familiar landmark, partially buried in snow, yet still visible from a mile out. The outline of a wooden roof and the lattice of a stone structure jutted out from the endless sea of white. Weber turned to Mayer and Wynberg and identified it as the *Amberger Hütte*.

Built in the 1930s by the Alpine Club to provide shelter to skiers, the hut had been abandoned due to the war. The team trundled over to the stone structure. Weber noticed that the door was locked. The men searched for an opening. Luckily, Weber was able to jimmy open a window, and the team clambered inside. The lodge was quite spacious, containing nearly three dozen beds, blankets, and wood for the fireplace. Hungry, the men searched for food. The remains of some powdered eggs, dough for some bread, and an inviting jar of green tomatoes lay in the cupboard. Famished, Fred twisted the top off the Mason jar, pulled out a couple of the icy treats, and wolfed down the slimy pickled vegetables. Meanwhile, the other men attempted to bake some of the bread. Their culinary skills fell short; the bread was only crust, or as Mayer described it, "hard tack." Mayer soon suffered a stomach ache and diarrhea from the rancid green delights. Freezing, the men cast security concerns to the wind, and believing it highly unlikely for a German patrol or even wandering civilians to stumble upon the place, they built a fire in the hearth. To get over Fred's ailment and to cover their overall exhaustion, they holed up inside the Amberger's comforting stone walls and wool blankets for several days.

Meanwhile, Wynberg pulled out his SSTR-1 suitcase radio, designed by OSS technicians. The forty-four-pound shortwave radio had an operational range of three hundred to a thousand miles. It was absolutely critical to raise OSS headquarters and let them know that the team had survived the jump and was not in German hands. Though Wynberg tried everything to make the set work, nothing got the radio to come online. So he pulled apart the outer case of the radio and started to remove the glass vacuum tubes inside it. They appeared to be unbroken, yet he replaced each one with a spare tube. The last tube in the set got stuck, so he pried it out with his screwdriver. The tube shot into the air. If it landed on the stone floor, all chance of ever contacting base would be lost. Luckily, Wynberg caught the errant tube in midair and nimbly replaced it in the set. Still Wynberg tried repeatedly and unsuccessfully to raise base.

After Mayer had rested and recovered from his ailment, he and Weber set back out onto the glacier to recover some of the equipment they had buried at the ski pole. Wynberg had "succeeded in contriving a makeshift pair of snowshoes out of a metal floor mat." Equipped with the shoes, he helped Weber and Mayer carry Greenup's equipment back to the hut.

The men spent several days in glorious sunshine resting inside the hut. With Mayer recovered from his unpleasant bout with the green tomatoes, the team embarked on its trek. They also "buried their Eureka (a top-secret signaling device), one battery, and rations behind." The bulky Eureka would come in handy later since it was used to guide planes to a drop zone. Weber led the way dressed in his German officer's uniform and snow cape, which identified him as a member of the German Alpine Corps. Wynberg and Mayer trailed behind wearing American ski parkas, which closely resembled Alpine Corps uniforms yet only partially covered their distinctively American olive drab pants. Greenup's cover story was that Weber, a.k.a. Erich Schmitzer, had captured two American pilots and was bringing them into custody. In summertime, it would have been an easy stroll to the nearby mountain village of Gries, Austria; however, it was the middle of winter, and they were on the side of a glacier. The entire trip was perilous. Without a trained guide, they could fall into a crevasse or become snow-blinded by the never ending white panorama.

After six hours of tramping through the waist-deep snow, the team trudged into the tiny hamlet of Gries. Fortunately for Greenup, Weber knew the area like the back of his hand. The team confidently strode up to a house belonging to the town's mayor, a top Nazi Party official. A stout, middle-aged man came to the door. With calm confidence, Weber announced himself: "I am Lieutenant Erich Schmitzer, and I was accidentally detached from my Alpine Corps unit. I need your assistance to get to the bottom of the glacier." He introduced Mayer and Wynberg (with a new cover story) as Dutch collaborators who were also separated from the unit, and they all needed to get back as quickly as possible to Innsbruck.

The mayor rolled out the red carpet. He eagerly gave the team a sled and asked that they return it to a woman at the bottom of the valley when they were done using it. Mayer thought to himself, This looks like Santa Clause's sled. The sled had large, hornlike handles, and the mayor used it to transport goods. They moved the sled toward the edge of a three-mile, serpentine, ice-covered dirt road, which ran down the side of the valley. Part of it even included a perilous thirteen-hundred-foot drop. The men clambered on board the sled with all of their equipment. Franz seated himself at the front, while Hans sat in the middle and Freddie to the rear, the equipment interspersed between the three of them. With one large push, the sled careened down the side of the Sulztal Valley.

Moving down the winding, icy road, the sled hit sixty miles an hour. Luckily, it was being steered by Weber's experienced and steady hand. As they sped down the slope, a bump in the wrong place could have led to a deadly wipe out, and a wrong turn could have sent the team flying over a precipice. The white-knuckle journey was an experience that seared in Mayer's brain like a branding iron. "It was the ride of my life. It was the scariest part of the entire mission," recalled the spy. To guide and slow the sled, they dangled a ski pole out its rear. "I acted as the break man," Mayer remembered. "The tip of the pole glowed red and sparked as we went down the side of the cliff, which was very steep at several points."

About fifteen minutes later, though it seemed "like a three-hour journey," the sled miraculously made it to the bottom of the Sulztal. White as ghosts, Mayer and Wynberg lumbered down off the sled as Weber nonchalantly jumped off the front. Later, Weber described the winding, hair-raising journey as "routine."

Dutifully, the Greenup team returned the sled to a house at the bottom of the glacier. Franz knocked on the door, and a thirty-something Austrian woman appeared, several children not far behind her. Weber regurgitated the same story he had told the mayor earlier, informing the woman that they needed to return to their unit in Innsbruck. With a somewhat startled look, she said, "Come inside. You, of course, can't be partisans." The woman's house smelled like apples, and the men took comfort by the hearth. Offered a meal and invited to stay the night, the team accepted. The wooden walls of the chalet kept the men warm, and Wynberg was enthralled by the children in the house. The Greenup team spent hours playing with the youngsters. Fortunately, the team left the next day without incident and made its way toward Innsbruck.

## 11

THE COUNTERFEIT GAMBIT

Lowenstein eyeballed the man's papers, his *Soldbuch*, which read "Hermann Böckmann, 2nd Battalion Fallschirmjäger Regiment 3" and had Hermann Matull's photo emblazoned on the front. Everything had to be perfect. Lowenstein, the resident expert on the German order of battle knew all too well that even a minor mistake in one of the forged documents could spell capture and ultimately death for the OSS agent. The German-Austrian Section's counterfeit department worked mandatory overtime on the Deadwood mission.

Ideally, the department would use original documents. However, in order to fit a particular cover story, they generally had to fabricate papers, although forging documents was still the last resort. For this exercise in minutiae, the OSS brought out the best, brightest, and most cunning in the field. They employed executives in paper mills and even forgers and counterfeiters sprung from prison. The signature department at the OSS London office even completed a Gestapo pass for one "Wilhelm von Donovan" complete with the general's signature. When they presented him with the expertly crafted pass, Donovan was initially taken aback and wondered how his photo and signature could have fallen into Nazi hands. He later laughed it off when a forger said to him, "Sir, you know what we do here."

The forgers spent their time focusing on the seemingly inconsequential minutiae of fabricating German documents. Even the ink had to be authentic and obtained through an OSS contact in Switzerland who directly acquired it from Nazi firms. Once the documents fit Hermann Matull's cover story, the forgers aged the papers. They burned the edges with sandpaper. A typical aging trick entailed concealing the document under someone's armpit for an hour or two. Everything had to be perfect.

They created a suite of phony documents, which contained a *Soldbuch* bearing the name of Hermann Matull and a *Wehrpass* (war pass)* with the name of Hermann Schüett. Even rubber stamps for "RR control Munich, 2nd Battalion Fallschirmjäger Regiment 3," were laid out on Lowenstein's desk. Things were coming together in the usual manner for the Deadwood mission.

Behind the scenes, it was a different matter. Deadwood was unique because the OSS was sending a single deserter-volunteer agent behind the lines with his own SSTR-1 radio and even "the unbreakable one-time [code] pads." Of greater concern were his loose lips and checkered past, which had raised flags outside the German-Austrian Section. The issue was still roiling the OSS hierarchy: Could Hermann Matull be trusted? What were his motivations? Was it purely money? Would the former black marketeer, once he got behind enemy lines, become a double agent for the Nazis?

Numerous memos touching on the subject of Matull's reliability had crossed Ulmer's desk, and even Colonel Chapin had been advised. At one point Chapin went so far as to send the following message to Ulmer:

---

* The *Wehrpass* was a very comprehensive document issued to all conscripts at the time of negotiation for the military draft and kept by the potential draftee until his induction into the military. When the citizen became a soldier, he turned in his *Wehrpass* and received a *Soldbuch* in exchange, with the *Wehrpass* being turned over and kept at the unit where the owner was serving.

"Talked to Colonel Sloan on Mason [Matull] this afternoon, prospects look dim."

Headquarters also raised the fundamental question of whether obtaining ground intelligence in southern Austria and Germany was even worth their time at such a late stage in the war. To continue vetting Matull, the OSS questioned him further, going so far as to double-check his alleged partisan contacts.

About to explode from the foot dragging, Ulmer wrote a seething memo to OSS's X-2, or counterintelligence group: "Please do not jolly us anymore. As Col. Chapin pointed out in his memo one month ago, we want unequivocal answer with someone taking full responsibility therefore."

Eventually, the long-sought approval came on February 21: "Operation Deadwood has been unconditionally approved by (OSS) Caserta including One-Time-Pads and finances. We are instructed to mount it at soonest." Approval had come "reluctantly and begrudgingly."

With approval in hand and documents prepared, Lowenstein looked for the right drop zone and a crew to fly the mission. Final preparations included dressing Matull fully in his disguise. They raided the German-Austrian Section's supply room and equipped the deserter-volunteer with the following items: "Luftwaffe officer uniform, overcoat Luftwaffe, rucksack, one sweater, three pairs of German army socks, leather belt Luftwaffe." Surreptitiously woven into the mix were a money belt and a small compass.

Hermann Matull would go behind the lines a rich man, carrying $1,000 in five-dollar bills, £10,000, and RM 150. If cash was considered trash, OSS even outfitted Matull with a thousand dollars' worth of gold, including two heavy gold rings stamped "H. M."

Most importantly, OSS gave Matull their highly secret and heavily guarded cipher pad. OSS engineers developed the portable radio transmitter known as the Strategic Services Transmitter-Receiver (SSTR-1), or the "suitcase radio," which became the "standard sender-receiver for all branches in the field." The model operated on 220 to 110 ac or dc commercial power and had a range of several hundred miles. It relied on the dots and dashes of Morse code, which were enciphered in a one-time pad. Portable and easy to learn, the cipher is considered unbreakable, even by today's standards. Two unique, easily concealable rows of numbers and letters were printed on silken cloth. Next, they gave the agent a conversion table and enciphered messages using the pads and then transmitted in Morse code where they were before decrypting back at Headquarters using the one-time pad.

Although the OSS still had lingering doubts about Matull's character, they were ready to launch Operation Deadwood. Then the weather got in the way.

# 12

## TICKET TO RIDE

The smell of fresh-burning embers assaulted the men's nostrils as they looked at the bucolic scenery around them. The candescent, ivory peaks were bathed in the first light of morning; splotches of larch trees broke up the rocky landscape. The worn tires of the truck strained as the vehicle chugged down the icy, serpentine road, thick puffs of black smoke and soot spewing from its stack. Gasoline was precious in the Reich, so many of the natives had converted their vehicles to burn charcoal or wood. This wood burner belonged to a farmer who was making his daily morning delivery into the village of Oetztal Bahnhof over thirteen miles from Laegenfeld. A steamy vapor misted upward from the Greenup trio's mouths as they made small talk and tried to warm themselves next to the furnace in the bed of the truck.

The first light had crept over the mountains as the men hitched a ride. The night before, Weber had been able to arrange for their wheels after giving his familiar story that the men had become separated from their unit and lost their way, thus needed a ride to the train station. Luckily, during the early morning hours, the men didn't encounter any German patrols.

Rather, they saw only the routine of everyday German life—people heading to work and such.

It took over an hour to travel the distance between the hamlets Laengenfeld and Oetztal Bahnhof. As the farmer pulled into the village, Weber thanked him, and the rest of the team clambered out of the back of the truck. The team spied the nearby Oetztal railroad siding; the station was a hub along the rail line that led toward Innsbruck. Several uniformed men milled around the siding. The OSS spies looked at each other and quickly decided not to attempt to purchase tickets at this location. Keeping a low profile, the trio avoided the town and picked up the blackened, creosol-coated timber tracks leading toward Innsbruck. They walked for several miles and for two hours avoided passing trains.

At a nearby town, they purchased tickets to Innsbruck even though they intended to disembark one stop earlier at Inzing; tickets to Innsbruck fit their cover story of rejoining their unit. Weber pulled out several fresh reichsmark notes and paid the clerk for three tickets. They then waited for what seemed like eternity on the platform. Several Germans milled around the station with their children, and the men began joking around with the kids, playing hide-and-seek. Only Weber wore a German uniform; the other two wore the white ski parkas that covered their American uniforms only down to their knees. Several American bombers roared overhead in the distance, and one of the women shook her fist and screamed, "These damned Americans are bombing our cities!" Mayer recalled, "She probably had lost a house to a bombing raid." After two hours, the train finally pulled into the station.

Hooked to the dark, reddish-brown locomotive were several passenger cars. The men of the Greenup team nonchalantly stepped onto a coach car and made their way to the rear, which had an exposed platform enclosed by a guardrail. Rather than seating themselves, the men remained standing. Weber stood in the middle of the platform, while Wynberg stood with his back to the handrail. Mayer stood on the opposite side. This was in keeping with their training: They were ideally positioned in case they needed to jump the enemy and quickly escape. After all the passengers had boarded the train, it barreled down the tracks toward Innsbruck. The first half hour of the journey was uneventful as the men peered up at the Austrian peaks.

Suddenly, two uniformed German noncommissioned officers approached Weber through the door joining the two cars and, looking him straight in the eye, demanded, "Your papers."

Confidently, Weber reached into the pocket of his tunic and pulled out his *Soldbuch*, which had been manufactured by OSS's counterfeit department. The fake *Soldbuch* passed the test, and the two soldiers asked Weber to identify himself and his two white-caped comrades. Convincingly, Weber repeated their cover story of having been separated from their unit. The officers nodded and crossed into the adjoining car, checking the papers of other passengers on the train. With their hearts in their throats, the Greenup team had only a few more miles to travel until they reached their destination; hopefully, the Gestapo wouldn't stand in their way.

Then, the monotony of the ride was again disrupted, this time by three men clad in leather trench coats. They wore the signature attire of the Gestapo. The team now faced imminent death.

As the men strode over to Weber, one of them barked, "Show me your papers!" With nerves of steel and the confidence of a movie star, Weber looked the agent squarely in the eyes and stated, "We've just been checked." Miraculously, the agent blinked, and the three men nodded their acceptance as they moved to the next car. "It was pure luck at [that] point. We were in American uniforms, had our radio and codebooks. If they would have searched our papers, they would have picked us up and it would have been the end of the mission. Franz was a deserter. They would have shot him on the spot. It was all luck." They were lucky then, perhaps; but without luck, the Greenup team was prepared to shoot its way off the train.

# 13

## THE GAME

Greenup had dodged a bullet. After their encounter with the Gestapo, the team disembarked at the Inzing station. Franz Weber reasoned that Inzing would not have the checkpoints that a large city like Innsbruck would have. Once they were off the train, the team made its way toward a nearby pine forest. Finding an abandoned shed on the outskirts of the town of Oberperfuss, they sat down inside, opened their rations, ate, and waited for darkness to fall. After chowing down, they made their way along paths in the forest toward the town as fluffy white flakes of snow hit their faces.

After less than an hour on foot, the men reached Oberperfuss. Located approximately fifteen kilometers west of Innsbruck at the entrance of the wide-open Sellrain Valley, nestled between forests and snowy fields, the cozy hamlet is renowned for its world-class skiing.

Weber knew the paths here very well. After nearly four years of fighting, Weber had finally returned to his hometown. He figured that the best person to introduce him and the team to his family was the former mayor of the town, Koecheles Luis. Luis was anti-Nazi, and the Germans had deposed him after annexing Austria.

Mayer agreed to approach the former mayor in order to get a feel for him. As he crept toward the house, using the forest to hide his movements, he looked up and noticed the full moon illuminating the shadowy outlines of the village. With his heart racing, he stepped out of the forest and moved toward the door of the former mayor's house.

The OSS agent pounded on the door.

A groggy, gray-haired, fifty-something man answered the door, visibly annoyed. With his Swabian dialect, Mayer cautiously stated, "Franz Weber has sent us."

The mayor shot back, "I've never heard of him."

Dumbfounded, Mayer responded, "Are you sure?"

The man nodded in denial. As a final retort, Mayer stated pleadingly, "But aren't you Koecheles Luis?"

The man nodded and closed the door. Defeated, Mayer walked back to the other team members and described what had happened.

Koecheles Luis had good reason to fear for his safety: Nazi agents occasionally impersonated Allied spies in their attempts to discern citizens' loyalties to the Third Reich.

Weber, however, quickly recognized the problem. Mayer had used Franz Weber's formal name; in this region of Austria, individuals were known by the name of their property. Weber told Mayer, "You need to go back and tell him my name is Tomasson Franz and that I'm a friend of yours."

Mayer returned to the former mayor's house, knocked, and announced that Tomasson Franz had sent him. Koecheles Luis's icy demeanor melted away, and he smiled and motioned for Mayer to come in. Mayer signaled the other members of the team to follow him through the door. They were counting on the former mayor's hospitality for the evening.

Inside, they could see there wasn't enough room in the house for them. Luis had been forced to take in several refugees, including a Russian girl, a Yugoslav worker, and a family from Berlin whose house had been destroyed. Despite the crowded lodging, he put Wynberg up for the night and escorted Mayer and Weber a few houses down to the home of Johann Hoertnagl, a trusted anti-Nazi neighbor. After settling in, the men slept on benches in the warmth from the hearth.

Soon, Mayer became intimately acquainted with Johann's sister, Thomas Marie Hoertnagl, and after the first night sleeping on a bench, Mayer found more comfortable accommodations in Thomas Marie's bedroom. He immediately connected with the twenty-something woman, whom he later described as a "typical farmer's daughter," "very sweet and helpful" with long brown hair. She eventually became one of Fred's most trusted confidants.

Forgetting about the team's need for secrecy, Luis went into the town's center to a small guesthouse called Gasthof Krone. A typical Tyrolean Alpine chalet made of large timbers and white stucco, the tiny hotel remains a flourishing business to this day, accommodating skiers attracted to the area's abundant natural snowfall and steep vertical drops. There, Luis informed Franz Weber's fiancée, Anni Niederkircher, whose mother owned the Krone, that Franz had returned.

Anni's mother, Anna Niederkircher, whom Mayer fondly called "Mother Niederkircher," was a "very determined" woman who "made no bones about how much she hated the Nazis." A matriarchal presence in the hamlet, she had enormous influence in village politics.

After learning of Franz's return, Anni ran over to Johann Hoertnagl's house to greet her betrothed after his long absence. They enjoyed a long embrace, they kissed, and then "those two went on their own way."

Over the next couple days, the team moved around, hiding in different safe houses. Mother Niederkircher took Franz Weber in, putting him in a separate annex on the top floor of the Krone. The lodging presented a fair level of danger since itinerant Wehrmacht personnel occupied some of Krone's rooms.

Luis also moved Wynberg to the attic room of one of his neighbors, Herr Schatz, where he stayed for two weeks. Schatz and Luis strung Wynberg's radio antennae between their two homes to make it look like a clothesline.

During his stay, Wynberg was only seen by the Schatz family. Thus, as one might expect, he had time on his hands, which he spent reading a chemistry book and carving a chess set. He also created an underground newspaper with articles titled, for instance, "Roosevelt, Hitler, and the American Way of Life."

On the radio, Wynberg first heard from headquarters on March 7. The following day he was again able to establish contact and sent the following message: "All well. Patience until March 13. Hans."

While the team hid in various safe houses, Mayer designed a courier system of "cutouts." Using a small circle of family and friends, Mayer built a solid set of operatives to support the team. It was vital that the radio operator's whereabouts remain secret. Luis, Thomas Marie, and Anni, Weber's fiancée, were recruited as couriers, as were Weber's two sisters, Eva and Gretel. These individuals carried messages from Mayer to Wynberg, allowing Wynberg to remain hidden.

Eventually Mayer grew tired of being locked up in the Krone. Through the efforts of Thomas Marie, he was able to obtain a partial German officer's uniform. Anni Niederkircher's brother also gave him part of another German uniform. Piecing them together, Mayer created a lieutenant's uniform that carried the insignia of Germany's 106th Alpine. Through a nurse at the local hospital, Mayer obtained phony documents indicating that "he had lost all his credentials in a bandit action while on the road from northern Italy." The document appeared to have been signed by a commandant in northern Italy and stamped by the hospital "saying he had been admitted for treatment." The hospital stamp had been purloined from a friend of Eva Weber who was a nurse there.

Equipped with a phony uniform and phony documents, Mayer "circulated both day and night seeing local people."

After a while, Mayer, a Jew fully decked out in his German uniform, boldly ventured beyond the town into the heart of Innsbruck. Traveling by bicycle, he visited another of Weber's sisters, Louise, who helped him put the finishing touches on his disguise. Milling about Innsbruck, Mayer took note of his surroundings. He observed a "typical city crowd" going about its normal business and a few interspersed soldiers. As head nurse at the hospital in Innsbruck, Louise provided Mayer with papers certifying him as having been wounded in the head, which she bandaged up to complete the disguise.

Staying in the uniform of a German officer for the next three weeks, Mayer began talking to different people in Innsbruck, establishing contacts among the nascent anti-Nazi resistance in the area.

One of the first contacts he established was a village clerk, who in turn introduced him to the leader of the local *Volkssturm* regiment. A unit formed mainly of old men and youths, the *Volkssturm* became the Nazi's last desperate bulwark against the invading Allied forces. From their leader, Mayer gleaned new information, which he sent back via his courier network to Wynberg. On March 22, Wynberg radioed back to OSS headquarters: "Old Dolomite [*sic*] frontier of 1917 is being rebuilt and occupied by *Volkssturm*, already called up in south Tyrol. Source *Volkssturm* leader." Mayer was getting information about Hitler's legendary Alpine Redoubt.

He also met a truck driver named of Walnoefer, a former Nazi Party member who was nonetheless anti-Nazi. Walnoefer introduced Mayer to one Herr Niederwanger, the "self-proclaimed leader of a resistance movement of five hundred men." Naturally suspicious of this claim, Mayer asked Niederwanger to verify the existence of such an organization by destroying a designated antiaircraft battery. The battery was never destroyed, and Mayer had "no further dealings with this man."

However, Walnoefer turned out to be quite a valuable contact because he introduced Mayer to Herr Heiss, an assistant officer in the "Kripo," short for Kriminalpolizei, or criminal police. His unit comprised plainclothes cops who handled crimes like rape, murder, and robbery. Known for their anti-Nazi stance, in one famous incident, Kripo officers attempted to arrest the head of Sachsenhausen concentration camp on charges of sadism.

The only witness to the attempted arrest was murdered, and the Kripo officers were promptly escorted off the camp grounds.

The day after they met, Heiss took Mayer to the "officer of the Kripo," Herr Alois Kuen, the dedicated leader of an anti-Nazi element within the organization. Forming truly extraordinary relationships, Mayer penetrated Germany's vaunted security forces in mere days. The slightly older, stocky Kuen and Mayer hit it off, "becoming good friends" as Mayer later recalled.

Kuen also introduced Mayer to two businessmen, Fritz Moser and his uncle, Robert Moser; both men had ties to the nascent resistance movement in the area. Fritz had been appointed finance representative for a group of Wehrmacht deserters (about fifty) hiding out in a remote Alpine chalet. These men, armed with a wide variety of weapons, from pistols to rifles, were not overly active in the area and mainly focused on avoiding capture or detection. Robert Moser ran a contracting firm for "electrical technicians among foreign workers." Mayer was strengthening his ties to the local resistance. In his most audacious effort, he moved into a rest area for convalescing soldiers, the Offizierskasino. Decked out in German uniform and with his head bandaged, Mayer had placed himself into the very belly of the beast.

## 14

---

# IN THE BELLY OF THE BEAST

Fred Mayer raised the metal stein to his lips and downed a large gulp of ale as he gazed around the beer-hall-like room known as the Offizierskasino. Setting down his drink, he noticed several other wounded men seated around a table. One of them beckoned with his hand: "Come over. Join us." Mayer sauntered over to the group and took a seat at the rectangular mahogany table.

Mayer sat at a VIP table called the *Stammtisch,* reserved for regulars at the Offizierskasino. He had penetrated the inner sanctum of the officers club where wounded German officers convalesced before returning to the front. The Offizierskasino and barracks were an oasis from the horrors of war. The food was remarkably plentiful, and the drink was cheap. Within a couple of months, this entire way of life, along with the Reich, would cease to exist.

"I think they felt sorry for me; my head was bandaged and they saw me alone, so they asked me to join them," Mayer later recalled. An inebriated Austrian captain from the engineer corps dominated a rather raucous night of drinking among convalescing comrades—or so the revelers thought. The German staff had brought the engineer to Berlin to make improvements to Hitler's *Führerbunker* twelve days earlier. The thirty-something captain boastfully painted an amazing scene: He had witnessed a gaunt and haggard Hitler gazing from the balcony of the *Führerbunker* as Allied planes mercilessly pounded the capital of his thousand-year Reich. In his drunken tirade, the Austrian engineer incredulously spouted out technical details regarding the thickness of the bunker's walls, its depth, and its exact location in the heart of Berlin. Round-the-clock Allied bombing raids forced Hitler to live a molelike existence more than thirty feet underground. Remarkably, the captain also described Hitler's state of mind. He looked at everybody in the room and uttered the unthinkable: "Hitler is tired of living." Before he raised his drink and stopped speaking, he jokingly, obtusely remarked that Mayer was a spy.

Brushing off the jab with jaw agape, Mayer was amazed by the tale. He could not believe that the engineer had been so unguarded about revealing the most closely guarded secret of the Reich, Hitler's location. Perhaps even more amazing than the captain's words was what was taking place in the Offizierskasino. Frederick Mayer, a Jewish German refugee who had barely escaped Nazi Germany and emigrated to Brooklyn before the war, was now a U.S. Army sergeant impersonating a German officer. Mayer played the role perfectly. He recalled, "I blended right in and felt like I was one of them."

That evening, Mayer strained to remember all the details of the conversation as he walked back to the officers' barracks in the heart of Innsbruck. After checking into his room, he was greeted by an orderly, who polished his boots and made sure his uniform was pressed and organized. Mayer strained to remember all the details from the conversation as he wrote them on a tablet of paper on March 21:

> 1. Fuhrer HQ is one and a half km southeast of the Zossen Lager rail station/Zossen is at RZ-91/near Berlin, located in a group of five houses parallel and facing each other, with one house length-ways in the center of the east end; Hitler's house is the first one on the southwest end. The houses are built of reinforced concrete, the walls are

one meter thick and the lowest floor is 13 meters underground with four ceilings, each one meter thick, above it; their roofs are steep and camouflaged green, black and white. In the center of the house group is the air-raid warning tower.

2. Hitler is now at the Reichkanzlei, where he meets general of staff [*sic*] nightly at 2200 GMT.

3. Two courier trains [*sic*], each with 24 cars are kept constantly under steam, one at Pehbrueke (2 kms S of Drevitz, R7–63) and one with SS guards at Barhth.

4. Hitler's alternate HQ is not at Obersalzberg (Berchtesgaden) but in Ohrdruf (VJ-15, Thuringia).

5. Hitler is tired of living. He watched the last air raid/prior to March 21/from his balcony; but only the officer's club was hit.

Mayer spent the next week gathering more gems of information from the loose lips of the convalescing Nazi officers. He became the ultimate fly on the wall, picking up tidbits of conversation and crucial intelligence, which he recorded and then couriered back to Wynberg to radio back to base. On March 25, he reported the presence of Italian dictator Benito Mussolini, providing details even down to the hotel the Italian dictator was staying in: "Mussolini reportedly lives in Zurlsarlberg Hotel, Zueushof [*sic*] Zürshof." Mayer also identified another key figure held by the Nazis near Innsbruck, former French premier Eduard Daladier: "Daladier, Schlossitter near Brixlegg, guarded by a company of SS men: source, local teacher."

After exhausting the intelligence potential of the Offizierskasino, Mayer moved on to another of Greenup's missions: obtaining intelligence regarding the rail and road traffic moving from Germany to the Italian front.

THEY DARED RETURN

The Allied air force bombed the route around the clock to limited effect. Real-time human intelligence on the flow of supplies was Mayer's primary mission, and he was about to provide key information that could potentially change the course of the battle on the Italian front.

Through Leo, a black marketer and opportunist he had met weeks earlier, Mayer set up a chain of informants consisting of railroad workers who provided him with intelligence on train schedules as well as the rolling stock and locomotives that pulled into the rail yards at Innsbruck, the most significant terminus before the trains headed into Italy.

Mayer gathered perhaps his most valuable intelligence at the end of March and beginning of April. Decked out as a lieutenant of the 106th Alpine, he strolled into the yard with his bandaged head. The yard was a beehive of activity. Swarms of German soldiers milled about, along with railroad workers who were loading the trains and preparing the tracks. "I blended right in," recalled Mayer. Miraculously, he was lucky enough to walk alongside Innsbruck's yard master. "Oh boy, there's a lot of trains," Mayer said nonchalantly as he walked beside yard master, who wore gray overalls, a sportsman's cap, and a handlebar moustache.

The yard master volunteered, "Wait til tomorrow morning. Assembled at Hall, we have over twenty-six trains, each with thirty to forty cars, loaded with ammo and tanks, that will be leaving April 3 and going straight through the Brenner."

Mayer couldn't believe his ears. In addition, the rail master volunteered information about how the Nazis always managed to repair their bridges after bombings by the Allied air corps. He told the spy that the bridges were collapsible and were stored in tunnels scattered throughout the crags of the Alps during the day to avoid detection by the ever-present Allied fighter bombers. At night they were then rolled out to allow trains to move through the Brenner Pass.

Feverishly, Mayer penned what would be one of his most important intelligence messages: "26 Trains at Hall and at the Hauptbahnhof and Westbahnhof in Innsbruck. They comprise 30 to 40 cars each loaded with tractors, ammo, gasoline, ack-ack guns, light equipment. Leaving [for Italy] April 3 after 2100 GMT via Brenner."

Delighted by the quality of the intelligence, headquarters responded, "15th (Air Force) delighted your 21 [a reference to 26 trains] verified by photos. Heavy op against your target cancelled last minute by weather." Fortuitously, the weather broke, and as the trains rolled toward Italy, the U.S. Army Air Corps destroyed virtually all of them. After the war a source in Eisenhower's headquarters revealed that Mayer's intelligence leading to the destruction of the trains shortened the war in Italy by six months. While the claim cannot be substantiated, twenty-six trainloads full of tanks, ammo, guns, and fuel never reached the Italian front, negatively impacting the German forces ability to continue their struggle.

Additional information flowed to the OSS through Mayer's human intelligence network, which was made up largely of railroad workers and his own on-the-ground sleuthing:

1. Vest station *Ausbesserungswerk* [repair workshop], 150 locomotives are being repaired by 500 workers on a twenty-four-hour schedule.

2. "Main [Train] Station Betriebswerk," 65 locomotives are ready for service.

And later, Mayer passed via courier to Wynberg the following important message: "Average of fourteen trains are assembled nightly between 10:30 [p.m.] an 12:00 [a.m.] in yards right outside Hall." This intelligence contributed to the Allied air force changing its bombing schedule to coordinate with the time that German trains were rolling through Innsbruck. The information provided by a tiny handful of men was having an impact on the war itself.

# 15

## THE ELECTRICIAN

Mayer stared blankly at the radio message from Ulmer. Getting information on German jet production had become one of the OSS's highest priorities. He thought for a minute, How am I gonna pull this one off? Mayer knew he wouldn't be able to go into a jet factory posing as a German officer. He needed a new cover story and disguise. Mayer's natural creativity and daring would now reach new heights of brilliance. He was about to improvise something straight out of a Hollywood script.

Soon, events on the ground presented him with an opportunity. The war was coming to an end, the Reich was falling apart, and Innsbruck was becoming a magnet for displaced foreign workers fleeing the chaos and destruction of advancing armies. One of his established contacts was Robert Moser, an electrical contractor whose firm serviced a nearby jet-production plant. From Moser, he learned about an underground Messerschmitt assembly factory buried deep in the mountains surrounding Kematen. And Moser revealed that not only were foreign workers employed in the mountain facility but more were needed. Mayer decided to create a new identity by becoming one of the mass of displaced workers.

Due to heavy and persistent Allied bombing, the Reich had been forced to move much of its production underground. Germany accomplished this goal on a large scale: Entire factories—and machines—were moved into salt mines, caves, and underground galleries hollowed out of the earth. Thousands of civilians, as well as slave laborers, toiled on the assembly lines to produce the armaments that kept Hitler's war machine running. In Kematen, German engineers had hollowed out the side of a mountain and built an underground factory that produced the ME-262 jet. It was one of the factories the Germans built in the so called Alpine Redoubt. During World War II the ME-262 jet represented the highest level of technology— the equivalent of today's F-117 Stealth Bomber. With a top speed of well over five hundred miles per hour, at least ninety-three miles per hour faster than any Allied aircraft, the ME-262 was well ahead of its time, ushering in the age of the jet fighter. In the hands of experienced Luftwaffe pilots, the plane was deadly. Equipped with four 30 mm cannons embedded in its nose, it had a five-to-one kill ratio over Allied aircraft. Greatly concerned about its capability, the Allies needed to know how many of these jets Germany was producing.

With his classic Jewish chutzpa, Lt. Frederick Mayer became Frederick Mayer, French electrician. Piecing together a disguise from civilian clothes and a dark blue beret, Mayer hung up his German army uniform and donned workaday duds—in later years he fondly remembered, "I definitely looked French"—and set off, once again, to gather important information for the Allies.

To gain access to the plant, Mayer needed new papers, and they had to be legitimate. Audaciously, he waltzed into the labor office in downtown Innsbruck and cued up behind the other displaced workers. Slyly taking advantage of the present chaos in the Reich, he obtained a fresh set of identification papers for one "Frederick Mayer." In broken German, tinged with a fake French accent, he pleaded his case to the local labor official, who soon supplied him with the needed documents. Mayer then bicycled approximately eight miles to the factory.

He inconspicuously ditched his bike and strode toward the large set of double steel doors that guarded a long, tunneled entrance into the plant. After presenting his paperwork to the guards, Mayer made his way down what appeared to be a mineshaft into the heart of the mountain. Walking through a tunnel that opened up into a large gallery, he saw dozens of civilians and slave laborers milling around lathes, hydraulic presses, and other large industrial machinery. As he glanced around one of the massive underground galleries the Germans had hollowed out of solid rock, he noticed an assembly line, which included the partially built fuselages of several ME-262 jet fighters.

Noticeably missing, however, was the noisy hum of production; the line was eerily quiet. Nevertheless, Mayer reported to the foreman, presented his qualifications, and was soon assigned to work in the factory. For the next week, he worked in the machine shop responsible for maintaining the electrical guts of the assembly line. After speaking with some of the workers, he learned that there weren't enough raw materials to complete production, and that, hence, the factory assembly line was idle. Mayer sent this vital information back to Wynberg who keyed in the following message: "Production zero in Messerschmitt-Kematen because of lack of resupply for the past three months. Made parts formerly for assembly plant in Jenbach. Trustworthy worker is source." Mayer contemplated sabotaging some of the machinery, but with the plant idle, he wisely decided it wasn't worth risking the mission and his capture.

# 16

## WHERE THERE WERE NO BORDERS

Franz Weber couldn't believe his eyes when he carefully opened the plain white manila envelope addressed to him. It was as though he had seen a ghost. He was deep behind the lines, secreted away in an attic room in Oberperfuss. Who could have possibly known his whereabouts? As he scanned the text, he noticed the letter was signed with a familiar name: Paul Kröck.

March 1945, Maribor Artillery Barracks, Slovenia.

Paul Kröck dove for cover as he tried to avoid the howling screech of a five-hundred-pound bomb headed directly for him. Miraculously, his life was spared, but the bomb obliterated the barracks in which he had recently been confined. Amid the chaos and confusion, Kröck slipped away into the night.

Kröck, a deserter-volunteer, was a member of the OSS's Operation Dania, along with two of the Jewish five, best friends Alfred Rosenthal and George Gerbner. His code name for the mission was George Mitchell. The

Dania team had as its mission the penetration of southern Austria in the area of Graz (near Kröck's hometown) for the purpose of exploiting clandestine intelligence possibilities. However, the Polish air crew had overshot the intended drop zone to the south by twenty-five miles, and the team landed in very rugged territory.

Gerbner recalls the drop:

> You go out and it seems like an eternity before the parachute opens. The wind from the slip stream hits you like a hammer. As I was parachuting down, I landed in a tree. And instead of an open field, I landed in a steep valley between two snow-capped mountains. I freed myself from the tree and found myself in about six feet of snow. We had snowshoes, but they tore apart after I walked on them [so I] threw them away. I kept going downhill towards the lights of a village. A truck passed by on the road to the village. I heard voices, they weren't German, I figured I was in Slovenia, in northern Yugoslavia. I flashed my flashlight, to signal the other men on the team. All of a sudden, the streetlights went on in the village, I stopped flashing. I assumed that the [Yugoslavian collaborators] must have seen the plane circling the village. So I hightailed it up the mountain several miles from the village. I was climbing as fast as I could, hours seem like minutes.

The Dania mission report summarized the subsequent events:

> Shortly afterwards, Gerbner heard whistles. Descending the mountain, he eventually found Rosenthal in one of the gullies. The meeting occurred about 0430 on 8 February—more than four hours after the drop. The two soldiers again climbed the mountain, in order to have a view of the terrain when daylight broke and to see if Mitchell could be found. As the sun rose, they were huddled in a bush near the peak. They could see men from some nearby farmhouses walking toward the town, and later, six men who they suspected constituted a guard patrol.

With Rosenthal missing gloves from the jump and possessing only an air force escape kit that included a crude map, a small hacksaw, and a tiny compass, they continued searching for Kröck and their supplies. After finding no sign of Kröck, they set out south to attempt to make contact with the partisans. After walking for several days, the men happened upon a peasant family whose son had been killed by the Germans. The family linked them up with a band of local partisans who led them along steep mountain trails for several days until they arrived at Partisan Fourth Zone Headquarters. There they found another OSS team, Mansion, and were finally able to contact OSS headquarters in Bari with their location.

In the meantime, suspended from a tree in his *X*-type parachute, Kröck cut himself free and fell into the four-foot-deep snow uninjured. After twelve hours of attempting to find Gerbner and Rosenthal in the bowels of the dark Slovenian forest into which they had been dropped, he realized he had landed south of his drop zone, in a no-man's-land, or so he thought. The area was ostensibly controlled by Tito's partisans. Unfortunately, Kröck was wearing the wrong uniform—that of a German sergeant.

Kröck immediately headed toward the Drava River, a major landmark with which he was familiar. Crossing the border, he arrived in the southern Austrian border town of Marienberg at the end of the following day. There, dressed in German uniform, he found it rather easy to get around in the heavily garrisoned town. But his luck ran out when he was detained by an SS junior lieutenant named Salmhofer, who was prepared to release him because his papers were in "good shape." In a darkly ironic twist, however, Kröck's luck then took a second turn for the worse as he was leaving Salmhofer's post. A sleigh pulled up containing two Gestapo men looking for a deserter rumored to be in the area.

The Gestapo men hopped out of their sleigh and accosted Kröck. His *Feldwebel* insignia ruled him out as the man they were hunting; nevertheless, the Gestapo men took him to nearby military post.

Kröck's phony German documents didn't hold water: A keen-eyed sergeant noticed that the papers, supposedly from Deutschlandsberg, utilized a circular stamp rather than a square one. Having just been transferred from

Deutschlandsberg, the sergeant knew that all papers from the town were furnished with a square stamp. He called Deutschlandsberg and discovered that the name of the city official on his papers was also phony. Armed with the damning information gleaned from the telephone call, the German sergeant accused Kröck of being a spy. Miraculously, however, the Gestapo did not believe either Kröck or the sergeant. Instead, they believed that Kröck was merely a slacker trying to falsify his documents in order to obtain an unauthorized furlough. Accordingly, the Gestapo escorted him to the city of Maribor, charged him with a relatively minor military offense, and administered a slap on the wrist—light imprisonment in the artillery barracks there.

Like a cat with nine lives, Kröck recovered his luck on the eighth day of his "light" imprisonment. American bombers targeted the barracks where he was held, and avoiding the bombs, he escaped in the ensuing chaos and walked toward his hometown of Frauenthal, Austria, where his wife and family were living. He hid in his own house and in that of his parents, a decision that would nearly prove disastrous for him.

With his house located on the perimeter of an abandoned chemical factory, Kröck was in a veritable wolf's lair. His father, mother, sister, and niece were all ardent Nazis. Additionally, to his utter horror, his sister and niece were "on more intimate terms with SS and Vlasov Cossack troops in the neighborhood than mere political sympathy would seem to indicate was necessary." The two girls were constantly inviting these soldiers into their home, a practice that Kröck wisely understood was "endangering his life."

Needing a way out, Kröck grasped at a straw. He remembered that his old friend and fellow deserter-volunteer, Franz Weber, went to a school in Oberperfuss. He boldly wrote a "vague letter" to the rector of the school Weber once attended "inquiring about Weber's address." Miraculously, considering the devastated state of Germany's infrastructure, the German post office ran like a well-oiled machine. He received a reply a "few days later" from the rector with Weber's old family address.

Upon receiving Kröck's letter, Weber passed it on to Wynberg, who then radioed Bari the good news: "George Mitchell alive and working. Letter contact established."

Ulmer responded the same day to Wynberg and informed him of the fate of the other two members of the team, and of the Jewish five: "George [Gerbner] and Al [Rosenthal] ok too. Will Mitchell join you? We can drop Henry Hague and Cole to him with radio if you send us necessary info."

Kröck's letter eventually allowed him to maintain contact with OSS headquarters throughout the rest of the war, and they were able to extract him from the Russian zone soon after the war ended. The fortunate efficiency of Germany's wartime postal service would eventually result in Kröck's reuniting with the group after the war.

Dania team members Rosenthal and Gerbner, meanwhile, had managed to link up with Tito's partisans by moving from one partisan brigade to another. Surviving multiple ambushes and a German trap, as the Dania mission report describes, "the group decided to affect a crossing of the main road, on which German guards were stationed at 200-meter intervals and a number of units were encamped. Three of the party were able to make a successful dash across the highway, but heavy machine gun fire prevented the Dania team members and an English flight officer from following them. Accordingly, the trio turned back into the hills." The band eventually made its way northwest toward Trieste. At least two of the Jewish five were on their way home, albeit by a circuitous and perilous route.

# 17

# FLY IN THE OINTMENT

With Lowenstein driving like a maniac, the olive-drab jeep bounced and jolted down a winding dirt road into the Italian countryside.

"Hey, Lieutenant Dyno," Matull said, "I want to get to the airfield, not the hospital."

The operative displayed good spirits, considering he was about to jump back into the most brutal police state in history as a traitor. The key figures of the German-Austrian Section were all in the speeding jeep to see him off. Lt. Al Ulmer sat at Lowenstein's side, and OSS jumpmaster Walter Haass was in the back with Matull. They had come a long way to get to this point. Despite his misgivings about Matull, Ulmer had finally received approval to kick off Operation Deadwood. Ulmer looked at the operative.

"Have you forgotten anything?" the lieutenant asked.

Matull grinned. "Yes, a handkerchief."

They soon arrived at the airfield and exited the vehicle. As part of Deadwood's cover story, OSS had provided Matull with a German paratrooper uniform. Inside his pocket was also a tube of the irritant he could apply to the wound he had received on his left hand in North Africa, giving him the appearance of a wounded soldier returning from the hospital to his front-line unit. To ensure he had the proper uniform and insignia, the OSS had outfitted him with false paperwork and raided the German-Austrian Section's equipment room, which was stuffed to the gills with militaria gathered from the battlefield and taken from captured German soldiers—everything from corpse tunics to camouflage German helmets to the proper insignia and decorations worn by the other side. The devil was in the details. Using the wrong pocket litter, for instance, could lead to disaster for an Allied agent behind the lines. With the rest of the quartet standing around him, Matull pulled on the camouflage "striptease" overalls, which were equipped with hidden compartments to store daggers, pistols, and other spy-craft paraphernalia.

Ulmer and Lowenstein bid Haass and Matull farewell as they climbed into the rear hatch of the blackened B-24 Liberator. Experienced with dropping hundreds of agents behind the lines, the intrepid airmen of the top-secret 885th crewed the plane. Matull and Haass were in good hands. At 7:40 p.m. the pilot pulled back the throttle of the B-24, and the twin-row, fourteen-cylinder Pratt & Whitney Wasp engines roared into action. The plane shot down the runway.

Crammed into the back cabin of the plane, Haass looked over at Matull. As the bomber climbed into the sky, the agent remained in good spirits, though the frigid air began to affect him. Haass tried to comfort the freezing man, handing him the clothes from the plane's escape kit.

The B-24 continued toward its destination, a patch of land on the border of Italy and Austria. Matull would drop blind; there would be no reception committee to meet him. He would then make his way north toward Munich, gathering intelligence on German jet production.

After they had been traveling for over two and a half hours, Haass warily looked out the window of the Liberator. The sky was completely clear, the moon not even having yet risen. A moonless night was perfect for parachuting an agent behind the lines. After Haass had double-checked the two target pinpoints, Matull was ready for the jump. "Tell everyone that they are all a nice bunch. . . . In the beginning, I thought you just wanted me to do a job, but now I consider you friends."

For the last several months, Matull had become aware of the air of distrust surrounding him and the mission. He shot Haass one last confident look. "I know you bastards don't trust me, but I am going to prove you wrong."

Peering out into the sky from the Joe hole in the belly of the bomber, Matull gave a final thumbs-up. Since the striptease suit couldn't carry all the critical gear for the mission, Matull held a canvas leg bag, roughly three-quarters the size of a duffle, topped with a hemp rope linking the bag to Matull's ankle. In an ideal jump, as the agent's chute opened, he would drop the leg bag, which would remain tethered about ten feet below his ankle, and both bag and agent would land safely; however, many jumpers' ankles had been bruised by a runaway bag that crashed to the earth, its valuable contents shattered. Once Haass saw Matull disappear into the darkness and the mushroom of his canopy pop open, he quickly dumped the package containing the radio after him.

Matull and his package floated to the earth and landed on a patch of snow atop a mountain ridge seven miles north of the town of Jenbach, Austria. This placed the operative seventeen miles northeast of Innsbruck, not far from Mayer and Wynberg. According to plan, the plane circled the area as the entire crew strained their eyes, attempting to spot the pre-arranged ground signal from Matull's flashlight. Quick "dits" signaled "all okay"; long flashes signaled that something had gone wrong. Haass and the rest of the crew breathed a sigh of relief when they saw Matull that had made it down.

A light scattering of flak and flares glowed in the distance as the plane banked for its return and sped back to Italy. On the ground, Matull buried his chute, rucksack, and suit in a shallow hole he carved out of the snow.

Only two hours after the drop, Matull felt he was being followed. According to the postwar mission summary, "Reports from the area indicated a German garrison in the vicinity likely witnessed the drop." But

Matull finally made his way to Jenbach and took a train to Munich, arriving at 6:30 p.m.

Initially he proved a convincing spy; the authorities checked his papers and found them satisfactory. Realizing the necessity of keeping a low profile, he hustled his way into a "private home" for the evening, all the while wary that he was possibly being tailed.

The next morning, the operative noticed a detail of soldiers following him. He quickly boarded a train to the small German town of Gehrmach, where he boldly stayed in the one place the authorities would never look for him: the *Soldatenheim*, a German army recreation center.* The next morning, he awoke, and to his amazement the same soldiers who had stalked him the day before appeared as though out of thin air. Matull's efforts at evasion had all been for naught; somehow, he sensed, the soldiers were on to him. He then began a long trek south back toward Allied lines in Italy and, more importantly, toward a beautiful and willing acquaintance of his in Milan.

Upon reaching a small hamlet in southern Germany with a railway terminus, Matull boarded a train to Innsbruck. After arriving at the station, he took to the streets, passing an air-raid shelter in which he managed "to hide his radio set which he was carrying on his chest." The operative continued heading south in order "to come back to Italy and then try again." However, his motivations were most likely carnal, for, as he later told authorities, he "planned to blow the money the OSS gave him on a girlfriend in Milan." After getting through the Brenner Pass, which connected Germany with Austria, Matull took a train to Vipiténo and once again decided to spend the night in the one place authorities would not look for him: the barracks of an SS detail. He reasoned that "nobody would have suspected his being there." However, the SS turned him away, and he was referred to the local *Soldatenheim*, where, amazingly, the same group of soldiers he had been evading for the past two days joined him. Stunned, the operative fled and jumped a freight train to Franzensfeste, Italy, near the Brenner Pass.

---

* *Soldatenheim* typically included a library, a bar, and even billiard tables.

In spite of his exceptional guile and a series of near misses, Matull's downfall resulted from a simple mistake: He smoked American cigarettes and lit them with American matches. After he had evaded the local security apparatus of the Third Reich for nearly a week as not only a deserter but a deserter turned American agent, it was remarkable that he tipped the Germans off to his real identity with such a trivial error. Matull was now in the hands of the Gestapo.

# 18

---

# *ALPENFESTUNG?*

In his cramped attic room, Wynberg tapped out the last sentence of Mayer's most audacious proposal to date on his SSTR-1 suitcase radio. For Mayer, an American staff sergeant, the proposal would require all of his underground contacts and relationships and culminate in his most daring coup. He proposed to capture Innsbruck. The message Wynberg sent on behalf of the bold Mayer was simple but direct: "If desired, can take Innsbruck and area ahead of airborne landings. Political prisoners would need five hundred pistols. Details await answer."

His plan was no pipe dream. Kuen, the German Kripo officer whom Mayer met several weeks earlier, would furnish the muscle for the coup by offering to free five hundred political prisoners held in a camp near Kematen. Kuen had also introduced Mayer to a Maj. Warner Heine, a Knight's Cross winner and the officer in charge of the 136th Mountain Reserve Battalion. Heine had offered to place his troops under Mayer's command. The combined force would secure drop zones and other key installations in the Innsbruck area.

According to Mayer, Warner Heine was not so much an anti-Nazi as "someone who saw the handwriting on the wall." Previously, Heine had offered to mine all of the bridges leading into Innsbruck; however, Mayer vetoed this idea since the Allies would need them to capture and secure the area. Mayer instead proposed capturing key drop zones and creating roadblocks ahead of an Allied airborne assault—not a completely unrealistic proposition, considering that the Allies had the Thirteenth Airborne Division as well as other airborne units in reserve.

Mayer's chutzpah-charged scheme never got off the ground. Speculation about the redoubt itself, as well as anticipation that SS, panzer, and parachute formations would act as guerilla groups in southern Germany's highly defensible Redoubt area, contributed to Eisenhower's decision to change the Allied campaign's strategic goal in Europe from capturing Berlin to eliminating Germany's ability to make a final stand in the Alps.

Eisenhower and Army Chief of Staff George Marshall reasoned that there would be no clear-cut surrender. Feeding off Goebbels's propaganda and other intelligence sources, the Allies had gathered evidence suggesting that the Redoubt was filling up with crack troops and supplies. "[These fanatical troops] will have to be taken by the application of or the threat of force. This would lead into a form of Guerilla Warfare, which would require for its suppression, a very large number of troops," wrote Eisenhower.

The entire western offensive was pivoting southward toward the Alpine Redoubt area rather than Berlin. Had Mayer's intelligence on the general weakness of the German defenses in the Redoubt been properly transmitted to the highest levels of Allied headquarters, the course of the entire Allied offensive might have changed.

However, intelligence had painted a mixed picture. Allen Dulles, OSS spy chief in Switzerland and later director of the CIA under Eisenhower, also hedged his bets with conflicting statements. In February 1945 Dulles wrote, "It now seems generally accepted that a delayed defense fortress will lie in the Bavarian and Austrian Alps." Later, on March 3, he stated correctly, "A critical analysis of data received so far it does not appear that the preparations have as yet progressed very far." The very uncertainty of the Redoubt compelled Eisenhower to expect the worst and eliminate the threat before it occurred.

Nevertheless, back at the German-Austrian Section, Lieutenant Ulmer brushed aside Mayer's plan to take Innsbruck. Rather than dismiss the plan altogether, Ulmer attempted to let Mayer down easy by responding, "No airborne landing currently scheduled. If you have top-notch plan, give complete outline to AFHQ, otherwise continue YR [*sic*] intelligence program which G-2 likes."

On the run with the Gestapo breathing down his neck, Mayer hardly had time to craft a full-blown plan to capture Innsbruck through an airborne assault.

Most likely, SS troops stationed in the vicinity could have crushed Mayer's proposed force, comprising the political prisoners and Heine's unit. Even so, a full-strength airborne division dropped into the area would have provoked chaos and potentially cut off supplies traveling from Germany to the Italian front by effectively choking off the Brenner Pass.

Though Chapin and Ulmer ultimately scotched Mayer's plan to take Innsbruck, they agreed on a supply drop nonetheless. They inquired whether Greenup needed an additional radio operator and if they could pass an intelligence team from Mayer's glacier drop zone and utilize his contacts within the nascent Austrian resistance movement to move the team deeper into the Reich. Because of his friendship and close working relationship with Wynberg, Mayer vetoed the additional radio operator but acquiesced to the proposed intelligence teams.

The drop consisted of eight large cylindrical containers, each weighing up to 275 pounds and holding everything from a German contact's camera, pistols, ammunition, a radio, and fifty gold pieces to ten tubes of insulin for a desperate diabetic Nazi who had agreed to work with Mayer in return for access to the life-saving serum. "I don't remember his name, but he was willing to make a deal," recalled Mayer.

Mayer, Wynberg, and Weber, along with Mayer's girlfriend and top agent, Thomas Marie, and several other confederates, making ten in all, assembled at 11:30 p.m. on April 14 to await the first attempt to deliver supplies. As they waited on the side of the mountain with a truck, Mayer looked up into the night sky's inky blackness. The cold mountain air pierced his clothing's thin fabric. Eagerly, they awaited any sign of the plane. A few minutes later, Mayer flipped the black plastic knob of the Eureka Mk III C. Silence. This meant the supply plane was not close to the drop zone. The transponder emitted a radio signal that worked between 214 and 234 megahertz, and the small homing beacon's frequency had a range of about two miles. Correspondingly, the supply plane was equipped with a unit known as the "Rebecca," which honed in on the Eureka's signal when close enough, creating "blips" heard at Morse code intervals.

The plane never arrived. The following night, to hedge his bets in case the plane showed up late, Fred decided to stay at a nearby hotel in Sellrain. While waiting alone near the drop zone, he spied a white flare that illuminated the area. A British intelligence team unknown to Mayer had launched the flare in an attempt to resupply its mission. As a result, the drop zone was compromised. "The whole area was alerted and searched [by the SS and Gestapo] the following day."

Despite SS troops combing the area, Mayer managed to slip back into Innsbruck, where Wynberg informed him that Ulmer had rescheduled the supply drop for Monday, April 16. OSS also indicated that a confirmation code would be broadcast over BBC Radio Austria at 1:45 p.m. on the night of the supply drop. They should expect to hear, "Achtung Alice Moll. Florence Nightingale geht Krankenhäuser."

When Monday finally came, Mayer's ten-man crew once again arrived near the mountaintop drop zone with a truck. Fred made a light show of the drop zone with several lighting beacons: two steady white lights, a blinking white light, and a green light that definitively identified the drop zone as Greenup's. Mayer flipped the switch of the Eureka at 11:00 p.m., the prescribed time for the plane's approach. He heard the faint crackle of the plane's approach. After a few seconds, the contact ceased, and he saw no sign of the plane.

Meanwhile, a thousand feet above and several miles away, Walter Haass circled in a B-24 piloted by the 885th Squadron of the Fifteenth Air Force. Though smoke billowed from the plane's right engine for the entire flight, Haass and crew soldiered on. To his dismay, he made no definitive contact with Mayer's Eureka on the ground. At 1:11 a.m., as the pilot circled over what he thought was the drop zone, the crew saw several lights but could not positively identify the all-important green light. After the sixth pass over the drop zone, the B-24's second engine burst into flames, and the bomber ominously nosed downward toward the formidable crags below. To avoid careening into the mountainside, the pilot ordered all cargo immediately jettisoned to lighten the plane's load. A near panic erupted in the rear fuselage of the Liberator as the men hurriedly tossed seven cylindrical containers into the blackness below.

Unbeknownst to Mayer, the cargo landed on the side of a mountain, miles away from the drop zone. After dumping the containers, the plane continued to lose altitude. Feverishly, Haass attempted to save the radio and its rhomboid-shaped container; however, thirty miles southwest of the drop zone, he had to toss it too. Lighter now, the plane limped safely back to base, but this was not to be Haass's only brush with death.

After returning to Innsbruck empty-handed, Mayer remarkably gained enough authority to order Heine to dispatch two squads of Alpine troops to search the area for the lost cargo. No one found the supply containers until the war was over and the snow had melted. Weber later ended up using some of the parachute material for his fiancée's wedding dress.

Back at base, Ulmer tersely memorialized the drop: "On Greenup resupply, one engine of B-24 burned out."

In the same memo, Ulmer recorded the apparent success of the resupply of another mission: "Dillon mission body and supply drop a success to reception last night." Ulmer couldn't have been more wrong. On April 16, 1945, Bernd Steinitz, the fifth member of the Jewish five, was the "body"

referred to in Ulmer's memo. The air crew had delivered him directly into
the arms of an MP-40-wielding Gestapo reception committee waiting at
the drop zone.*

Somewhat disheartened by the lack of supplies, Mayer returned to what
he did best: gathering intelligence. "Two special trains with Fuehrungstab
(der) Oberst Reichsbehoerden [High-Ranking Operation Staff] left Berlin
April 14, members now in off-limits area, Imsterberg. Eighteen members of
Ministry of Interior in hotel post. Undersecretary of State, Von Bergsdorf
in Garmisch Partenkirchen. Source, copy of secret order."

Next, Mayer delivered a bombshell, claiming that Nazi Germany's second-
highest-ranking official had arrived in the area: "[Heinrich] Himmler arrived with staff, night of 17th in Ingalls near Innsbruck in hotel, Gruberhof.
Three SS divisions expected, but so far, only one regiment, of which Company A is rounding up all politicals [sic] possibly dangerous, source Kripo."
However, while Mayer furnished some excellent intelligence, this source
had failed him. Himmler was still in northern Germany. Nevertheless, it
did appear that some elements of the Nazi hierarchy were moving south
into the phantom redoubt.

Mayer's Kripo contact, Kuen, also provided him with a complete book
of all Gestapo agents in the area. The material was too voluminous to transmit over Wynberg's radio, so Ulmer determined that Mayer should meet
one of Allen Dulles's couriers near the Swiss border. Ulmer devised an elaborate cover plan and code to make the drop, none of which came to
fruition.

Meanwhile, Walter Güttner and August Schiffer were closing in on Fred
Mayer. On the afternoon of April 20, Güttner captured one of Mayer's

---

* Refer to appendixes B and C for the original report of the Dillon Mission.

black market contacts, Leo, and also apprehended Mayer's Kripo contact, Kuen. Through his various underground contacts, Mayer found out that Leo had been apprehended, so he wisely decided to avoid going near the apartment building he had shared with his shadowy contact. That night, Mayer walked down Innsbruck's dimly lit streets toward Weber's sister Gretel's apartment.

# 19

CAPTURED

A gleaming Mercedes command car pulled up along the side of the road in Franzensfeste, Italy. Two muscular SS thugs got out and confidently strolled over to a group of German soldiers holding a noticeably distressed Hermann Matull. They nodded to the troops and then shoved the OSS agent into the back of the command car.

The SS men drove the Mercedes down the winding mountain roads toward Bolzano, Italy. After a short trip, the vehicle pulled up in front of the grey, utilitarian, fortresslike building in the heart of the city known as the Corpo D'Armata. The squat brick-and-stone building, formerly an Italian military headquarters, now housed the Gestapo section tasked with crushing the resistance in northern Italy and part of Austria.

For Heinz Andergassen and Albert Storz, it was regular day on the job as they guided Hermann Matull down a long, dark stone corridor to a nondescript office. After opening the door, the duo greeted their boss, a German officer with tightly cropped black hair and steel grey eyes sitting behind a desk. Remaining seated, he cast a brutal poker-faced glare at Matull and ordered him to sit down. Matull was sitting in the office of notorious Gestapo major August Schiffer.

As Matull obeyed the order to sit, he noted that in the corner next to the officer sat a beautiful brunette with a notepad in hand. When either Matull or Schiffer spoke, she dutifully recorded every word. Known as Christa Roy, the woman was August Schiffer's stenographer and mistress. Referred to around the office as "the queen," she was a "female without feelings . . . [who had] attached herself to Schiffer just . . . so that she could enjoy the trappings that came to her through her boss." Schiffer went to great lengths to satisfy her. More than once, he ordered the arrest of rich Italian women with the sole purpose of acquiring their fur and jewels and bestowing them on the buxom Fräulein.

A professional interrogator, Schiffer seemed to know Matull's background even before the former black marketeer opened his mouth. He furrowed the deep crease in his brow and asked smugly, "Are you also coming from Bari?"

Matull recoiled, responded yes, and gave his alias, Hermann Schuett. He knew that he was in a precarious position—perhaps the most dangerous position of any Allied agent. Considered a traitor, he would be executed if he did not cooperate.

Seemingly pleased with Matull's candor, Schiffer shot him another icy glare: "Do you want to play ball with us?"

Matull knew he had only one option, to consent, and he did so with remarkable confidence. Having limited time to come up with a foolproof cover story for his true mission, he wove a detailed web of believable lies and half-truths. He revealed to Schiffer that he had been sent to develop contacts within the Austrian resistance movement in the Munich area. In reality, his destination was Hamburg, but he was protecting his friends in that city's black market, including Charley.

Matull's web of small prevarications eventually led to his greatest lie. The OSS operative falsely claimed that his true mission was to recruit high-level Gestapo agents to the OSS to fight the Russians after the war. Known for being skeptical and a fact-checker, August Schiffer put Matull through the mill—the torture mill. Not satisfied with Matull's answers even under torture, they eventually hung the young spy by his feet and thrashed him repeatedly. During the beating, Schiffer asked, "Do you know Lieutenant Jewels and what his functions are in school [the OSS spy school]. Teacher?"

Matull's voice cracked as he answered, "I do not know."

"Do you know radio teacher Walter Haass?"

"Do you know King, Foster, Stone?"

Now Matull responded yes. Schiffer then asked, "Where did they go?"

"I don't know."

Schiffer finally laid down his trump card by placing a picture of Matull's parents in front of him. Acidly, he threatened, "If you do not talk, they will be killed."

It's likely that the Gestapo had the family photos of many of Germany's deserters on file. Schiffer continued the grilling, and Matull reiterated that "the mission was not to give targets to the air force, but instead was a long-range political project. [He] want[ed] to form a group of people who would work with the Americans after the war."

He was brilliantly and confidently, despite the torture, giving the answers Schiffer wanted to hear, and soon the Gestapo major began to "loosen control and became very interested in doubling Matull."

With the war drawing to a close, Hermann Matull was slyly offering a ray of hope to Schiffer, who was otherwise a war criminal and would likely face the gallows. One of World War II's greatest liars, Matull fabricated a story so clever that it held water even against one of the war's most notorious and ruthless torturers, as well as one of the Gestapo's best counterinsurgency experts. His tale convinced Schiffer that it would be in his own best interest to "double" Matull and even facilitate his mission.

Schiffer doubled the OSS agent at the point of a gun and played the "radio game," or *Funkspiel*. With Schiffer's gun to his head, Matull was to radio OSS headquarters while the Gestapo carefully controlled his messages. The plan could not go forward, however, until Matull recovered his radio. Shortly after parachuting into the Reich, the operative lost the haversack that held part of the device. Matull knew Schiffer's game, and so he brilliantly fabricated more details for his story. In order to link back up with the OSS, he would go to a certain restaurant in Milan, sit at the table, order two glasses of beer, drink one, and leave the other half full. Next, he would leave an open fountain pen in front of the glasses and wait until his contacts arrived.

Accompanied by Schiffer, Matull first returned to the area where he lost his haversack, which they found. Next, the Gestapo took him to the café that he claimed was his contact point for OSS agents in Milan. No one showed up.

Nevertheless, Matull's lies held up, and Schiffer went forward with his own plan. He assigned one of his men to handle Matull when he went on the air as a double agent. Schiffer also made a phone call to Walter Güttner and informed him than an Allied agent would be operating in the Innsbruck area.

## 20

### THE *KRIMINALRAT*

On the dreary morning of April 20, the Führer's last birthday, Kriminalrat Walter Güttner had reason to be optimistic. He had received a hot tip about illegal operations in Innsbruck. That afternoon, armed with a contingent of men, Güttner followed up on the lead, and the detective and his team burst into Fritz Moser's flat located in the heart of Innsbruck. The *kriminalrat* did not immediately reveal the nature of the arrest. Stunned and caught off guard, Moser allegedly collapsed like a house of cards.

Güttner's men punched and slapped him around for a few minutes. The beating produced results beyond his wildest dreams. "Not knowing under which charge he had been apprehended and after a slight beating [Moser] gave away several addresses."

Moser allegedly revealed much of Mayer's network, including Moser's brother, Robert, Kripo leader Kuen and several other Kripo men, the truck driver Leo, and an American agent.

# 21

---

# DOWNFALL

April 20, 11 p.m. Harsh pounding shook the door of Eva and Gretel's tiny apartment located in the heart of Innsbruck on Schillerstrasse.

Mayer heard men's voices in the hallway of the one-bedroom flat. He shot off the couch, burying his rucksack and .32 caliber pistol underneath a cushion. He looked at the bright embers glowing in the potbellied stove and knew instantly that he must throw the incriminating documents into the fire. He opened the latch and chucked them in. There was pounding at the door. Mayer knew he was in grave danger. As Eva nervously reached for the door, it flew open, and six men, two in plain clothes and the rest in uniform, with MP-40 machine pistols drawn, burst into the room.

"Are you Frederick Mayer?" one of them demanded.

Mayer glanced up.

"Oui."

"At this time I thought they were picking me up because I was not working at the foreign workers' camp," Mayer recalled. "I didn't think they suspected I was an American agent. I decided to play it cool."

A shifty-eyed plainclothes Gestapo agent, thin and wiry and no more than 5'4", came into his view. Mayer thought to himself, He's just a little rat.

"Put on your shoes," the Nazi barked.

With their machine pistols drawn, the agents told Eva to prepare to leave also. The woman pleaded and begged, insisting someone had to watch the children. Initially, the Gestapo did not buy it, but Fred corroborated her story, claiming they had just met at the movie house that evening and that she did not know anything. Fortuitously for Mayer and his team, the Gestapo showed mercy and allowed Eva to stay with the children; shortly after they left, she ran off to Oberperfuss to warn the other two members of the Greenup team. As Mayer was roughly escorted out of the apartment with a machine pistol to his back, he glanced over at the potbellied stove knowing that, had the burning documents reached Nazi hands, they would likely have sealed his death sentence. Despite nerves of steel, Mayer, an American Jew, was now in the custody of the most ruthless police state in history, a state bent on the extermination of his race.

Outside the apartment, Mayer was stuffed into the backseat of a green van that whisked down the darkened streets of Innsbruck to the Gestapo headquarters located in an old cultural building across from the opera. When the vehicle came to a stop in the courtyard, Mayer was let out of the side door and escorted, with the barrel of an MP-40 trained on his head, into an austere interrogation room. The room contained two tables, a bottle of schnapps, and a pitcher of water. Mayer's arrest was part of a series of raids aimed at disrupting the local Austrian resistance movement in the Innsbruck area. Several of his contacts had been picked up, though he did not know this at the time.

In his mind, Mayer still thought that perhaps his captors didn't know he was an American agent. He clung to his story, stating he was merely a French electrician. He knew he needed to buy time in order for Eva to return to Oberperfuss and warn Wynberg and Weber. Politely, confidently, and in French, Mayer answered each question of the interrogation, which was led by Güttner, who now engaged in the age-old game of good cop, bad cop.

Everybody in the room, unbeknownst to Mayer, was "quite jubilant" that they had captured an American agent, so Güttner started the interrogation playing good cop. He focused like a laser on extracting several key pieces of intelligence: "Nationality, landing site, persons who accompanied him, radio operator, place where the sender [radio] was located, and contacts."

The interrogation went on for four hours before Güttner finally revealed his ace in the hole. The door to the room opened and Leo, Mayer's black market contact, entered the room. Rounded up a day earlier by Güttner, Leo had cracked early. He showed no signs of mistreatment.

Looking directly at Mayer, he said, "They know everything. Tell them everything, or they are going to hurt you more."

With a straight face, Mayer stared at Güttner. "I don't know the man."

Leo told Mayer that his associates had confessed, then hung his head as he was escorted out of the room.

Knowing he would no longer be able to maintain the ruse that he was a mere electrician, Mayer decided to change tactics. He claimed to be an American agent who had traveled alone to Austria from Switzerland. Güttner once again searched Mayer, ordering the guards to strip him naked. As they cut his clothing to ribbons in order to find any hidden pockets, their efforts yielded bounty. In his belt, they discovered $600 in gold coins— damning evidence.

Güttner gave the money belt to Friedrich Busch, his superior and chief of the Gestapo in the Innsbruck area. Güttner, Busch, and the other men had been draining the bottle of schnapps the whole night and had begun to lose steam. "I was very tired," Güttner later explained, "having not slept for several days." Nonetheless, Busch insisted they continue the interrogation but shift their tactics from good cop to bad cop. According to Güttner, Busch ordered, "Use extreme measures in your questioning."*

After Busch left the room, Güttner and several of the SS men started slapping Mayer in the face. An SS man by the name of Beringer "hit Mayer

---

* Güttner would later claim that he did not relish his role as "bad cop."

in the face several times and quite strongly." Mayer remembered Beringer as "the tall one."

The abuse continued. And now they believed Mayer to be a Jew. "The more they hit me the less inclined I was to talk," Mayer would later say.

In between the beatings, one of the goons shoved a pistol into Mayer's mouth, breaking his front and back teeth. His genitals were also bloodied during the beating from the use of a cowhide whip. Next, the tall one and the other SS toughs hurled him to the floor and jammed his arms and legs against his body before lifting him like game on a spit. Then they dunked his head in a bucket of water.

"Where is the radio operator?"

"Where is the radio operator?"

Another man held his mouth open, shutting his nose, and poured water down his throat. Mayer had the presence of mind and mental discipline to remain calm and feigned unconsciousness. The tall one lashed him again with a cowhide whip.

"Where is the radio operator?"

A pool of blood grew under Mayer's suspended body.

Suddenly, the door swung open, and several men, including Busch, entered the room. The beating momentarily stopped. Another officer, adorned in full Nazi regalia, exclaimed, "Put him down! He is unconscious."

Two SS guards grabbed the rifle from which Mayer was suspended, lifting his battered, balled-up body from the table and placing him on the ground. His open wounds smarted against the cold stone floor. Through the slit of one swollen and bloodied eye, he spotted the hardened toe of a jack boot about to collide with the instep of his foot. He moved his foot away. The tall one, clearly upset that the beating had stopped, again grabbed the whip to beat Mayer, but the mysterious officer grabbed his arm.

Mayer did not see the first rays of early light seeping through the windows of Innsbruck's Gestapo headquarters since he lay on the cold, damp floor of the unheated cell into which his captors had thrown him, bloodied, beaten, bound at the hands, and naked. The weather was freezing: "It was probably the coldest I had ever been in my life," he would later recall.

Ironically, the freezing cold likely saved him by preventing his wounds from becoming infected. In a random act of kindness, one of the guards, an old man, approached the cell. With pity in his eyes, he reached through the bars and loosened the rope that bound Mayer's hands; then, reaching into his pocket, he drew out and handed to Mayer a handkerchief to wipe his bloody penis. He then gave Mayer half a ham sandwich, but Mayer's teeth were broken, and he could not eat.

## 22
---

# *FUNKSPIEL*

On the bright and sunny day of April 22, Schiffer's command car roared down the only thoroughfare through the Brenner Pass. With Albert Storz at the wheel, SS major August Schiffer rode in the backseat with important cargo at his side, managing to mask his jitters with a veil of self-confidence. At his side, he had his trump card, or so he hoped. With the Reich crumbling around him, yet still an ardent Nazi, he was drawn deeper into Hermann Matull's lie. The SS major had agreed to transfer Matull to the state police bureau in Innsbruck and give him the opportunity to continue controlling his radio game.

After the war, Schiffer described his plan: "It was agreed with Matull that he would organize in Innsbruck a few resistance cells, which, however, I would infiltrate with my own confidants." Schiffer had intended to use thugs Andergassen and Storz for this purpose.

With the approval of his superiors, Schiffer handed Matull over to a Gestapo radio handler and Walter Güttner. They took Matull to the Innsbruck apartment of one Hans Butz, a childhood friend of Schiffer, now also a fellow henchmen. Butz's apartment became a makeshift hideout where Matull would continue the *Funkspiel*. Under Gestapo control, Matull went back on the air. His first messages were broadcasted from Bolzano on April 16 and indicated to headquarters that he was okay. Interestingly, on his third message, his Gestapo handler told him he was free to warn his headquarters that he had been captured. It was all part of Schiffer's plan to curry favor with the OSS, to get in their good graces as the Gestapo agent who would help fight the Russians, which Matull had led him to believe was the focus of OSS activity now. To alert headquarters that he was really under Gestapo control, Matull inserted extra word groups into his messages— something OSS had warned him never to do.

Unfortunately, OSS was asleep at the switch and didn't interpret Matull's message correctly and failed to grasp that he'd been captured. In fact, they sent back a rather upbeat message: "We are proud of you old boy. Bad penny always turns up. Go to Munich fastest, if this is absolutely impossible, proceed immediately to other strategic southern Germany." Believing they would eventually catch on, Matull persisted in inserting extra words into his radio messages. OSS remained clueless to the *Funkspiel*, the same critical error that occurred in the Dillon mission.

While Matull tried to convey his capture to OSS headquarters, Schiffer outlined the details of his own harebrained plan to Matull and Güttner. He would go into hiding in town under the name "Bruder." Matull could get in touch with him through a family in Arzel, and he would be presented to the Americans as a friendly Gestapo agent they had previously been acquainted with named "Leone."

Hitler's Third Reich was in its final days. To the east, the Russian army was fighting in the smoking ruins of Berlin, and American and Russian forces had already met at the Elbe. The Allies had advanced up the spine of Italy and now approached the Alps. And America's Seventh Army, including the 103rd Infantry Division, was advancing on Innsbruck from the west.

Despite the collapse of the Reich, Schiffer was pleased that everything was going according to his plan, or so he thought. He did not know that Matull had a plan of his own, and he could not know that Frederick Mayer did as well. All their plans were fatefully about to converge.

Frederick Mayer, a German refugee of Jewish ancestry who dared to return to the Third Reich as a U.S. spy, was inspired by patriotism to his new adopted country. Behind enemy lines, Mayer impersonated a German officer of the elite 106th Alpine. As the team leader of the OSS's Greenup mission, Mayer's intelligence-gathering efforts resulted in finding the exact location of Hitler's infamous Berlin Führerbunker, and led to the destruction of dozens of Nazi trains. At the end of the war, Mayer personally accepted the surrender of Innsbruck and the thousands of German soldiers who were stationed there. (Fred Mayer)

Fred Mayer flexing his "guns" while attending spy training in Italy. (Fred Mayer)

Hans Wynberg, shown here in a postwar wedding photo, was Greenup's radio operator, whose quick and daring thinking helped Fred Mayer's team on more than one occasion. Like his best friend Mayer, Wynberg was a fellow Jewish refugee. He had escaped the clutches of the Germans before they overran Holland in 1940, yet, with the exception of his twin brother, the Nazis rounded up the rest of his family and sent them to Auschwitz, the infamous extermination camp. (Fred Mayer)

Hermann Matull, a twenty-six-year-old German soldier, conman, and black marketer who became a "deserter-volunteer" for the OSS and dared to return behind the lines on a secret Allied mission, named Operation Deadwood. Codenamed "John Mason," Matull operated as a one-man team—his heroic actions and convincing "lies" profoundly impacted Operation Greenup and Fred Mayer's life. (National Archives)

Franz Weber, an Austrian patriot and German army officer who fought on the Russian Front and in Germany's Polish and Yugoslavian campaigns, renounced the Nazis and became an OSS "deserter-volunteer" agent. He was an important member of Fred Mayer's Greenup team. (National Archives)

Soaking up the spoils of victory, all three members of the Greenup team (Fred Mayer, Hans Wynberg, Franz Weber) pose for the camera in May 1945. (National Archives)

Wartime photo of the area around Greenup's parachute drop zone shows some of the 9,500-foot Sultzer Glacier, located outside Innsbruck, Austria. In a scene similar to the movie *Where Eagles Dare*, Greenup dropped by parachute onto the mile-high-plus mountaintop, landing in chest-deep snow. (Fred Mayer)

Greenup's landing required pinpoint precision—crosswinds and a missed drop meant certain death for the team on the icy crags. (Fred Mayer)

In order to leave the snow-capped peaks of the mountaintop where they landed, Mayer and Greenup made a white-knuckle sled run down the steep side of the glacier on their way to their mission in Innsbruck. (Fred Mayer)

Fred Mayer's Greenup team recruited several local Austrian women to help with the mission, including Thomas Marie Hoertnagle, who became one of Mayer's best local agents, as well as his girlfriend. (Fred Mayer)

Frau Niederkircher (called "Mother Niederkircher") was the matriarch of the small Austrian village of Oberperfuss, and bravely quartered some of Greenup's team at her inn, Krone. (National Archives)

Postwar photo of the Greenup team with some of the local women who risked their lives to shelter the team and act as couriers. (National Archives)

WALTER M P HAASS
PVT

Walter Haass, an expert interrogator in the OSS who helped recruit numerous "deserter-volunteers," was the jumpmaster for countless spy missions. In 1933, Haass' family fled Germany and took up residence on the Belgian-German frontier, where Haass was employed as a "border secretary." In this capacity, he "performed extremely valuable work in maintaining underground contacts." In 1940, Haass immigrated to America and joined the U.S. Army. In 1943 the OSS plucked him from the army. In the final days of the war, Haass miraculously survived a crash-landing of a flak-attacked plane carrying him and his agents to a mission drop-zone site. (National Archives)

Lieutenant Al Ulmer ran the day-to-day operations of OSS's German-Austria Section. The unit was largely staffed by Jewish refugees, who had become naturalized American citizens and vowed to return to the Third Reich in service to their adopted country. (Fred Mayer)

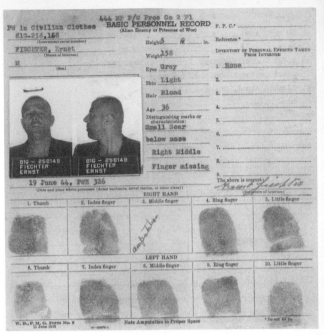

Julio Prester, American citizen-spy who heroically helped save the Dillon mission from death at the hands of the SS. (National Archives)

U.S. Army's personnel record of Ernest Fiechter, a German prisoner of war who became a "deserter-volunteer." Fiechter dropped by parachute into Nazi-occupied Austria with the ill-fated Dillon mission. The mission included another Jewish refugee-turned-spy, Bernd Steinitz, who along with others on the team, was captured by the Gestapo a few weeks after landing. (National Archives)

The drop zone of the Dillon mission. (National Archives)

An inmate of the infamous Mauthausen camp electrocuted on the electrified wire in the camp. The Nazis executed numerous Allied agents within the confines of Mauthausen. (National Archives)

Fred Mayer, eighty-nine years young, is ever the optimist. The former spy chops wood every day, cooks his own meals, and volunteers his time serving hot dinners for the Meals on Wheels program. Looking back on his life, he offers several quips of wisdom: "If you don't risk you don't win"; "Life is about doing your best"; "Control what you can and don't sweat the rest." (Author Photo)

## 23

# GENERAL FRED MAYER

"Do you know an American agent by the name of Fred Mayer?" Güttner pressed his new prisoner, Hermann Matull. Startled, Matull raised his eyebrows, showing signs of recognition.

"I know a Fred from Bari."

Güttner furnished a detailed description of Mayer.

"He's probably the one that I know," Matull stated flatly. "I need some more information, but [you] have made a good catch."

Matull assured Güttner that if shown a picture, he could provide a positive identification. The Gestapo agent said he would return later that evening and left the cell.

Lying on the bare, freezing floor, Mayer slipped in and out of consciousness for several hours only to be awoken by the lanky figure of his tormentor. The shifty-eyed Güttner held a ragged pair of pants and a jacket. He untied Mayer's hands and ordered him to dress. Neither piece of clothing fit, and the rough material irritated his raw wounds. Crimson seeped through the fabric.

To conceal his identity from the other prisoners, Güttner put a raincoat around Mayer's shoulder's and escorted him down the long corridor to a room with a photographer. They placed the hunched figure before the shutter. Snap. The crack and sizzle of the flashbulb startled the weary Mayer, who was then escorted back to his cell.

Güttner returned to Matull with the developed picture and shoved the black-and-white photo of the bruised and battered man into Matull's hands. The Gestapo agent looked him straight in the eyes.

"Do you know this man?"

"Yes, [I] have been together with him in Italy."

With a sudden stroke of genius, Matull concocted a cunning story to add to the web he had already weaved. He would embellish Mayer's stature, painting him as "a 'Big Shot' with the Americans, with a rank of colonel or even general." And, Matull ominously warned Güttner, he and all of them "would all be killed by the Americans if they shot Freddie." Furthermore, he insisted, "Freddie [should] only be interrogated by the Gauleiter personally."

Taking advantage of his tormenter's fear of Allied retribution at the end of the war, Matull had cleverly turned the tables on his captors by implying that the "big shot" operative should be released. Güttner assured Matull that he would take personal responsibility for the prisoner.

Matull's plan was working, and it would dramatically change the course of the Greenup mission. Ironically, a former German soldier's successful manipulation of a fellow German would help ensure the success of a bold and daring Jew—Frederick Mayer. And Matull's lies were soon to become an unforeseen reality.

# 24

## INTO THE HILLS

The blare of an air-raid siren pierced the silence of the dank prison. In a show of remarkable and unusual compassion, the guards rushed the inmates, including Fred Mayer, into the prison's cellar where they would be safer. In the chaos and confusion, Mayer recognized one of his fellow prisoners, Alois Kuen, the Kripo officer who had done so much for the OSS agents. Kuen's arm was in a sling. Though the prisoners were under strict orders not to converse with each other, Kuen whispered to Mayer that a day earlier he had attempted to escape by jumping out a second-story window of the prison, breaking his arm. He had briefly made his way down the dark streets of Innsbruck but could not get far with his injury, and Güttner's men had quickly caught up with him. Mayer also saw Robert Moser, who looked like a dead man walking. Severely beaten, Moser would die from Güttner's torture later that night.

From the preponderance of evidence he had gathered, including Mayer's association with Gretel and Eva, Güttner calculated that Mayer had based his radio operator in Oberperfuss. It is possible that one of the detainees, under sever duress, may have provided information. Armed with this intelligence, Güttner hastily threw together a posse of various police and SS elements. The next morning at the crack of dawn, Güttner and his band forcibly aroused Mayer and threw him into the back of a green lorry destined for Oberperfuss.

Upon arrival in the village, Güttner's crew disembarked and began going from house to house in search of the radio operator. When they reached the home of the farmer who quartered Wynberg, "they found the spare parts for the radio, extra equipment, gold pieces, a chemistry book and three chemistry theses." With the damning articles in hand, the Gestapo investigator interrogated the farmer and his nineteen-year-old son, pressing them for more information. Under his intimidating gaze and facing the barrels of several MP-40s, the young man "lost his nerve and said that he knew Fred, that Hans and Franz had left the night before accompanied by Thomas Marie."

Güttner quickly tracked down Thomas Marie and threatened her with execution on the spot, barking, "Lead us to the radio operator or you will be shot!"

Confronted directly by his girlfriend and top operative, Mayer looked her straight in the eye and winked. The Gestapo didn't catch on. She led them on a fruitless chase around the mountain for about five hours. Güttner later hissed that with "the time that he wasted in telling his lies, [Mayer] was able to warn his comrades and make it possible for them to escape." The search continued in the village, and Güttner further whined that "while Mayer was fed by villagers," he and his patrols "remained without food." Frustrated, Güttner did not arrest any further people in the town and returned to Innsbruck the same night.

That evening, in full defiance of the Gestapo, the village did something truly extraordinary. Organized by Mother Niederkircher, some sympathetic villagers went to the local church and prayed that Frederick Mayer would be delivered from the clutches of the Gestapo. There, in the heart of the Third Reich built around an ideology of racial hatred, Austrian villagers were praying for a Jewish spy.

After Gretel was almost arrested in the apartment and then released, she immediately traveled to Oberperfuss. She could feel her heart pounding against her chest as she raced against the clock to warn Weber and Wynberg about Mayer's capture. First, she stopped at the Krone and found Weber, who immediately rushed over to the safe house where Wynberg had set up the radio operation.

"We don't have much time. Pack everything," Weber blurted to Wynberg after bursting into his attic room.

Quickly the two men packed their radio and most of their belongings into their rucksacks and barreled out the back door. In their haste, Wynberg left behind his beloved chemistry book and some radio parts. They looked up at the sky and saw the moon shining through the wispy, rapidly racing clouds as puffy, fresh snowflakes pelted their faces. Weber knew the trails in this area where he had grown up and wanted to move as quickly as he could to the west. Realizing that Mayer's arrest had taken place in Gretel's home, the two operatives assumed that the SS would soon be in Oberperfuss because of her close ties to the village. Leaving footprints, they could only hope that the falling snow would cover their fresh tracks. As the two ran for their lives, they made their way down winding paths through the thickly forested hills west of Oberperfuss. Fir and larch trees closely lined their route, giving it a tunnel-like feel as they made their way toward the village of Ranggen.

Luckily, Mayor Luis Koecheles knew a farmer who could be trusted and earlier had recommended to the two operatives that in the event of trouble they hide in his hay loft. That night the men took turns posting watch for the SS and the Gestapo patrols, which were combing the area.

"There were only a few moments when I became mildly religious," recalled Wynberg about that night. "One of those moments was when there

was a knock on the door and four uniformed German firemen entered."
Weber and Wynberg had drawn their weapons, and peering through the
cracks, they could see the uniformed men below talking to the farmer.
Adrenaline rushed through their bodies when they placed their fingers on
the metal triggers of their weapons. They were prepared to shoot their way
out. Luckily, the farmer was able to convince the uniformed Germans to
leave. "They were merely part of the German forest service on a routine
patrol. The firemen were merely checking on the facilities [which were]
very vulnerable to fires," recalled Wynberg and were not associated with
the Gestapo or SS.

As Güttner's patrols relentlessly searched the nearby villages and farmhouses throughout the course of the week, Wynberg and Weber remained
in the safety of the loft, right under their noses.

# 25

# THE TABLES ARE TURNED

The heavy metal bars of the cell door clanked open on the sunny afternoon of April 24. Güttner stepped through the entrance along with a mysterious, uniformed Nazi whom Mayer vaguely remembered as the man who stopped the vicious beating he had received days earlier. Bearded and bearing the visible bruises of torture, while wearing only an oversized tunic, pants without underwear, and shoes that didn't fit, Mayer looked up at the two Nazis.

The uniformed Nazi stared back and said, "Follow me."

He escorted the American agent through the halls of the Gestapo headquarters and out to the courtyard to his black BMW convertible, where Franzl, his chauffeur, dutifully waited at the wheel. In the backseat of the convertible, the Nazi told Mayer who he was—Dr. Max Primbs, deputy to Franz Hofer, the Gauleiter of the entire area. With far-reaching and immense power, Hofer's was essentially the governor of the area and controlled its troops and defenses. Primbs then admitted to Mayer that he and several other Germans had admired him for his courage during the three days of torture he had endured.

Mayer placed a glimmer of hope in this individual. Several days earlier during the torture session, it was Primbs who had stopped the beating. Mayer flashed back to a few days before when he had feigned unconsciousness. He learned that not only was Primbs a medical doctor who had known that he was faking, but he was a renowned plastic surgeon, well-known and respected in the region. A small part of Frederick Mayer began to trust Dr. Primbs. While the good doctor was talking, the BMW cruised eastward through the bucolic Alpine countryside toward the small town of Hall. Primbs told Mayer that they were heading toward the Gauleiter's mansion, Lachhof. Within twenty minutes the ride was over, and the black BMW rolled up the winding driveway of the estate. Mayer got out of the car and was escorted by Primbs through the foyer and into a dining area inside the house, filled with several guests.

The doctor told Mayer that he was to meet Franz Hofer, Gauleiter of Tyrol and Vorarlberg. Mayer did not know it at the time, but the meeting would never have taken place had it not been for Matull's brilliant lie convincing the SS that Mayer was a powerful figure in the U.S. military.

As Mayer and Primbs entered the room, the doctor introduced Fred to the entire group: "This is Frederick Mayer. He's an American agent." There they were greeted by the infamous Franz Hofer. Blond with a closely cropped haircut and a chubby face that masked his symmetrical features, the rotund Hofer then introduced his beautiful blond-haired, blue-eyed wife. Next, he introduced Mayer to Rudolph Rahn, the German ambassador to Mussolini's rump state in northern Italy, and several other dignitaries. Rahn approached Mayer, extending his hand and greeting him before introducing the other people in the room. On top of the large fine wooden table in the main dining area was a cornucopia of fine food. Hofer then offered Mayer a seat as the rest of the guests sat down for the meal. A large bowl of soup and a glass of wine were placed in front of Mayer. His stomach ached; he was famished. Over the last several days, he had hardly eaten anything. Nevertheless, after the vicious beating he had just endured, he felt that the food could be a ruse to persuade him to reveal information or possibly even to poison him. While the other guests began to eat, Mayer remained motionless.

Hofer and Primbs looked over at him, and in German reassured him, "It's okay."

Mayer didn't move a muscle. Finally, Hofer came over and plunged his silver spoon into the steaming bowl of broth, took a sip, and smiled at Mayer, reassuring him the food had not been poisoned. Mayer then eyed the crystal goblet of wine. Primbs understood, took a sip, and smiled. The other guests at the table laughingly assured him it was okay. With Mayer's mangled teeth, the best he could hope for was to down some of the soup. Reluctantly, he dipped his spoon into the amber-colored liquid and gingerly sipped the red wine, which tingled the exposed nerves in his teeth.

The men at the table began to discuss the war and eventually touched upon the possibility of Germany's joining the Allies to fight the Russians. Brazenly, Mayer asked how Germany could be trusted after it had broken all of its prior treaties. The table uniformly responded that the Russians were the only real enemy. Privately Mayer sensed a softening of their attitude and felt that he might be able to turn this weakness to his advantage.

As the discussion moved forward, Ambassador Rahn, a thin, distinguished man, rose from the table and reintroduced himself to Mayer, mentioning that he had lived in Los Angeles at one point prior to the war.

He looked at Mayer and said, "I'm going back to Zurich, and I plan on contacting your people and letting them know that you're alive." Somewhat surprised, yet still sensing a trap, Mayer silently nodded. Hesitantly, he agreed to Rahn's suggestion to contact the OSS in Switzerland since it was the only way he knew to get his message out without revealing to the Nazis the whereabouts of Wynberg and the hidden radio.

Over the next hour, the guests continued to dine. Eventually the conversation tapered off, and the dinner came to an end. As a parting gift, Hofer handed Mayer a sausage and a roll of bread, neither of which was much help considering the condition of his teeth. On his way out the door, Rahn reiterated to Mayer that he would deliver the message. In the back of his mind, Mayer wondered if the elaborate dinner was merely a ploy to get him to reveal the location of Wynberg and the Greenup radio. Nonetheless, Rahn was true to his word and delivered the message to the OSS office in Berne, Switzerland, led by Allen Dulles. Dulles then cabled OSS headquarters in Caserta, Italy: "Fred Mayer reports he is in Gestapo hands but cabled 'Don't worry about me, I'm really not bad off.'" It was a remarkable statement coming from a Jew in the hands of the Nazi hierarchy, classic Mayer chutzpah.

Primbs and Mayer got back into the convertible and drove to Innsbruck where Mayer was once again placed behind bars at Gestapo headquarters.


On April 27, Güttner's bellowing voice awakened Mayer in his jail cell. Dropping a bag of cookies into Mayer's lap, Güttner remorsefully explained, "I did not mean to torture you. I was just doing my job."

Mayer's incisors throbbed with pain, the exposed nerves poking through what was left of his cracked enamel. Obviously lacking a sweet tooth and in pain, he placed the bag in the bed.

Güttner then explained that the entire jail in Innsbruck was being evacuated and the inmates moved to another location. Surrounded by armed guards, Mayer was marched out to the courtyard where he was whisked away by car to Reichenau concentration camp. Before departing, Mayer gave the bag of cookies to the old guard who had treated him so kindly.

Reichenau was established in 1941 as a transient camp for the Third Reich's "undesirables." The camp's inmates included many Jews from northern Italy, as well as members of the Austrian resistance who had been captured in recent raids by the Gestapo. Like most concentration camps, Reichenau was the scene of multiple atrocities that occurred on a daily basis. For sport, SS guards forced Jewish women to walk in a circle with sand cupped in their hands and a machine gun trained on them. If any of them dropped even a grain of sand, the SS would open fire. At Reichenau, Mayer found himself bound by the very system he sought to end. He was now a mere number among the millions of Jews and other victims of the Reich.

Güttner and his goons escorted Mayer underneath the wrought iron gateway. As he glanced up, he noticed the words *Arbeit macht frei* ("work shall set you free"). It was not a sign that anyone believed. Rather, it announced a portal to hell; many inmates didn't survive to pass back through. He continued to a room containing multiple rough-hewn wooden bunks stacked up to the ceiling. Mayer sat on the edge of one of the bunks and pondered his fate. He did not linger long, however, in the bowels of Reichenau. Hours after his initial internment, Primbs boldly walked through the iron and barbwire-laced stockade that surrounded the camp, found Mayer, and when questioned by SS guards, curtly replied, "He is in my custody now."

Primbs took Mayer back to the Gauhaus, where he escorted Mayer into his own office, which was next to Hofer's. For the first time since he was picked up by the Gestapo, Mayer was left alone while Primbs dashed out of the office to take care of pressing business. He could have escaped, but Mayer reasoned that he was better off in Primbs's hands than on his own. Shortly after Primbs departed, the phone in the office rang. Without missing a beat and to satisfy his curiosity, Mayer picked up the black Bakelite receiver and placed it to his ear: "Ja?"

The caller on the other line identified himself as a Nazi Party official and was under the impression that he was speaking directly to Dr. Primbs. "Should we open up the doors of our warehouses so that civilians can help themselves?"

"Under no circumstances, we are going to need them later," Mayer barked.

As Fred gently placed the receiver back on its cradle, Primbs sauntered back into the office and asked with surprise, "Who were you speaking to on the phone?"

Mayer relayed the conversation to Primbs, who shot him a devilish look and replied, "That's exactly what I would have said."

On April 30, 1945, Hitler and Eva Braun committed suicide. However, the man Hitler appointed as his successor, Adm. Karl Doenitz, compelled all of Germany to fight on to save the Reich from the Russians. With an air of urgency, Primbs explained to Mayer that Hofer was about to make a radio speech to the population of Innsbruck and the thousands of SS soldiers defending the *Alpenfestung*. He was preparing to gird the defenses as well as implement plans for the "Werewolf movement," an underground insurgency to be led by fanatical SS men and Hitler Youth who would continue the struggle in occupied Germany and Austria. He was going to exhort the population and the troops to make a last-ditch stand for Germany.

Primbs looked directly into Mayer's eyes. "Go talk some sense into him. Make him declare Innsbruck an open city."

Though he was battered and bruised, Mayer confidently pushed his way into Hofer's office, where the Gauleiter was putting the finishing touches on his most important speech yet. The speech drew upon an earlier speech to the German nation by Joseph Goebbels, Reich plenipotentiary and Propaganda Minister:

> Hard times need hard people. Our age is the hardest that mortal men have ever had to face. We have faced setback after setback, but that is no reason to resign and let things take their course. They will not give up if we give up. We face bloodthirsty and revenge-seeking enemies who want to realize their devilish threats if we give them the chance. No one may deceive himself about that. One side wants to deal with the German people through executions and deportations to Siberia, the other to decimate and exterminate us through terror and starvation. It would be foolish to believe it will not be all that bad. It would be even worse than that, should we give it a chance. We therefore consider it our national duty to warn against the danger, and to repeat it even if it becomes boring over time, to make our people aware of an alternative more threatening than ever before that stands before us. When the burdens of this war are finally taken from us, we will devote ourselves to the new tasks of peace. But as long as they rest on our shoulders, we all have but one command: to resist the enemy with silent determination, to resist at any price, not to waver or grow weak, and to hold the flag of our faith all the more firmly the

more it is threatened, the more tattered that holy banner flies through the storms.

Hofer was planning to speak over the radio shortly. With the zeal of a trial lawyer, Mayer appealed to Hofer's pragmatic side as well as his heart. Mayer told Hofer that if the Germans decided to make a last stand, American air power and artillery would flatten Innsbruck. Did Hofer not have any regard for the lives of Innsbruck's civilians? Mayer continued, "Once armored troops break through the mountain passes, Innsbruck will be destroyed. It is insane to order a last-ditch effort. If you love Innsbruck and its people, why destroy it? You haven't got a chance [against American forces]."

Visibly anguished, Hofer hemmed and hawed and searched his soul. His stern disposition suddenly melted away. "I need fair treatment," he responded.

Mayer pounced at the opening and shot back, "I will make you and your staff my prisoners and guarantee your lives."

"You're right," Hofer sheepishly responded.

"I had no authority to take anyone prisoner or guarantee their safety, I just thought it was a good idea," Mayer modestly recalled sixty-three years later.

With Mayer in the room, the Gauleiter got on the radio and made the announcement that Innsbruck was an open city and that forces around it should lay down their weapons. Thousands of SS and regular army troops garrisoned in Innsbruck could have slowed the Allied advance and caused hundreds, if not thousands, of deaths on both sides. The dream of a last stand at the Alpine Redoubt had died. And Mayer's plan to effect the surrender of Innsbruck was becoming a reality.

# 26

## TO THE END

After Hofer departed from his initial script for the radio broadcast and declared Innsbruck an open city, the Nazi governor and Primbs agreed with Mayer's suggestion that Wynberg was critical to getting the message to the Allies that the city of Innsbruck was ready to surrender. Accordingly, Mayer jumped into Primbs's staff car, and they drove to Oberperfuss. Not wanting to implicate any of the Austrian civilians who hid Wynberg, Mayer asked Primbs to remain in the car while he went into a house near the Krone. His first stop, however, was to find Thomas Marie. When he located her, the two embraced, and she took him to Wynberg. She was his top operative and "something much more."

The sun was beginning to set as Franzl drove Mayer and Wynberg in the black BMW toward the mansion Lachhof where Hofer had made his home. The two best friends were together again, but in the most bizarre of situations. After they made their way through the foyer, Wynberg was now treated to dinner with the Hofers. Dr. Primbs, quite disconnected with reality, discussed allowing Mayer to fly his airplane, which sat in a hangar at a nearby airfield. Mayer wisely demurred considering the heavy presence of Allied fighters. Wynberg recalled the scene: "There was high tension. I had trouble putting the spoon up to my lips without shaking. I was twenty-one years old, in front of some of the most powerful Nazis of the Third Reich." Wynberg was not too overawed to recall, "They were fat slobs, all trying to save their own necks."

Before they got to the farmhouse, the group came upon a large automobile overturned in the road. Fred and Hans, the least scared of the group, got out and checked for booby traps before pushing it away.

Also present at the dinner table was Major Alfred von Frauenfeld, former Gauleiter of Vienna. He discussed his postwar plans to write a historical treatise about the fall of the Nazis. All at the table agreed that Mayer somehow needed to get through to the American lines to relay Hofer's message of the pending surrender of Innsbruck. With the sun down, though, it was too dangerous to travel at night. That evening, the group retreated to a farmhouse protected by a police force of fifteen men. The Nazis now feared for their own safety and wanted to place themselves in Mayer and Wynberg's care.

Wearing pieced-together American uniforms, the two spies armed themselves with MP-40 machine pistols. Hofer was the first to retire, while the rest of the party stayed up until dawn debating and arguing the course of the war. Wynberg recalls the surreal discussion: "Why did America have to mix herself up in a completely European affair?" the Germans bizarrely demanded.

The Americans' answer: "[The] word of Hitler meant nothing and *no country* was safe from the aggression of the Nazis."

Still clinging to their own fabricated history, the Nazis responded,

How can you say that we invaded neutral countries? First of all the Poles murdered 60,000 Germans in August, 1939; we have documented proof of that. And when the Führer with his unparalleled vision, destroyed Poland in 28 days and offered peace to the western allies they refused and prepared to attack Germany in the back by invading Norway. The Führer waited all winter hoping for a peaceful settlement but when in the spring of 1940 it became obvious that England was going to use Norway as a springboard for their attacks against Germany, he attacked first and thus forestalled any British attempts. The same [happened in] the Low Countries.

Mayer and Wynberg deftly parried the German arguments, putting them in their proper context and putting the Nazis in their place. Later, Wynberg considered the late-night discussion:

> The remarkable thing about [their] answers is that [they] believed what they said. [Their] faith in Hitler seemed something more than fanatic and was also very noticeable in Hofer and all of his helpers. Until the very end, they claimed that Hitler had been betrayed by his staff and that he died for his country in his fight against Bolshevism. When Hitler died, their will to fight died also.

That night, the Nazis had also hinted at the coming of the Cold War, citing numerous examples of "friction between the Russians and Western Powers." "They kept on warning us of the menace of Russian domination of Europe," recalled Wynberg.

The discussion turned next to the question of Austria itself. Wynberg remembers that "they wanted to know if we had decided to split Greater Germany again into its [pre-1938 components]." The OSS spies assured them that it was the intent of the Allies to re-form an independent Austrian state. The men then asked if the Allies "expected this [independent Austrian] state to act as a buffer against the Russians," then sternly vowed that they were willing to fight on the side of the Allies against the Soviets.

Groggy from a night of spirited debate that would have made most modern talk show hosts squeamish, Mayer awaited a call from an American officer, Colonel Mueller, who was to acknowledge the Gauleiter's capitulation of elements of a German army group, which occupied the entire region.

Lachhof was a beehive of activity as it maintained direct radio and telephone lines with Innsbruck. Without outwardly showing their emotions, the two friends shared a proud moment. In their own small way, two Jews returning to the Third Reich to make a difference had changed the course of World War II. They lingered in the farmhouse until early afternoon when Hofer once again approached the two OSS operatives, emphatically stating his "order of unconditional surrender and his declaration that Innsbruck was an open city."

He had also given an order to save the bridges, public utilities, and airfields, and he told Mayer that the Alpine Redoubt was fantasy. With Hofer having fulfilled his end of the bargain, Mayer assumed command, placing Wynberg in charge of the fifteen-man police guard and the other Nazis, including Hofer, under house arrest. Mayer then boldly set out toward the American lines to relay news of the surrender officially.

## 27

MATULL'S PLIGHT

At noon on April 30, 1945, Storz, Andergassen, and Schiffer left Bolzano. The three Gestapo thugs piled into the black Mercedes and made a one-way trip to Innsbruck. The men wore uniforms but, like chameleons, were ready to change their colors. Schiffer had two pin-stripe suits with him. One was dark blue and single-breasted, with very thin white stripes; the second was gray and double-breasted. He also had two hats, one gray and one black. The Gestapo major was prepared to go underground and wait for the right opportunity to surface and show himself to American troops. As he changed into his single-breasted, blue pin-stripe suit, Maj. August Schiffer, counterinsurgency expert, became the actor known as "Leone." In front of Matull in Hans Butz's apartment located in Innsbruck, he staged a fake argument with Butz, claiming that he wanted nothing to do with the SS or Gestapo and was going over to Matull's side. Schiffer's secretary recalled the scene: "[Schiffer] pass[ed] over to Matull's side. . . . Matull was to be convinced that Schiffer had completely changed his mind and that he wanted nothing to do with the SS, the police or the entire Nazi clique."

Always one step ahead, Matull saw through Schiffer's phony guise. The final nail in the coffin came when Matull received the following radio message from Bari: "Stop all further activities and await the occupation by American troops."

The following day, Matull met with Schiffer, but this time instead of a fake argument, it was a shakedown. "How much U.S. money and gold do you have?" Schiffer glared at Matull.

Matull took off his hidden money belt, which contained gold coins and American dollars. Still believing that Matull could serve as a bridge to the Americans, Schiffer allowed him to keep a "small sum." Ever the micromanager with a high attention to detail, Schiffer then said, "You should tell the Americans that you used [the money] up."

As he was leaving, Schiffer handed Matull a "small, closed package containing money and some personal items," then left the room for the last time. Matull craned his neck and barely heard Schiffer mention to Güttner in an adjacent room where he was going to go into hiding, a suburb of Innsbruck called Mühlau. Under questioning, Schiffer later elaborated:

> I drove April 30, 1945, with Andergassen and Storz, to Innsbruck and also wanted Hans Butz to join us there the following day. . . . I had in my possession documents made out in the name of Emil Bruder and . . . for the time being I was using this name. I had given Matull, as late as April 30, 1945, the opportunity to communicate with his base in Bari from the apartment of Hans Butz in Innsbruck. . . . From Bari, he received the order to stop all further activities and to await the occupation by American troops. Thereafter I had the feeling that Matull did not agree with my plans any more and that he wanted to follow his own plans.

28

—

# THE SURRENDER
# OF INNSBRUCK

Armed with an MP-40, Mayer told Primbs he was setting out toward Allied lines to alert them that Innsbruck was an open city and Hofer had essentially surrendered. Mayer requisitioned Primbs's official car and chauffeur, Franzl, and unfurled a white bed sheet, which he hoped would be recognized as a flag of truce as he made his way toward American lines.

Puffy-faced but victorious, Fred Mayer felt the wind hit his face as he drove down the verdant winding roads toward the American lines to the west, avoiding several overturned cars that partially blocked the road. He also spied pockets of still belligerent German SS troops manning flak positions and areas favorable for launching insurgency ambushes. Using the code name "Werewolves," these die-hard Nazis were ready to fight to the death.*

---

* In the late summer to early autumn of 1944, with Allied armies closing in from the west and the Soviet juggernaut advancing from the east, Himmler ordered SS Obergruppenführer Hans-Adolf Prützmann to begin organizing an elite troop of volunteer forces to operate secretly behind enemy lines, disrupt the Allied occupation

The journey was made perilous by strafing American planes prowling the skies above the road looking for targets and American and German ground units looking to open fire at any time on the enemy. After about twenty minutes on the road, Mayer noticed an American outpost and what seemed to be an MP standing guard. Fortunately, the American did not fire at the car, recognizing the flag of truce. Wearing the blood-stained and tattered remains of a standard olive drab GI shirt for his uniform, a pair of oversized trousers, and shoes that didn't fit, Mayer confidently sauntered over to the American outpost, white flag in hand. He then asked for the officer in charge and requested to speak with the division intelligence officer. A small contingent of American soldiers gathered around the spy from Brooklyn. They noticed his face was bruised and battered. Someone chimed in, "How'd you get your face smashed in?"

Mayer chuckled, "Hit by Gestapo, truck, I think."

An officer arrived and used a field phone to call the 103rd Division headquarters. Maj. Bland West from Norman, Oklahoma, arrived on the scene shortly thereafter. The 103rd was the tip of the spear for Gen. Alexander Patch's Seventh Army pushing east toward Innsbruck. The "Cactus" division was led by Maj. Gen. Anthony C. McAuliffe, who had become famous at Bastogne for replying, "Nuts," to a German request for surrender during the Battle of the Bulge. West did not even know about the OSS, so

---

of Europe, and conduct irregular warfare against the Allies. A veteran of the eastern front, Prützmann studied the tactics of Russian partisans in the Ukraine who were cut off and effectively operated in small pockets deeply behind German lines. Initially, the Werewolves were to be uniformed and trained to conduct sabotage, arson, assassination, and sniping attacks. The German populace was exhausted from six years of war, millions of deaths, and overwhelming numbers of Allied occupation troops which curtailed the majority of Werewolf activities after the war. However, in a practically forgotten footnote to history, an interesting Werewolf-like organization sprang up in the east: members of the 20th SS Division (1st Estonian). Thousands of Estonians fought for the SS like some Cossaks and Ukrainians. The Soviets viewed them as collaborators and executed them on capture. The men fled to the forests to protect their homes and families. The "Forest Brothers" continued the fight into the 50s, causing thousands of casualties among the occupying Russian forces.

he contacted McAuliffe directly. McAuliffe was familiar with Donovan's spy agency and authorized West to confirm Mayer's story.

With a small contingent of troops from the 103rd, West jumped into a jeep and accompanied Mayer back through German lines to the Gauhaus. The roads were sloppy; a recent late-season snowfall was melting, making the roads difficult to traverse. Mayer and West arrived at the farmhouse and there discussed the surrender of Innsbruck with Gauleiter Hofer.

As the talks started, the major received a radio message informing him that three pieces of German flak artillery were holding up the 103rd's advance in front of the city. German antiaircraft guns, such as the 88 mm, were renowned for their ability to puncture holes in any tank in the Allied arsenal. Several well-concealed and dug-in guns could stop an entire attack. Startled by the news that German units were still fighting, Hofer insisted he had "given orders for them to pull back beyond the city of Innsbruck."

To remove the threat to both the 103rd's advance and the surrender process, Wynberg, along with an SS major, traveled via Volkswagen toward the flak units to convey Hofer's order. About a mile east of the city, Hans came upon the flak units, which were by now retreating eastward in accordance with Hofer's orders.

So close to American lines, Wynberg now had his turn to link up with American forces. With the white flag of truce fluttering in the wind, the Volkswagen drove approximately eight miles west toward Zirl, where the group approached the American lines and an olive-drab M4A3 Sherman tank accompanied by a platoon of American infantrymen. Wynberg recalled, "They had their BARs trained upon me; it was a tense moment. Luckily the lieutenant in charge of the outfit believed me." He wondered nervously if his false tags with the cover name of Hugh Wynn would somehow raise the Americans' suspicions.

Wynberg leapt out of the car, carrying the flag of truce toward the tank. Blond-haired and wearing the remains of an American uniform, he shouted that he was an American and requested to speak with the unit's commanding officer. A short time later, a lieutenant colonel approached. Wynberg quickly summarized what had occurred and revealed he was part of the OSS. "There is nothing here between your present position and Innsbruck. Innsbruck has been declared an open city," Wynberg stated emphatically. The officer nodded and agreed to advance. Acting upon Hans's advice, the lieutenant colonel jumped into a jeep followed by several Sherman tanks, and the column roared into Innsbruck.

With the sun setting behind them, Wynberg and the SS major returned to the farmhouse. The capitulation talks were finished, and West promised Hofer fair treatment. An American platoon was sent to guard the house. True to his word, Mayer had insisted that West's platoon keep Hofer under house arrest rather than take him prisoner. Nevertheless, tempers inside the house started to heat up as American heavy machine gun fire began reverberating through the distant woods. Hofer and many of his colleagues were noticeably distressed.

With the sounds of combat in the distance, Mayer left the safety of the farmhouse and made his way into Innsbruck, returning with a platoon of American soldiers. A rather dry letter, written by Major West, memorialized the event:

> On the afternoon of 3 May 1945, Lt. Fred Mayer performed a very valuable service for the Army as a whole and for the 103rd Infantry Division in their attack in the INNSBRUCK Valley. The following recital of facts illustrates the foregoing statement: 'At approximately 1630 3 May 1945, advance elements of the Division were moving East from ZIRL to launch an attack on INNSBRUCK. German troops had withdrawn and taken up positions on the western edge of the city. At this time, Lt. MAYER crossed the INN River in a civilian sedan and contacted Major Bland WEST, AC of S, G-2, and Lt. Peter RANDON, and offered to lead them to a farm South of HALL where he was holding Gauleiter Franz HOFER and his staff in custody awaiting the arrival of the American troops. LT. MAYER led a small party to the Gauleiter and through this contact it was possible (1) to

order the German troops on the western edge of the city to cease all resistance and admit the American troops in the city of INNS-BRUCK without opposition, (2) to obtain a statement from the Gauleiter HOFER for a radio broadcast exhorting the Standschutzen [*sic*] of the TYROL-VORARLBERG Area to lay down their arms. In addition, the Gauleiter gave much valuable information on the disposition of troops and non-existence of defenses throughout the area.

The officer in charge of the platoon acquiesced to Mayer's request, assuring him that they would treat Hofer diplomatically. Meanwhile, Hofer had a "long talk with Fred and Hans," who convinced him to make an additional radio speech telling the people and the SS and army garrisons surrounding Innsbruck that "the war was absolutely lost, not to participate in Werewolf activities, and to cooperate with the Americans." Through Mayer's efforts, Hofer gave the speech that prevented further bloodshed and curtailed any potential Werewolf and guerilla war activities. They had secured Innsbruck, and Mayer and Wynberg looked forward to their first night of sleep in three days.

29
———

# TURNABOUT

May 4 was turning into a glorious day. The 103rd was occupying Innsbruck, and General McAuliffe's headquarters had summoned Mayer and Wynberg to congratulate them—and to exchange their ratty uniforms for fresh olive drabs. Shortly after the agents' meeting with McAuliffe, Ulmer and Lowenstein arrived in Innsbruck. They quickly caught up to Mayer and Wynberg, embracing them emotionally. Franz Weber also came out of hiding, and the Greenup team was finally reunited. With the exception of Ulmer, they were all refugees, ordinary men who had bonded together and changed the course of events in their homeland. Not much was said, but it was understood that Lowenstein and Ulmer were very proud of Mayer, Wynberg, and Weber. Greenup was clearly their most successful mission, perhaps one of the most successful OSS missions of the war.

Another scene was unfolding in the Innsbruck suburb of Mühlau in an apartment that Schiffer had assigned to Hermann Matull. Matull and his small band of resistance fighters burst into a room holding his former captor,

Maj. August Schiffer. Matull's posse arrested Schiffer and threw him into the very jail that had once housed Mayer's bloodied and bruised body.

Desperate, Schiffer broke a glass bottle he found in his cell and used a shard to slit the arteries in both of his wrists. He preferred death to capture. Upon discovering him, Matull had Schiffer transported him to an Innsbruck hospital, where he convalesced. Later he was able to falsify his papers and eventually escaped. He was on the run for several weeks until apprehended by the Allied Counterintelligence Corps (CIC), which finally brought him to justice as a war criminal.

Back at the farmhouse, members of General McAuliffe's 103rd Division's CIC attachment arrived in an open-back half-ton truck. Hofer and his henchmen were swiftly escorted onto the flatbed and placed under arrest. The men also searched Lachhof and quickly secured RM 15,000 and other personal items of value.

Wanting to remain true to his word, Mayer was dismayed by the arrest. He demanded and received from Maj. Bland West a letter promising Hofer he would be treated fairly. While in CIC detention, Hofer pulled off a remarkable escape. He managed to flee to Germany, where he continued his former trade as a salesman in Mulheim-Ruhr. Unrecognized and using his true name, he died in 1975. In the meantime, Kriminalrat Walter Güttner remained on the run.

30
---

# THE DOUBLE AGENT

After completing his mission and bringing August Schiffer into custody, Hermann Matull felt as though he was part of the victorious Allied campaign. The black marketeer, former deserter, partisan fighter, Allied OSS agent, and even potential double agent felt pretty good; he had somehow survived. He needed a vacation.

OSS did not see things quite the same way. Lowenstein knew Matull was a hustler. Potentially in it for the money, was he also a double agent? In a debriefing shortly after the capture of Innsbruck, Lowenstein put Matull under his rhetorical knife. He searched him and found on his person four Louis Dior gold coins, $30, and an IOU for a debt Matull claimed to have incurred—using Deadwood mission funds—to bail someone out of German custody. The OSS certainly did not consider him a hero; however, without his lies, Greenup would have failed. Yet Lowenstein remained skeptical.

When asked about his plans now that the war was over, Matull stated rather flatly, "I'm willing to stay anywhere in central Europe. I'll stay with the OSS until you throw me out."

Lowenstein and Ulmer still had a hard time buying Matull's stories and shamefully devised exercises to further test his loyalty to the Allied cause:

> 1. Mason [Matull] watches Schiffer and [informs OSS] as soon as Schiffer is strong enough to talk again. Then OSS should interrogate him and get confirmation of [Matull's story] told to me.
> 2. Mason, in connection with CIC, goes on a search raid … where he knows the hiding place of several Gestapo people.

Upon successful completion of these tasks, Matull would be "cleared of any suspicion and brought to Salzburg for discharge from the organization." Despite all the blatant snubs and obvious distrust, Matull accompanied the CIC group to Vipiténo and through "his close association with the Gestapo, helped track down many more of its members who had gone [underground] in the area." He did not end up watching August Schiffer because the SS major escaped from the hospital in Innsbruck before he could be interviewed. After proving his loyalty once again, Hermann Matull was discharged by OSS with the stroke of a pen. On June 1, 1945, he received a final payment of approximately $650 without so much as a thank you. Hermann Matull then disappeared from the annals of history, never to be heard from again.

## 31

# "WHO DO YOU THINK WE ARE, NAZIS?"

Shortly after midnight on May 7, 1945, Adm. Karl Dönitz authorized the chief of staff of the German armed forces, Col. Gen. Alfred Jodl, to surrender all German troops still resisting in Europe to the Allies. Jodl signed the instrument of surrender in a drab brick schoolhouse in Rheims, France, which temporarily served as SHAEF headquarters.

With Germany's official surrender, life slowly began to return to normal in Innsbruck. The local paper returned to press, businesses gradually reopened, and Hans and Fred attempted to get their first good night of sleep after the surrender. A few days after Hofer's arrest, they had procured the keys to a villa belonging to the assistant Gauleiter of the region; however, the high living did not last long. As Wynberg recalled, "Our second night [at the villa], soldiers burst in while we were on the couch and told us to get out." Despite the appearance of normality, the hunt for Nazis continued.

Across town, the CIC closed in and ensnared Walter Güttner. Remarkably, inside Güttner's pocket was a souvenir photo of the bruised and beaten Fred Mayer. Later that day, a CIC officer approached Mayer and asked, "We've got Güttner. Do you want to see him?" Mayer nodded yes.

For Mayer, Güttner's capture represented the culmination of all of his efforts. The Gestapo officer personified the hatred he felt toward the Third Reich. With his adrenaline surging, Mayer briskly walked through the very halls of the Gestapo jail that had once housed him. He made his way through the dank corridors to the cell that held his nemesis. Upon seeing Mayer, Güttner froze, cowering in the corner. Mayer noticed that the Gestapo man was bruised and beaten, just as he had been only days earlier. In a bizarre turnabout, captive had now become captor.

"CIC had already roughed him up," Mayer recalled. "[I was] upset because he was already beat up. I wanted to beat him myself."

Trembling, Güttner stammered to Mayer, "Do anything you want with me, but don't hurt my family."

A sense of calm came over Fred Mayer. He looked Güttner directly in the eye and responded, "Who do you think we are, Nazis?" Then he turned his back on Walter Güttner for the last time.

# EPILOGUE

On May 17, 1945, things wound down in Oberperfuss, and Mayer and Wynberg said goodbye to many of their close friends. Fred embraced Thomas Marie one last time, and Mayer and Wynberg shook hands with Franz Weber. A few days later, Weber and his fiancée traveled back to the glacier and located the white silk from Greenup's parachute canopies, which she used to make her wedding dress. Before departing Innsbruck, Hans tapped out a final Morse code message: "Gadsen to base; close my circuit net, taking over this morning. Many thanks for three months cooperation. Best Regards from Fred and Hans."

That afternoon, after saying their goodbyes, the team traveled to Salzburg, Austria, where the OSS had established a new headquarters closer to the newer threat that was emerging: the Soviet Union. That evening, in a hotel located on the outskirts of town, the men were reunited with the three other members of the Jewish five. Bernd Steinitz, upon seeing his close friend Fred Mayer, embraced him and the men sat back, relaxed, and drank deeply from their beer steins, quietly reflecting upon their experiences. Lowenstein, Ulmer, and even Walter Haass, who until days earlier had been missing and feared dead, all joined them. In late April, filling his role as dispatcher and jumpmaster for a final mission into the Reich,

Haass's plane was hit by flak and crash landed behind enemy lines. Miraculously, he survived and was able to attend the reunion.*

With the war in Europe ended, the full extent of the Nazi regime's atrocities was coming to light. Auschwitz, Sobibór, Bergen-Belsen, Mauthausen, Dachau: The infamous camps had destroyed a large portion of the Jewish population in Europe. One by one, the men learned of their own families' the tragic fates. Wynberg learned that his mother, father, sister, and little brother were killed at Auschwitz. Most of Rosenthal's and Gerbner's families were also lost to the camps.

The five had sworn to bonds of secrecy, a promise they kept for years after the war. When they were discharged separately and returned home, they received hardly any recognition or hero's fanfare. The men quietly hung up their uniforms and returned to civilian life.

---

* On April 25, 1945, Walter Haass was part of the Hope mission, and he described what happened. "From Hope we went to [our] target . . . and no signals were seen. After we made a large circle we returned over the target area at 3,000 ft. and still did not see any signals. After I told the pilot to head for home, we turned our heading and gained altitude. This was 0100 local time. At this moment we received a direct hit in the bomb-bay. The waist was immediately filled with smoke and flames, and everybody fitted chutes." Haass bailed out with "the tail gunner and the waist gunner." He was captured but later saw two of the surviving men in a German hospital in Böehlerwerk, badly burned. Haass gleaned from his German interrogators that "four bodies had been found in the wreckage of a plane." Walter Haass was lucky to be alive.

# THEN AND NOW

**Chappell, Howard**: Arguably trained one of the OSS's most effective operational groups; many of his operatives did amazing things during the war. The team leader also had his own successful mission, Operation Tacoma, chronicled in *The Brenner Assignment*. Chappell went on to become part of the Federal Bureau of Narcotics. He fearlessly pursued and took down several leading mafia kingpins.

**Gerbner, George**: Became a scholar and later was dean of the Annenberg School of Communications at the University of Pennsylvania.

**Güttner, Walter**: Survived CIC detention, but in the mid-1950s was brought to trial for war crimes in Austria. However, charges were later dropped because key witnesses could not be found to corroborate the evidence. Ridiculously, the U.S. government failed to inform Mayer even though he was working for the Voice of America, a government agency.

**Haass, Walter**: Went on to have a successful career and raised a family.

**Hoertnagl, Maria** (Thomas Marie): Was happily married after the war and awarded the Austrian Liberation Medal for her heroic sacrifice during the war.

**Hofer, Franz**: Escaped CIC detention and lived a fruitful life as a pipe salesman and unrepentant Nazi. He died in 1975 from natural causes.

**Kröck, Paul**: Thanks to his letter, managed to link back up with the OSS and was spirited through Russian lines and discharged from the OSS without a thank you.

**Kuen, Alois**: Ever the intrepid anti-Nazi Kripo police officer, helped CIC round up die-hard Nazis and SS men during the occupation of Innsbruck.

**Lowenstein, Dyno**: Became the owner of a small graphics business and wrote several books on graphing techniques.

**Matull, Herman**: Never heard from again.

**Mayer, Fred**: Discharged from the OSS in 1945 and received the Purple Heart and Legion of Merit. After the war, he worked at General Motors and later worked for Voice of America as a supervisor where he traveled the world. He is now retired. In 1990, the Austrian government awarded him the Tyrolean Order of the Eagle in Gold. The author, who has interviewed thousands of veterans, strongly feels that Mayer is eligible for the Medal of Honor.

**Primbs, Dr. Max**: Spent several months behind bars following the end of the war before returning to his successful plastic surgery practice. After the war, Mayer became friends with Primbs and visited him several times while working in Europe.

**Rosenthal, Alfred**: Sadly couldn't put the war behind him and passed away during the 1950s.

**Schiffer, August**: Captured by CIC agents in September 1945, attempted to commit suicide again by swallowing sleeping pills hidden in his sock. Schiffer was brought to justice and hanged at the gallows in October 1946.

**Steinitz, Bernd**: After being captured during the Dillon Three mission, helped facilitate the surrender of German forces outside of Klagenfurt. After the war he finished college and became a certified public accountant. Semiretired, he still does accounting for high-level pension and benefit programs.

**Ulmer, Alfred**: Stayed with the CIA until the 1960s and later retired from an executive position at a bank.

# APPENDIX A

Over the past eight years, I have gotten to know the surviving members of the "Jewish Five." Initially, I was going to include all their stories in a single volume—it was impossible. Each team needed a separate book. Nevertheless, segues with the separate Dania and Dillon missions occur in this book. I'm providing the original mission reports, which capture their stories in the men's own words.

## REPORT ON OPERATION DANIA
German-Austrian Section, SICE
2677 Regiment OSS (Prov.)
APO 512, U.S. Army
20 May 1945

Based on interrogation on 17 and 18 May 1945 of Sergeant George Gerbner and Sergeant Alfred Rosenthal, Hq., 2677 Regiment OSS (Prov.), APO 512.

## I. INTRODUCTION

The following report is based upon extensive interrogation of Sgts. George Gerbner and Alfred Rosenthal, the two American military members of the Dania team of the German-Austrian Section, SICE, OSS-MEDTO. The team, which also included one Austrian deserter-volunteer named George Mitchell, was dispatched from Bari on the night of 7 February 1945 with the mission of establishing clandestine intelligence chains in the area of Graz, Austria, and of forwarding to this organization such information as it might obtain on military, political, economic, and social activities and institutions. This report will contain a description of the landing of the team at a wrong pinpoint (some twenty-five miles south of its goal), a record of the travels of Gerbner and Rosenthal between 7 February and 15 May when they returned to Caserta, and observations of interest made by the two soldiers during their three-month stay in Yugoslavia. It should be noted that this report does not contain any data received from the Austrian civilian, Mitchell, who was separated from the team at the time of the parachute drop and who, it is expected, will be interrogated by other members of this section in Austria.

## II. THE FLIGHT AND THE JUMP

The Dania team had as its mission the penetration of southern Austria, in the area of Graz, for the purpose of exploiting clandestine intelligence possibilities. A pinpoint near the town of Deutschlandsberg had been selected; aerial cover of the entire vicinity had been obtained and studied extensively by all three members of the team prior to the departure. Through a gross error of navigation, however, the team was informed that the plane was over the pinpoint when actually it was some twenty-five miles south, at a mountain near the village of Vuhred, on the south bank of the Drava River in northern Yugoslavia. That the two American members of the team were able to parachute without injury in this wild, inaccessible, and unexpected spot and eventually made their way to safety through the midst of one of the most violent guerilla warfare areas of central Europe is a tribute to the courage, stamina, and coolheadedness of the two soldiers.

The Dania team, which had waited through an entire moon period for good flying weather, was alerted at 1030 hours on the morning of 7 February 1945, at headquarters of the German-Austrian Section, SICE, Company B, 2677 Regiment OSS (Prov.). The team, after rounding up its equipment, left for Brindisi about 1600, accompanied by Pfc. Walter Haass, the conducting officer for the flight, and Lt. Dyno Lowenstein of the G-A Section. At Brindisi the team encountered the first of its unexpected difficulties. The original idea of the men, and of the G-A Section, was that the three men would each jump with a leg bag weighing approximately fifty pounds, into which all the men's personal belongings would be placed, their finances, and some of the radio equipment and rations. The remaining equipment was to be dropped in a single container attached to a parachute.

Upon their arrival in Brindisi, the men found that these plans had been extensively altered without notification of any sort. For reasons beyond their understanding, the Dania team members were told that they would not be permitted to jump with leg bags and that parachutes had been attached to each of the bags; in addition, plans to place the rest of the paraphernalia in one large container had been similarly changed, and the men found that instead four smaller packages had been packed and equipped with parachutes. None of these decisions to alter the packaging had been communicated in advance to the G-A Section in Bari by the OSS packing detachment in Brindisi; it was only a couple of hours before the actual takeoff that the changes were discovered. It was accordingly found necessary to revise the schedule for jumping over the pinpoint in order that the three men and the seven packages would not be spread out over the entire countryside.

Prior to the takeoff, according to the two American team members, it was arranged with the pilot and navigator that the Austrian civilian member of the team was to identify both the town of Deutschlandsberg and the pinpoint. The navigator assured the team that there was no cause for worry as to directions, and the pilot added that if there were any doubt about the pinpoint, there would be no drop.

The plane, flown by the Polish crew of the Royal Air Force, took off early in the evening and arrived at the "pinpoint" about midnight. Contrary to the earlier discussions, there was no opportunity for Mitchell to examine the terrain, and the team was forced to take the word of the crew that they were over the right spot. After being told that there were clouds over the pinpoint, the team asked for another spot nearby in which a drop would be feasible. The plane was already circling over the area (it spent about fifteen minutes altogether in the vicinity), and within a minute or two, the team received the green light to jump.

Mitchell went out first, followed by three packages dropped as quickly as the dispatchers could move them through the jump hole. The plane then circled for another five minutes, after which, at a signal from the navigator, Gerbner and Rosenthal, followed by the three remaining packages, were parachuted out.

For a moment after they jumped, both men saw a light on the ground, which they presumed to be Mitchell since he had been instructed to provide a light marker for the others. Neither Gerbner nor Rosenthal saw each other or any of the packages once they left the plane. Gerbner went down uneventfully, but Rosenthal was caught in an ascending airstream, and despite all his efforts to "play" the chute, it took him almost five minutes to negotiate the thousand-foot drop. Rosenthal reported that as he parachuted to earth, the absence of bare patches of snow on the terrain below first caused doubts in his mind as to his presence over the right pinpoint.

The area into which both Gerbner and Rosenthal descended was a rugged piece of badlands at the foot of two mountains blanketed in three or four feet of snow. The land was torn into a series of steep gullies, each about thirty feet deep and about forty to sixty feet across the top. Through the bottom of several of the gullies ran small brooks, which flowed out the only open side. The other three sides were extremely steep and covered densely with evergreens and snow. Rosenthal spent the next several hours vainly looking for an escape route from his snow-filled gulley, while calling and whistling a prearranged signal from time to time. He heard nothing, except a plane, probably his own, flying overhead about ten minutes later. Gerbner, more fortunate, managed to find a way out of the gulley into which he had descended; unable to find either of his companions, he climbed to the top of the mountain to get better orientation. A short time later he saw a light flicker to the north. Assuming it was one of his teammates, Gerbner lit three or four matches. At that moment, however, the street lights suddenly were turned on in a village about two miles north, even though the pilot had assured them there was no town for eight miles in any direction. Had the men delayed their jump for another minute or two, they would have descended into the middle of the enemy-controlled community of Vuhred on the south bank of the Drava River.

Shortly afterwards, Gerbner heard whistles. Descending the mountain, he eventually found Rosenthal in one of the gullies. The meeting occurred about 0430 on 8 February, more than four hours after the drop. The two soldiers again climbed the mountain in order to have a view of the terrain when daylight broke and to see if Mitchell could be found. As the sun rose, they were huddled in a bush near the peak. They could see men from some nearby farmhouses walking toward the town and, later, a group of six men who they suspected constituted a guard patrol.

Since they had been unable to find their packages, the two men had almost no supplies. Between them they possessed only one air force escape kit; they had no extra clothes, and Rosenthal had lost his gloves when he jumped; and they carried on their persons only $200 in U.S. currency and an extra watch for trading purposes. Throughout that day and the next, they searched unsuccessfully on all sides of the mountain and on an adjoining hill for trace of Mitchell and their supplies.

## III. ESCAPE ROUTE

Sometime during the day on 9 February, the two military members of the Dania team realized, through conversations overheard from their hiding places along the road and later from talks with the local peasants, that they had been dropped in Slovenia rather than in Austria. Without equipment or food supplies, they realized that it would be necessary at once to make contact with the Yugoslav partisans in order to get back to Bari and have another opportunity to penetrate Austria. Since their evacuation from Yugoslavia did not occur until 13 May, that second chance never materialized. Instead, for a period of three months, the two men lived with the partisans in the areas just north and south of the Sava River, were kept almost constantly on the move by the presence of German forces and were able to leave the hinterlands only with the evacuation of enemy troops after the European surrender.

On 9 February, having been unable to find any trace of Mitchell or of the six supply packages, Gerbner and Rosenthal started to move south. At night, they entered the stable of an old Slovenian peasant woman, who gave them a meal of stew, a flour dish, which was their first real food since leaving Brindisi two days earlier. The next day, about noon, they walked to another farm and were again provided food. On 11 February, the two men spent the whole day walking west through the woods. At night, they found a friendly farmer but because of a warning that the Germans were only a 15 minutes' walk away, they continued hiking for another three hours. The night was spent in the haystack of a mountain peasant's farm. In the morning, in the house, they found two women and a bunch of children. The reception was extremely cool at first, until the women were certain that the men were not members of the Gestapo; they explained later that many Gestapo officers, using American military uniforms, had been in the area for some time. Satisfied with the identity of the Dania team, whose cover was that of escaping American fliers, the women sent one of the children to contact a brother, who served with the partisans. He returned shortly and promised to lead them, after dark, to partisan contacts in the mountains. In the evening, the two men and their escort walked to a cabin high in the mountains, which was occupied by a peasant family whose son had been killed by the Germans. From there, contact was established with the partisans. On the evening of 13 February, two partisans came to lead them to a military outpost. The men were asked for military identification and were asked to surrender their pistols, which were returned to them when they reached the commanding officer's hut; the partisan post, which they reached earlier in the evening, was a courier station; the commander, a boy of nineteen, was dressed in civilian clothes, was cordial, and offered them a meal.

At 0230 on 14 February, the men walked another two hours with the commander to a hideout near the top of Mola Kapa. There they were given medical care, and the partisans sewed up rips in their clothes and repaired their shoes. Until 16 February, Gerbner and Rosenthal divided their time, along with the partisan couriers, between the two huts on the side of the mountain. On 16 February, the team, together with two escorts, crossed the big Kapa Mountain and headed south, where they slept at a partisan courier station.

After four hours of walking on 17 February, the team reached Partisan Fourth Zone Headquarters, at that time located in the mountains. Through Major Owens of the British Military Mission, who proved most helpful at all times, the men filed a cable to Bari giving their location. There, also, they met Mr. Bob Perry of the OSS Mansion team, who was working closely with Major Owens. The next day a radio message from Bari ordered them to return to Italy by most expeditious means possible. It was decided that they would attempt to reach Crnomelj, site of the partisans' Slovenian HQ, of 7th Corps HQ, and of an airstrip. A snowstorm prevented any further move on 17 or 18 February, but on the next day the Dania team, with its escort, started walking east. For the next few days, the presence of German forces in the vicinity made progress difficult; the men walked through the mountains at night and slept during the day. On 21 and 22 February, further reports of a German column and of SS men added to the confusion. On 22 February, they saw a German patrol on the road; the partisan escorts wished to remain in hiding in the woods, but the party, now increased by seven, wanted to keep moving. Accordingly they dashed across the road, amidst scattered firing from the Germans, and wandered through the wooded sides of the mountains. At one farm-house they were refused succor by a peasant woman, who feared retaliation from the Germans in garrison across the valley. In the morning, shortly after the group left the farm, they saw a patrol of fifty Germans march by the house they had left only a few minutes earlier. It was not until 1900 hours on 23 February that they found the partisan courier station which they had been seeking for two days. The next evening they accompanied the couriers over some steep mountain trails. Hav-ing spent one night en route in a stable, the group crossed the bridge over the Sav-inja River at Radmirje during the night of 25 February. Later the same night, they crossed the Drava River on a bridge.* There were no Germans to be seen at the time, though they held positions nearby. The area, previously occupied by the par-tisans, had been taken by the Germans during the January offensive.

Once south of the Drava, the group climbed steadily in the direction of the Menina Mountains to the southwest. The group spent the morning of 27 Febru-ary in Motnik, which at the moment was free of German garrison troops. During the evening of the same day, they crossed the main east-west road and met couri-ers from the next station to the south. Shortly afterwards, the presence of a German patrol caused the group to scurry into the hills. Although they had been advised that most of the area southwest of Motnik was unfriendly, they found an old cou-ple who gave food to the group. Before dawn on 28 February, the group went up into the hills to hide from the enemy; Gerbner, walking down the slope during the morning, was passed by a German column less than a hundred yards away. The Germans ransacked the home of the elderly couple, apparently in retribution for their suspected aid to the partisans.

The group lived on the mountain side until 5 March, occasionally hearing the sounds of battle in the neighboring valleys. On that morning, there were sounds of heavy fire from dawn until noon; from dusk until midnight the group marched to-wards the Sava River. At 0190 on 4 March, they again met the Partisan Fourth Zone HQ, this time accompanied by the 1st (Tomasic) Brigade. Fourth Zone HQ had also been attempting to cross the Sava towards the south, and the Dania team met them as they were retreating north after encountering heavy gunfire and ca-sualties near the river. The entire group spent the day on a nearby mountain; dur-ing the evening they marched back north to a small village. Informed that the Sava was heavily guarded by the enemy, Dania determined to leave the zone HQ and see if a small number of persons could be more successful in affecting the

---

* This section report contains geographical errors and inconsistencies. The author did not make the corrections.

river passage. On 6 March, four Liberators came over to drop supplies for the British mission, for Bob Perry of the OSS Mansion team, and for the partisan brigade; the Dania team accordingly received badly needed food supplies and ammunition. In the evening, the team moved off, searching the same mountain on which they had stayed earlier. They planned to move west from Motnik across the main road at a lonely spot and wait in the mountains for an opportune moment to cross the Sava. Instead, heavy German patrols along the road necessitated their waiting north of the road. On 10 March, when the group was contemplating a return to the partisan courier station near Motnik, they learned that that village was now in German hands, so they returned up [a ridge]. On 11 March 1945, while walking west along the ridge, they met the Partisan 6th and 11th brigades. These two units, which had been ordered to proceed south, had been battered by the Germans, who had caught them between two roads. The brigades were planning to move south towards the Sava, but the Dania team decided to stay back and search for their couriers, with whom they had lost contact two or three days before. Early on 12 March, they met the couriers, and it was decided to return again to Motnik. About noon the next day, they again met the two brigades; their efforts to cross the Sava had been repulsed, and German units were moving up into the hills. These patrols were later turned back by partisan gunfire. In the evening the Dania group continued its trek toward Motnik. Throughout 14 March, the group with which Dania was hiking was forced to hide from German groups, among them, a unit of fifty border police.

On the evening of 15 March, the group decided to conduct a crossing of the main road, on which German guards were stationed at two-hundred-meter intervals and a number of units were encamped. Three of the party were able to make a successful dash across the highway, but the ongoing machine gun fire prevented the Dania team members and an English flight officer from following them. Accordingly, the trio turned back into the hills, where, after some hours, they met, for the third time, the Partisan 6th and 11th brigades. They were told that the partisans' six hundred men had run into a German force estimated by the partisans to number six thousand and that for a period of forty-eight hours, they had fought a defensive battle, and in the course of it, the Germans had suffered two hundred deaths to only five casualties for the partisans. During the night of 16 March, the partisans slipped out of the mountaintop trap, which the Germans were preparing, and managed to dash across the main east-west highway eventually reaching a hill north of Sg. Ozbald [sic]. The Dania team stayed with the brigades on the hillside until 19 March, when the units attempted to cross the Sava, but they found the current too fast. Two days later, in the same vicinity, a battle with several German patrols lasted through the morning and afternoon. On that day, the Dania team secured permission from the brigade HQ to go with a small group to the courier station closest to the Sava, in the hope of making a quick crossing of the river. During 22 March, the group of five proceeded south of the Sveta Mountains to a point near Tirna in order to wait for an auspicious moment for the crossing. At the rivers' edge, a courier, who had paddled over from the south bank, notified the group of eleven that courier lines to the south had been broken and that a shortage of food made living difficult. Accordingly, the group returned to the hills and remained in hiding from both Germans and Slovenian White Guards until 30 March. A second effort to cross the Sava that night was foiled by the nonappearance of the couriers from the south bank.

On 1 April, the men made another contact with three partisan brigades, which they had encountered at various times in the past: the 1st (Tomasic), 6th, and 11th. Carrying barges constructed by local partisans, the column of some 750 men reached the river about 0200. Just as the units reached the river's edge, the Germans opened fire with small arms, mortars, and artillery, and the column had to about-face. Fearing that to stay with the brigade would involve another unnecessary hide to the north, the Dania team arranged through an officer of a local partisan group to be escorted to a point near Tirna, where they planned to wait still further for a chance to move south across the river. The decision was wise, for they learned subsequently that the brigades had been ordered to abandon the trek south and had been instructed instead to proceed to the vicinity of Maribor.

From 6 April to 13 April, the team waited near Tirna. There were occasional shots from roving patrols nearby but no actual battles. On 7 April, the team sent a message via a courier to Bari; they asked that supplies, a radio, and directives be dropped so that the time might be utilized to advantage. The message, like two subsequent ones, was sent though partisan channels but due to cipher difficulties was never received in intelligence form.

The Sava was finally crossed on the night of 13–14 April. Six persons were ferried across the river in a rubber boat and then escorted by the couriers into south of the Sava. That day the team reached a headquarters of the Dolenski Odreda, an organization comprising three battalions, which had, as it mission, the servicing of partisan communications in the region between the Sava River and the Austrian-Yugoslav border established by the Germans in 1941. Because of the presence of the White Guard troops to the south, the Dania team was informed that progress in that direction would be slow, a prediction borne out by the fact that the commissar of the 9th Corps, who tried to get through to Crnomelj, was forced to return to Odreda headquarters.

The team stayed with the Odreda headquarters from 14 April until 7 May, remaining almost constantly in the neighborhood of one small area. On 3 May, the team heard reports that the Germans had capitulated in Italy and asked permission to move out, but they were informed that the Slovenian White Guards were still fighting vigorously. Three days later the Odreda battalion surrounded a nearby German fortress and presented a surrender ultimatum to the enemy forces. When the Germans refused to yield, the partisan battalion withdrew. Reports that the partisans had moved into a number of villages hitherto occupied by the Germans reached Odreda, and heavy firing could be heard in the direction of Ljubljana, about twenty miles west.

During the evening the Odreda HQ and its battalions moved out in the direction of Litija, a village a few miles to the west, which was still in the hands of an SS unit. It was arranged that they would join with other partisan battalions en route. At noon on 8 May, the partisans marched down the main highway leading west, the first time they had dared use a principal thoroughfare. Near Litija the SS opened up with heavy fire, and the partisans swung south into Smartno, moving from there into the outskirts of Litija. German firing ceased in the village about 2200 hours on 8 May, and when the partisans entered the community the next morning, they discovered the Germans had withdrawn. The village was filled with partisan flags, some hastily converted from swastikas, and the soldiers received a warm welcome from the populace. In the previous days' fighting, both Gerbner and Rosenthal had taken an active part in the battle for the village.

The partisans provided the Dania team and two accompanying English fliers with a horse and wagon on which they proceeded west to Ljubljana. They were the first two Americans to reach that city, arriving there at 2100 on 10 May, the day after its liberation. The team remained in Ljubljana overnight, eventually being given a car, which had been requisitioned for them by the Partisan 4th Army. In contrast with this army, which was well equipped with British uniforms and weapons, the Croatian Partisan Corps, which entered the city on 12 May, was a ragged, tattered outfit. It was garbed in motley German uniforms and carried both German and Russian weapons. Many of the marchers were boys as young as sixteen, and a large proportion were walking without shoes.

During the two-and-a-half-hour drive to Trieste, the men passed long lines of partisan motor transports and tanks moving towards Ljubljana from the west, as well as jeeps with American and British officers. At Trieste, the Dania team contacted a representative of OSS and then, in company with the British fliers, flew to Udine. The next day an RAF advance squadron placed a B-24 at their disposal and flew them to Foggia, Italy. From that point they returned to Bari on 13 May in a B-17 and on 15 May 1945 reported to the chief, SICE, OSS-MEDTO, at Caserta.

Both soldiers expressed keen admiration for the manner in which the partisans, who were fighting a desperate battle to hold their ranks against much larger numbers of Germans, were constantly cordial and helpful to the team. Every courtesy that primitive conditions would permit was shown to the two men. It should be noted, of course, that the men preserved their air force officer cover throughout their entire stay with the partisans. The men thereby avoided some of the subtle surveillance which other OSS teams working in Yugoslavia have encountered, and they were permitted free access to partisan officers and enlisted men, as well as to the native peasants. Without the assistance of the partisans, the Dania tem felt certain it could never have survived the three-month period, and despite the delay in returning to Italy, they felt that the partisans had utilized all their slender communications resources in an effort to move the team to safety.

# APPENDIX B

## DEBRIEFING REPORT ON OPERATIONS
## DILLON AND DILLON III

### I. INTRODUCTION AND SUMMARY

The Dillon team of the German-Austrian Section, SICE, 2677th Regiment, OSS (Prov.), was assigned the mission of effecting clandestine penetration of the Villach-Klagenfurt area of Carinthia for the purpose of securing secret intelligence about the enemy and of establishing friendly chains, which would serve as reception groups for additional teams to be dispatched by the section. The team was sent into the field on the night of 27 December 1944.

The team consisted of the following five persons: Second Lieutenant Miles Pavlovich, USA; Mr. Julio Prester, a Yugoslav civilian who had been recruited by OSS in the United States; and three Austrian deserter-volunteers: Ernst Fiechter (described in this report as "Victor"); Karl Steinwender (known as "Karl"); and Helmuth Kinzian (known as "Hans").

At 2130, on the night of 27 December the team dropped successfully, but because of deep snow and rough terrain, the supply packages were not found until approximately a month later. Due to the damaged condition of the batteries and radio receiver, contact with the home base was unsuccessful. On 18 January 1945, photo reconnaissance of the area was made at the request of the German-Austrian Section, and subsequent study of the pictures by Lt. Hart Perry of the section revealed a V in the snow. This, by prearrangement, was a request for radio and other supplies. Four containers, including supplies and new radio equipment, were dropped to the team on 30 and 31 January 1945, but because of high winds the parachutes were torn in descent, and much of the equipment was badly damaged.

During January the deserter-volunteer known as Karl proved increasingly unreliable; he had stolen personal property of his companions, failed to carry out assignments, and cheated friendly contacts of the team. He was tried by a court-martial established by Lt. Pavlovich, found guilty, and put on probation. When on 2 February 1945 he returned to the team after an unexplained absence of forty-eight hours, during which he had acquired a new German uniform, he was executed in accordance with the sentence of the court.

On 16 February, Prester and Hans were arrested in their hideout ski hut, after having been betrayed by a local peasant. The next day, on information supplied the police by Hans, enemy authorities surprised Lt. Pavlovich in his hideout. In the ensuing fight, Pavlovich was shot and killed. Victor, who had been in the house with Pavlovich, was captured the next day.

The three remaining members of the team—Prester, Hans, and Victor— together with some twenty friendly contacts were taken to the jail at Klagenfurt. Starting on 18 February the Dillon radio circuit was worked by Prester under the control of the Gestapo, and though he transmitted the danger signal in each of the next thirteen messages, that fact was never adequately reported to the German-Austrian Section, nor its implication appreciated. Consequently, a supply drop originally planned to provide Klagenfurt Gestapo officers with candy and cigarettes and to improve Prester's position with certain of these officials, who were showing an increasingly friendly attitude, was developed into a drop of both supplies and personnel.

On the night of 16 April 1945, an operation called Dillon III was laid on by the German-Austrian Section. It comprised Cpl. Bernd K. Steinitz, who used the cover of an air force first lieutenant and the name Peter Hartley, and an Austrian deserter-volunteer named Otto Langer, whose cover name was Oscar Langston. These two men made a successful drop to a "reception committee" of police officials and were apprehended within fifteen minutes of their landing. After two days, these men were placed in the same jail in Klagenfurt as the original Dillon team and its local contacts.

During the latter part of April, the impact of the Allied military successes upon certain of the local police and Gestapo officials made possible rather frank discussion by Prester and Steinitz concerning the future role of these officers in the probable event of German collapse. On 4 May, Prester was permitted to notify the

German-Austrian Section that he had been incarcerated for the past two months. On 5 May, Prester and Steinitz were given their freedom in order to be available for possible surrender negotiations, and the following day they secured the release of the deserter-volunteers Hans, Victor, and Oscar, all the local contacts of the team, and all other political prisoners.

Steinitz subsequently notified OSS of the desire of the Germans in Carinthia to surrender to the Anglo-Americans rather than to the Yugoslavs. A few days later he served as an escorting officer for two representatives sent by the Klagenfurt Gauleiter to the American military authorities at Salzburg for possible surrender conversations. Upon their arrival the completion of general surrender negotiations for all German military forces in eastern and central Austria had obviated any necessity of talks with the two representatives, and they accordingly returned with Steinitz to Klagenfurt.

During the period immediately following the liberation of Carinthia by elements of the British Eighth Army, Prester Steinitz, Victor, and Oscar provided G-2 of the British Fifth Corps with a steady stream of intelligence reports concerning the whereabouts of SS units, the names of local Nazis and war criminals, and other data of a similar nature.

## II. THE FIRST PHASE OF THE OPERATION (27 DECEMBER 1944–18 FEBRUARY 1945)

The five members of the Dillon team—Lt. Pavlovich, Prester, Victor, Hans, and Karl—left the airport at Brindisi, Italy, on the night of 27 December 1944 at 1800 hours in a Halifax bomber flown by a Polish crew of the Royal Air Force. The pinpoint originally selected for the team was 13 34′ 55″–46 58′ 10″, but according to the report of the pilot, when the point was found to be woody and rocky, the dropping area was changed to a spot approximately one half mile west of the original target. The plane circled three times over the point. On the first round, Hans jumped from an altitude of one thousand feet, and four of the team's five packages were dropped. The fifth, containing arms and ammunition, failed to drop because of mechanical difficulties. Eight minutes later, Lt. Pavlovich and Karl parachuted out, and on the third circle, at 2138 hours, Prester and Victor jumped.

According to Prester, who is the source of information throughout this section of the report, the landing was effected with ease. The men found about two meters of snow on the ground but had no difficulty in assembling themselves. They were unsuccessful, however, in locating the packages. On 29 December, Karl was sent into a nearby village in search of food. He came back empty-handed the next day, and it was subsequently discovered that he had made no efforts to find any, having spent the time with a girl [most likely, Martha Fraus].

After three days had passed, the team moved to a house recommended by Karl. The walk, through chest-high snow, took eight hours, and upon arrival the team was quartered in a stable, was provided by Karl with tea and bread, and was told by him that they must leave at once because the house was occupied by a German family. This was another of Karl's falsehoods; the place was actually owned and inhabited by his brother.

On the following day the team passed the village of Eisentratten and moved to the village Treffenboden, which is located about a mile north of Gmünd (for this and all future map references, see 1,250,000 Italy Sheet 7–11, Trieste, 765–713). Because of Victor's foot, which had frozen during the hike, it was impossible for the group to continue, and they were put up for the night in a small hut. In the morning, they went to the first house in Treffenboden, occupied by a Mrs. BERTHA KRABATT and her daughter, MARIA WINKLER. One of these women had previously been to jail for three months for some political offense, and they gave the team a cordial reception, provided food, cleaned and washed the men's clothes, and promised full cooperation. Throughout the next few months, these two women proved constantly helpful. They were eventually rounded up by the police with the other Dillon team contacts, and MARIA WINKLER gave birth to a baby in the Klagenfurt jail. The risk of sheltering the team in their home was great, since a Nazi official lived in the next house, only ten meters away, but the two women kept the team for four days.

Eventually, MARIA WINKLER went to Gmünd for help. She returned with two other contacts who provided assistance on many future occasions: GEORGE HASLITZER and GUSTAV FILITZIG. These men brought an eight days' supply of food, a pair of skis, and treatment for Victor's frozen foot. In addition, HASLITZER led them to a more secure spot—a ski hut on top of a mountain near Treffenboden. While Lt. Pavlovich and Victor remained in the ski hut, Prester, Hans, and Karl returned to the original dropping point to continue the search for the missing packages. The trio stayed at the hut near the dropping point for eight days, eating very little. Prester fashioned a *V* signal in the snow with a German flag he had discovered; the *V* was a prearranged signal with OSS to indicate the need for a new radio.

Unsuccessful in their quest for the packages, Prester, Hans, and Karl returned on the eighth day to the ski hut near Treffenboden to rejoin Lt. Pavlovich and Victor, and the same day Hans and Karl were sent back to the home of Mrs. BERTHA KRABATT in Treffenboden for food. Throughout the ensuing two months, this home served as the collection point for food brought by the team's various contacts.

During the next four weeks, Hans and Karl made several trips to the dropping point in further search of the packages. They would return to the ski hut at Treffenboden to rest for a day or two before going back for further searching. On the twenty-eighth day, one of the rucksacks was discovered at the dropping point; it had no parachute attached to it. The following day the radio batteries were found, similarly without parachute. Eight days later, the radio set was located; its package was tied to an unopened parachute, and the receiver had been damaged in the crash.

With the radio equipment in his possession, Prester, together with Karl and Victor, who was ill, went back to the house of Mrs. BERTHA KRABATT, where Prester sent two blind messages on the guard channel requesting a new radio receiver. (About this time in late January, the German-Austrian Section in Bari was notified that a guard channel contact had been established with Dillon, but in the effort to change it over to one of the team's regular radio frequencies, the contact had been broken and lost. This was obviously due to Prester's lack of a workable receiver.)

Prester and Karl then left the KRABATT home to join Lt. Pavlovich and Hans, who had gone to the ski hut at the dropping point to await the new supplies requested by ground panel and by radio. On 30 January, a P-38 carrying a belly load of containers came over the pinpoint and dropped some of the supplies—a new radio and signal plan, as well as food and PX supplies. Through a mechanical error one of the containers did not fall, and a return trip was made on 31 January. (The container dropped on the second day was apparently never found by the team.)

The drop was made about noon in a high wind, Prester reported, and the parachutes were ripped in the descent. Even more serious, the course of the plane and the dropping of supplies were witnessed by observers at an air-raid warning post located on the peak of a mountain near Kremsbrücke. They immediately flashed a warning to police at Eisentratten and Gmünd. The team, meanwhile, was able to find one package, containing smashed batteries, but before they had time for further search, they saw lumberjacks working in the woods nearby. Accordingly the team returned to the KRABATT home in Treffenboden, where they learned the police, *Volkssturm*, and *Hitler Jugend* were searching the woods for the containers. It was discovered later that the other packages had been found by these searching parties and turned over to the Gestapo at Spittal.

During the remainder of that day, the five men of the team waited in the KRA-BATT home. There they met a visitor, one MARTHA FRAIS, who Prester knew had been intimate on a number of occasions with Karl. She told the men that she had food for them in Gmünd. In the evening, the entire team moved back to the ski hut near Treffenboden. On the following day, Karl was sent back to the KRA-BATT home at Treffenboden, to get the food about which MARTHA FRAIS had spoken. Karl did not return for two days; when he did, he reported that the bread, fat and meat which he brought cost him some 700 marks. Prester, suspicious, went to visit MARTHA FRAIS two days later and was informed that the food was a gift from her and a number of other contacts of the team, and that no reimbursement had been sought or given.

On Prester's return to the ski hut, a summary court-martial was formed by himself and Lt. Pavlovich to hear the various charges against Karl: fictitious payments for food, protracted visits to town, petty thievery among the men, etc. The other men testified that they feared Karl's unreliability and had no desire to work with him. As a result of the testimony and evidence, Karl was sentenced to death, but at the conclusion of a three-hour talk with Prester, during which he promised to reform, he was placed on probation. Later that day, Lt. Pavlovich, Prester, Hans, and Karl returned to the KRABATT house; Pavlovich and Hans remained there, while Prester and Karl secured a horse and wagon to bring food and the team's radio set to the ski hut. About 0100 Karl returned to the village, at Prester's direction, with orders to give the horse back to its peasant owner and to return immediately to the ski hut. Instead Karl remained away for over forty-eight hours, and when he returned to the ski hut, he was garbed in a new Wehrmacht uniform. Convinced by now that Karl would never reform and that he was becoming an increasing menace to the security of the team, Prester at once carried out the sentence of the court-martial. This occurred on 2 February at about 1700 hours. About two hours later, Lt. Pavlovich and Hans arrived at the ski hut from the KRABATT home, where they had been staying for the past few days. They reported that Karl had disobeyed Prester's orders to return the horse to its owner and that as a result this peasant had notified the police that bandits living in the hills had stolen his animal. Lt. Pavlovich had seen Karl at the KRABATT home and ordered him to notify Prester and Victor immediately that the area was becoming hot. Karl had again disobeyed an order and, instead of notifying the two men in the ski hut, had spent the next twenty-four hours with MARTHA FRAIS at her home in GMÜND before returning to the ski hut.

The four remaining members of the team prepared immediately to leave. They buried Karl's body, hid the radio equipment in the deep snow, and proceeded to Gmünd to the home of a peasant named FINATZER, with whom contact had been made some time before. During the next few days' stay, a number of places were discussed as possible future hideouts. It was éventually decided to stay in a hut on the farm of a peasant named JOSEF WEGSCHEIDER-GEISCHLER at Maltaberg, who Hans said was one of his good contacts. The radio equipment was brought back from its hiding place near the Treffenboden ski hut, and late that night the team followed its peasant escort to the WEGSCHEIDER home. In the pitch-black darkness, however, Lt. Pavlovich disappeared somewhere along the route. It was not until four or five days later that Prester learned from MRS. KRABATT that Lt. Pavlovich, having become separated from the others, had returned to the MARTHA FRAIS house at Gmünd where he stayed. During the four- or five-day intervening period, Prester and his companions rested two days at the WEGSCHEIDER home and then moved to a ski hut about five kilometers distant. There the radio was set up, and a message asking again for new radio equipment was sent to OSS, Bari, over the guard channel. This message was never received by the base.

When Prester found Pavlovich at the FRAIS home, there was some discussion of future plans; and in in the next day or two Prester and Hans made a return visit to the WEGSCHEIDER's ski hut from their temporary quarters in a stable at Gmünd. Eventually Lt. Pavlovich ordered the team to move in to a spot in the mountains above FLIEGERHOF, some five kilometer west of Malta; Pavlovich said they would be transported there by HASLITZER and Dr. Wallner, a friendly contact who had treated Victor's frozen foot from time to time. Prester disliked the plan outlined by Lt. Pavlovich and expressed belief that the ski hut at Maltaberg would continue to be the best hideout. His doubts were increased that many of the arrangements outlined by Lt. Pavlovich were not altogether carefully planned. Prester eventually accepted the orders however. On the same night, 17 February, Prester and Hans left the home of MARTHA FRAIS in Gmünd for the Maltaberg ski hut to pack their belongings for the trip to Fliegerhof, while Lt. Pavlovich and Victor remained behind at the FRAIS home.

En route to the hut, Prester said goodbye to the Wegscheider family, to whom he announced that he was leaving for the Karawanken Alps. For unknown reasons, Wegscheider, having heard that Prester and Hans were preparing to leave the ski hut on his property, notified the police. What motivated him to take action, after he provided shelter for the men during a five- or six-day period, was never learned by members of the Dillon team.

Thus, while Prester and Hans waited in vain from 0600–1500 hours on 18 February for HASLITZER to appear, the police had already been alerted. At about 1500 hours, the team members were preparing to leave Gmünd to inquire about the delay when they suddenly heard shouts outside the hut, and into it stomped three policemen armed with submachine guns and a few *Volkssturm* members. The *Ortsgruppenleiter* from Malta, a brutal man, conducted the search of Prester and Hans, tied their hands, and led them on a stumbling descent of the mountain through chest-high snow. As they proceeded through the village of Maltaberg to Gmünd, a passerby shouted, "Shoot the bandit dogs." During the walk, Prester sought to reassure Hans: "Don't worry. It's the fate of war; and since so many soldiers die on the front, if they shoot us, it won't matter. Keep your mouth closed, and don't say a word." Hans promised to reveal nothing. About 2000 hours, the party arrived at Gmünd police station, where Prester discovered he was carrying the text of a radio message giving the location of a new pinpoint and asking for a radio set; he quickly swallowed the wad of paper.

The chief of local police, who was quite friendly, placed a call to the Gestapo at Spittal to notify them of the arrest. While they were awaiting the Gestapo's arrival, one of the police noticed Hans's *Soldbuch* lying on the table. Before he asked any questions about it, Hans volunteered it was a fake document and the name it contained was not really his own. From that moment on, Prester was certain that Hans would talk, although he didn't appreciate how fast or how much Hans would furnish the Gestapo with all details of the operation.

At midnight, the Gestapo chief of Spittal arrived. An hour later, the police captain from Spittal came in—a far more friendly person who ordered some *Volkssturm* people out of the room in which Prester was being held, untied his hands, and furnished him with cigarette.

At 0300, Prester, sitting in the Gmünd police station, heard shots somewhere in the village. Although he did not know it at the time, the shooting resulted in the death of Lt. Pavlovich. Although the entire neighborhood knew within a couple of hours that an American officer (Prester) and a "bandit" (Hans) had been apprehended, Lt. Pavlovich apparently did not realize how dangerous the situation had become or how quickly Hans would talk. Lt. Pavlovich and Victor were staying at the home of MARTHA FRAIS until they, together with Prester and Hans, could be transported to the newly chosen hideout near Malta. After the arrival of the Gestapo official from Spittal at the Gmünd police station, Hans agreed to lead the police to Lt. Pavlovich's hideout. Tied by a ten-meter rope to his captors, he conducted them to the home of MARTHA FRAIS and knocked on the door with a signal customarily used by the team. Victor, hearing the knock, roused Martha, who opened the door. Standing in the doorway was a police officer, who fired a shot into Lt. Pavlovich's stomach as the latter reached for his own pistol. He then withdrew from the doorway. A moment later shots were fired through the window, and two grenades tossed through the window exploded in the room. MARTHA FRAIS became hysterical and begged Lt. Pavlovich to kill her to prevent vengeance upon her by the Nazis. Lt. Pavlovich fired a shot through her brain, and almost immediately afterwards a shot through the head killed Lt. Pavlovich instantly.

The police made no effort to enter the house until morning. Victor sat in the room with the two bodies until daybreak and contemplated a possible escape, but at 0700 a crowd of police and SS men, led by a young boy, entered the house. One of the SS recognized Victor [Ernest Fiechter was native to the area along with fellow DV Karl Steinnender] and addressed him by his correct name. They searched him for weapons, without doing any bodily harm, and then led him to the police station where Prester and Hans and twenty of their local contacts had already been incarcerated.

It was learned subsequently, that the gendarme who shot and mortally wounded Lt. Pavlovich was JOSEF HARTLIEB of Bergim Drautale. His name and address and those of others who acted in a particularly hostile manner to the members of the Dillon team have been turned over to the British military authorities in Carinthia for appropriate action. Among these is JOSEF OBERLECHNER, mayor of Gmünd, who ordered the bodies of Lt. Pavlovich and Martha Frais to be buried without coffins. Small holes were dug and the bodies of the two were interred in a crumpled position. Oberlechner was reported to have kicked Lt. Pavlovich's body several times to force it into the grave. After the liberation, Prester personally superintended the disinterment of the bodies by a group of local Nazis who had been most hostile to him and his colleagues. Pavlovich's body was placed in a coffin and the grave was properly marked and decorated. The body of Martha Frais was removed, at the request of the family, to their own burial plot.

### III. IMPRISONMENT

During the morning of 19 February, Prester, his hands tied again by the Gestapo authorities, was driven to the Gestapo jail at Spittal and placed in solitary confinement. About noon a young Gestapo official entered the cell, tied Prester's hands with a thicker rope, and brandished a knife while warning Prester that his heart would soon be cut out. About noon Prester was ushered into the office of the Gestapo chief. As he entered the chief's secretary, a Miss Winsberg, turned pale, for she had been one of Prester's valued contacts. Luckily, however, she was not known to Hans, who by now had informed the police about all the contacts of the team of which he was aware. In the office were a number of Gestapo men, among them HERMANN HELFRICHT and RUDI PIENITZ, both of whom were later to provide extremely helpful information to Prester and his colleagues. During the twenty-minute conference, the Gestapo chief told Prester that if he talked freely, he would be treated as an officer; if he refused—Prester heard the chief talk to his subordinates about the possibility of fever injections. Prester refused and was led back to his cell, his hands still tied, as they were for a total of three and a half days.

A day later he was again brought back to the chief's office. Arranged on the table were his radio set, codebooks, signal plan, and other equipment. During the questioning about the use of the codebooks, Prester said afterwards, he lost his respect for the Gestapo's alleged intelligence and concluded that their only effective method of obtaining information was through use of brutal physical torture. Prester also felt that the system of printing encoding instructions on the back of the OSS cipher pads was a serious mistake (it should be pointed out, however, that shortly after his entrance into Austria, considerable changes in encoding procedures were developed by OSS Communications, so that a person following the instructions as printed would have automatically been sending a form of danger signal). Prester again refused to answer questions and was returned to his cell. A few minutes later a guard entered and removed ten gold pieces, which had been sewn into the crotch of Prester's trousers; this money had escaped the police in the earlier search of Prester's effects but was later reported by Hans.

At 0300 the following morning, Prester was told to put on his shoes. Since his hands were still tied, Hans was brought into his cell to help him dress. At that point he was told they were to be marched to a railroad station. Hans was informed with regret by the Gestapo official that it would be necessary, for the sake of public appearance, to tie his hands during the march. At the station Prester found Victor, who told him for the first time about the death of Pavlovich and about the arrest

of some twenty of his contacts. When Prester sought to reassure them with prom-
ises that he would never disclose his connections with them, he was told by one of
the girls that many of the peasants, out of their fear of the Gestapo, had already
talked freely of their assistance to him. The train ride to Klagenfurt was cold, but
HELFRICHT, the Gestapo agent who had been present at the questioning at Spittal, was friendly and provided them with blankets. Prester saw that practically all
of his friends were in the group, including even MARIA WINKLER, who was in
the advanced stages of pregnancy.

Upon arrival at the jail, Prester was slapped on the side of the head by the chief
warden and then placed in a room with sixteen other men. For the next two weeks,
he saw no one from the Gestapo. During this time Prester worried that the Gestapo
would use his set to send false messages to OSS.

At the end of the fortnight, HELFRICHT appeared and took Prester to Gestapo
headquarters. The atmosphere there was friendly, and after some talk about the
state of the war, Prester was asked to send a message on his radio to OSS in Bari.
The request was indignantly refused. Later he asked what sort of message they
wished him to send.

"Well, we first need some cigarettes and chocolate," was the Gestapo reply.

"If you think that Germany can win the war with some chocolate and some
American cigarettes, I'll send the message," Prester replied.

Prester said his agreement to transmit the message was based on his hope of
being able at the same time to warn OSS of his predicament. After he had consented to use the radio, HELFRICHT introduced him to OBERSLEUTENANT
HERGER, the Klagenfurt Gestapo chief; Prester commented later that they
seemed very happy at the prospect of getting American supplies. Prester was then
returned to his cell.

A couple of days later, he was brought by HELFRICHT and two Gestapo radio
men to a villa outside Klagenfurt, on the banks of the Woerther See, and from there
he sent a message to Bari—the first received from the Dillon team—announcing
that Karl was dead, that Lt. Pavlovich was "missing in action," and that the remainder of the team was located east of Spittal. The message concluded with the
danger signal.

The radio communications that followed between that date, 25 March, and 4
May, when Prester was permitted to tell the true facts about his case just prior to
his liberation and cessation of hostilities, were filled with misunderstanding and
misinterpretation that almost ended in fatal results for an American soldier and
an Austrian deserter-volunteer working for OSS.

For reasons never fully understood by the German-Austrian Section, the section was not adequately informed—if it was informed at all—that Prester was using the danger signal in each of his first thirteen messages. Two members of the section remember that when they received that first Dillon cable, one of the sergeants at the message center said that he thought the team was employing the danger signal. When he was asked by the officers to ascertain definitely whether the signal was being used, he searched the file, consulted with another member of the message center, and then said that had been mistaken. The sergeant added that the Dillon operator was actually using the current danger signal but that a different system was employed at the time the operator was briefed, so presumably the current system would not be known to him. When, on 4 May, Prester's fourteenth message announced that he had been in jail for two months and that someone had made a "big mistake" concerning his encoded messages, a thorough check of the Dillon communications file was instituted. It revealed only a notation that Prester had been briefed in use of the danger signal, but there was no indication as to the precise signal to be used. No satisfactory explanation of the failure to recognize the danger signal during the thirteen messages or to communicate its use to the section in a formal manner was offered, other than the suggestion that the general change in danger-signal procedure early in 1945 had confused the situation and that when Dillon first came on the air on 25 March, the earlier signal was completely out of use and practically forgotten by the communications personnel. It is to be emphasized that this is scarcely a satisfactory explanation concerning a matter of the utmost security affecting a team in dangerous enemy territory. Had it occurred a few months earlier, at a more critical stage of the war, this mistake would have had the most serious consequences. As it happens, the results were serious enough: Two men were parachuted to a Gestapo reception committee, placed in jail for close to three weeks, and escaped death only through the stalling tactics of a friendly police official.

The first message received by Prester from OSS on 26 March had caused him worry and confusion. It asked about his intelligence contacts; further that radio base station also gave the danger signal, as Prester understood it. He felt that the station probably knew what it was doing since, as he expressed it, "there were many and I was alone in Klagenfurt," only added to the confusion. In his second message to Bari, Prester took a chance of getting information about his status through to the German-Austrian Section. While HELFRICHT and PIENITZ were conversing in the next room, Prester sent at the beginning of his message these uncoded words: "Miles (Pavlovich) dead," and in the middle of it he sent the words

"Klagenfurt jail," also uncoded. If the station received these interpolations, they failed to understand them, for they were never transmitted to the section.

When the German-Austrian Section received the request for supplies, it gave immediate consideration to sending addition personnel as well, in order to strengthen the team, provide it with late intelligence directives, and seek to procure messages of value from the team. This plan, when communicated to Prester by radio, caused him intense dismay, and according to later statements from HEL-FRICHT, it was equally disappointing to Gestapo circles in Klagenfurt, who were far more interested in cigarettes and PX supplies than in being bothered with the capture of additional American personnel.

The German-Austrian Section went ahead with its plans, while keeping Prester informed of developments. Prester was originally alerted for the drop on 12 April, but because of bad weather the flight was scratched at the last minute. A party consisting of HELFRICHT, PIENITZ, two soldiers, and Prester waited for the plane at the designated pinpoint on Tragenwinkler Alm. The drop was made a few nights later on 16 April with Prester not among the reception committee.

The men who jumped to join the Dillon team, in an operation designated as Dillon III, were Sergeant (then Corporal) Bernd K. Steinitz, who wore first lieutenant's bars; and Otto Langer, a deserter-volunteer. Their plane, which took off from Rosignano airport, Italy, in the middle of the evening, cruised over the dropping zone for some time past the appointed hour, and it was not until 0100 that the signal lights were spotted. The two men landed successfully, within a short distance of each other. Otto's parachute had tangled in a tree, and it was some minutes before he could disengage himself from it. Eventually he found Steinitz, who said that he had lost his leg bag and was going to look for it; Steinitz suggested that in the meantime Otto bury his chute. When Otto had finished, he waited for Steinitz, but this time the latter had already been seized by the enemy police who were awaiting him. Steinitz had encountered a man wearing an American air force flyer's jacket, who identified himself as a contact of Prester. While they were talking, one of the other members of the reception group jumped on Steinitz from the rear, and he was firmly tied and bound. His captors then identified themselves as members of the German antiparachute agency and promised that no harm would come to him. Otto, wandering through the area, noticed their fire and approached. Mistaking one of the German soldiers for Steinitz, he came forward, wondering about the lack of security involved in the roaring campfire. Before he could realize what had happened, he too had been jumped upon and bound.

The two men were kept lying by the fire all night, and in the morning their captors went to search for the packages. Steinitz and Otto commented ruefully that it had been a perfect drop, with all the packages in a line and in a small area, with the exception only of the leg bag, which contained some of Steinitz's personal belongings. In the morning, with their hands still tied, they were marched down the hillside, and after two and a half hours arrived at a farmhouse. There the gendarmes arranged to cart away the supply packages for the forty kilometer drive to Klagenfurt. Once there, they were placed in separate cells in the Gestapo jail. On the second day Otto was called in for interrogation by HELFRICHT and the local Gestapo chief. He was asked about his political and military past; it was not until some days later that he was asked about the nature of his mission. Otto's reply was that the two men had been parachuted into Austria to estimate posthostilities supply and food needs.

One of the principal questions asked by the Gestapo was the meaning of the initials "OSS." They said they knew the last two letters stood for "secret service," but they didn't know what the "damned 'O'" represented.

Steinitz, too, was being separately interrogated during this period. His treatment, as an American officer, was somewhat better than Otto's, and he received a slightly better grade of food—although it was far from first quality. During even the early phases of their interrogation, both Steinitz and Otto began to realize that HELFRICHT was "going easy" on them. This was largely the result of some conversations between HELFRICHT and Prester shortly after he started to send the radio messages to OSS. Prester told HELFRICHT that the war was quickly driving to a victorious close and that if he wished to see his wife and children again, he had best help the American representatives. After some further discussion HELFRICHT agreed to handle with as little speed as possible the papers and documents in the cases of Prester, his colleagues, and all their arrested contacts, and later, after the Dillon III drop, the cases of Steinitz and Otto. All the persons concerned vouched that HELFRICHT had been helpful, and Steinitz asserts that he owes his life to the activities of this Gestapo man.

## IV. LIBERATION

Conditions in the jail had been very difficult for Prester, and after a month he persuaded HELFRICHT to get him better accommodations. As a result, he was moved into a less crowded cell with DR. WALLNER, an old contact of the team who had been arrested at the same time as Prester. Likewise he was able to get HELFRICHT to release to him some of Lt. Pavlovich's old clothes to replace his own tattered uniform. In the lining of the trousers thus provided, Prester discovered a number of gold pieces, which he was able to use to have a guard buy food on the black market. This he distributed among all his friends and Steinitz and Otto. In addition, he arranged for DR. WALLNER to be appointed the doctor for all the prisoners and through him to reestablish contact with all his coprisoners.

The events that transpired during the final stages of the team's captivity may be better understood in the light of events known only after the liberation. A DR. SCHNEIDER, together with a few close associates, had been pressing over a period of some months for a peaceful surrender of Carinthia to the western Allies. Their influence had extended to several branches of the official service and had also had an effect on Gauleiter RAINER. The Gauleiter changed his mind frequently, alternately calling for last-ditch resistance and promising to preserve the province from war destruction. It was this "soft-peace" group that saw possibilities of using the Americans for liaison purposes and which probably helped to save their lives.

In the same cell with Prester and DR. WALLNER was RUDI BOCKALMANN, the mayor of Ottmanach. BOCKALMANN was released some twenty days before Prester. Early in May, as Prester and his guard were making their daily excursion to the radio cottage on the shore of the Woerther See, BOCKALMANN informed Prester that a "very important person wanted to see him about a very important matter." The three men then walked to a room where he met a DR. SCHNEIDER. SCHNEIDER proposed that Prester escape. Prester pointed out that he had numerous opportunities to do so but felt his duty lay with his twenty colleagues in the jail. SCHNEIDER then asked for another meeting later in the day, and on his return to the jail, Prester obtained permission from HELFRICHT for an afternoon trip. At the radio cottage he found SCHNEIDER, a *Hauptsturmbannfuhrer* and HELFRICHT. Also present were the guard and the radio assistant, PIENITZ, whom Prester had previously convinced of the wisdom of helping the Americans and their contacts. There Prester was told that he was free since he was to be an intermediary officer for surrender proposal negotiations. It was then suggested that they visit BERGER, the Gestapo chief, at his headquarters for further discussions. BERGER was out of his office when the party arrived, but a *Hauptmann* in charge confirmed Prester's liberation and asked what he wished to be done.

Prester replied that he wanted all the political prisoners freed immediately. The *Hauptmann* answered that he had "too many" political prisoners who had worked with "bandits," but that they would be liberated the next day. With some heat Prester retorted that these people had worked with him, not with any "bandits," and that he wanted their release effected immediately; and that further he wanted Steinitz and DR. WALLNER brought to him at once. They appeared in twenty minutes, and ten minutes later all the remaining political prisoners had been released from jail. It was then that Prester met Steinitz for the first time. Victor, Hans, and Otto, together with four Russian parachutists and two Italians, were kept in jail while Otto was kept even longer.

Otto had been in the death cell for some time and had been sentenced to be shot on the morning of 5 May. Through Prester's intercession, HELFRICHT had had the case turned over to the divisions in order to gain time; on 5 May Prester heard that the court had refused to accept the case and that Otto, Hans, and Victor were to be executed on the morning of 6 May. Prester immediately went to the jail and ordered that the men be freed. The warden at first refused, but when Prester pointed out that the Nazi political situation had almost completely deteriorated and that the death of Otto and the others would be regarded seriously by the Allies, the warden consented to their release. Steinitz, who had been released earlier, was also facing execution.

After the liberation of the team and its contacts, Prester instructed Hans—who had been responsible for the death of Lt. Pavlovich and the arrest of the contacts— to stay around his home in a nearby village. Subsequently he was handed over to the CIC officers at Salzburg for detention and formal charges.

Upon his release from prison, Steinitz played a leading role as intermediary in the surrender negotiations for Klagenfurt. He was informed by an intermediary that RAINER, the local Gauleiter, had expressed a willingness to surrender unconditionally to the Americans, although he claimed he would resist the forces of Tito until the bitter end. When a cable to OSS from Steinitz announcing this fact and suggesting that an officer with full authority be flown to Klagenfurt for surrender discussions failed to produce action immediately, Steinitz left Klagenfurt by car for Salzburg to meet the American military forces there and present to them the representatives of the new Carinthian "government," DR. SCHNEIDER, the man who had talked with Prester a few days earlier, and SS Hauptman RHINEHOLD VON MOHRENSCHILDT, serving as a military representative of the "government."

The trip from Klagenfurt to Salzburg was delayed by the party's being arrested by an SS colonel, who threatened the entire group with execution, but the intercession of a Wehrmacht general who was himself in the midst of surrender negotiations saved their lives. By the time of the arrival of Steinitz and the two representatives at Salzburg, however, the British army had already entered Klagenfurt, and the general surrender of all enemy forces in central and eastern Europe had obviated the necessity of any localized surrender. Accordingly the party returned to Klagenfurt on 10 May.

On 13 May an OSS field detachment assigned to the British Eighth Army by the German-Austrian Section arrived in Klagenfurt and channeled to British intelligence authorities considerable data gathered by Prester, Steinitz, Victor, and Otto concerning the activities and whereabouts of leading Nazi officials throughout the area.

Suitable rewards were given to the many peasants of Gmünd who had aided the various members of the Dillon team and who had been placed in jail through the testimony provided the Gestapo by the deserter-volunteer Hans. Under the personal supervision of Prester, leading Nazis of Gmünd and neighboring villages were assigned the task of disinterring the bullet-ridden bodies of Lt. Pavlovich and MARTHA FRAIS. With many friendly townspeople in attendance, Lt. Pavlovich was honored with a formal funeral service and his new grave decorated with flowers and with the flag of the country for which he sacrificed his life.

# APPENDIX C

**MEMO: BERND STEINITZ DEBRIEFED BY**
**DYNO LOWENSTEIN 8 MAY 1945 AT SALZBURG, AUSTRIA**

[Note: Some sentences are incomplete, since they are Lowenstein's original notes.]

Peter [Steinitz], when dropped on April 16, landed ok and was able to hide his leg bag and parachute, which are still at the spot and can be found. Pinpoint was missed by drifting about 50 feet; almost missed plateau. Otto got hung over a cliff in [a] tree. Parachute was hidden. Peter started going up the hill alone, and Otto followed 100 feet behind. On top of the plateau he saw light signal flashing "ok." Reception party also had fire at about same place. Then Peter saw men clothed with U.S. flying jacket, walked up and Peter put his gun away. Peter asked him for his name. Otto said that his name was Hans. He told Peter that Julio and the other guys were further down the mountain waiting for party and supplies. Peter asked him how many bundles he had seen dropping. Answer: Six. Peter: We better put the fire out. Answer: Ok. That time two men came from behind the fence, one of them with a machine pistol. Peter: "Who are they?" Answer from Hans: "People from the village who will help us." Two others had been sitting at the fire who were introduced to Peter as people from a nearby [village]. This place, according to them, was also a hiding place for TRC set. Hans asked Peter whether he had any mail for Julio from his wife. Answer: "No." At that point, Peter waved for Otto to follow him. Then, Peter, while he bent down to find his flying jacket, all four

men, including Hans, jumped on him. Wrestling for some time, a few of the
Gestapo people were hurt. Then Peter was roped and brought back to the fire
where he found Otto in the same condition. Then both were promised that nothing would happen if they behaved ok. Interrogation of Peter: "What did you know
about Julio?" Answer: "Never seen any of the boys." Searched personnel (Germans searched Steinitz, a.k.a. Peter, and found the following): Emergency code
with BBC message, also packing slip prepared by Ulmer, German money. On bun-
dle, Gestapo found packing list marked "OSS, OSD, Dillon 3 itemizing contents!!!!!" Next morning interrogation: Neither Peter nor Otto said anything.
Then left plateau and arrived in farm around noon with "supply bundles" arriving
around noon. Bundles were taken down to valley. Stayed in farm about four to five
hours, were fed and guarded by three machine guns. Peter read his Yank maga-
zine. Six in the evening arrived at the first village in the valley. Three Gestapo men,
one spoke English, waited for them. "Interrogation in village Gasthof." Interrogation in English: Gestapo had great knowledge of team because one of Julio's men
had confessed and turned over local contacts. Gestapo told Peter that Otto would
be shot. Peter's case supposedly was different because he was working for his own
country. If he would be reasonable, he would be safe. Peter refused to talk because
he was a U.S. officer.

Then proceeded to Villach on truck. Took ropes off. Population assembled.
Luftwaffe soldier walked up to them and said it was silly because plane was heard
widely, too low. Everyone was watching plane. From village, proceeded to Klagenfurt (April 17) arrived evening. Were delivered at Klagenfurt Geheime Haf-
tanstalt. Both remained in single cells. From that time on, Peter did not see Otto
until three days before release. Next interrogation April 20th: Same interrogators.
Told Peter that one of them was head Gestapo for enemy parachutists. Asked Peter
if he was treated ok. Peter stuck to cover story. Interrogator believed it. Interrogator: "How long were you in the OSS." Peter: "Short time." Next interrogation
April 24th: One letter (the Gestapo brought up a letter they found stating that
Peter was team captain). What was the reason? Peter answered, "This was for-
mality for drawing rations, real reason liaison officer for other armies." Peter was
fed (at the prison) with U.S. rations. Received also lard given courtesy of Julio who
was sitting in other cell (prison food very bad, little bread, soup). April 25th: Warden Franz Cogler approached Peter and told him he was politically unreliable.
Brought him together with British corporal Albert Smith from Barnhurst. He had
been POW and was brought to prison because he had listened to BBC in his sta-

lag. Through Cogler, Peter was able to send message out to Julio and Otto. Himmler had personally signed death sentence for Otto. Also Cogler had told him that Otto had given full confession, including how he was recruited, schools, name of Lieutenant Ulmer and Dyno Lowenstein, everything about Bari, but not Curcinella. Peter got in touch through Cogler with leaders of Communists in Villach, of Socialist Communists in Klagenfurt and Jonas Mikola (Catholic minister of all inmates in the prison). Among outside people he met were Dr. Schurz Radetzkistr. Who was used by the team as meeting place and letter box. Cogler got a friend of his and agreed that in case the Gestapo wanted to shoot Peter or Julio, they would get them out that day and get them to the partisans. Peter did not want to go and see partisans unless he absolutely had to. Wanted to keep contacts going. Twenty people in prison were taken because of confession of one of Julio's men. Contacts between Julio and Peter; Dr. Wallner, inmate, who was also prison doctor. Also through prison barber who was a Frenchman. Julio was taken out of prison on May 1st to send a message. Gestapo chief Helmuth had at all times been working for Julio, which Peter knew only after release. Helmuth also helped so that Otto would not be shot. Suggested that execution be postponed until Allies took over control. While Peter was in prison, he got his money all back (3 May). Was released from prison on May 3.

# APPENDIX D

## REPORT OF GESTAPO ANTI-PARACHUTE
## CHIEF IN KLAGENFURT

On or about February 20, 1945, I received from the foreign department in Spittal/
Drau a telephone dispatch stating that in the Gmünd/Maltaberg area, an American agent group was captured. I went to Spittal the next day in order to make the
necessary inquiries myself. When I arrived, the following men were already under
arrest: the American, Lt. Prester, the German soldiers Helmuth Kinzian, cover
name Hans Schwager, Ernst Fiechter, cover name Ernst Fuchs.

As far as I heard from the chief of the foreign department in Spittal/Drau, Julio
and Kinzian were arrested in a hut in Maltaberg. The report was made by the "Ken-
schler" Josef Wegscheider from Maltaberg. Kinzian told the gendarmerie during
his first questioning that the leader of the group, Capt. Miles, and one other member of the team, Ernst Fichter, were staying in the apartment of Martha Frais in
Gmünd. With this information at hand, the arrest of all persons was tried during
the night from February 19 to February 20, 1945. Kinzian led the gendarmerie
and one officer of the foreign dept. Spittal/Drau. Kinzian knocked on the door,
whereupon Martha Frais opened the door, and Gendarme Hartlieb from Gmünd
jumped into the room with a pistol in his hand, calling "hands up." Miles pulled his
pistol anyhow, whereupon Hartlieb fired a shot. Miles offered resistance with his
weapon. The troops left the room but kept the house occupied. As shots continued to come from Miles's room, hand grenades were thrown into the room but
caused no damage. The next morning the troops again occupied the Frais apart-

ment. Capt. Miles and Martha Frais were lying dead in bed. According to Fichter, Miles was hit in the stomach by Hartlieb and was in great pain. He then shot Martha through the heart and shot himself through the head. Fichter was arrested and brought to the court prison in Spittal/Drau. The following persons were also under arrest: Berta Krabatt, Anna Sornig, Gustav Philipzig, Josef Finatzer, Luise Finatzer, Elisabeth Finatzer, Johann Pichorner and wife, Ferdinand Bandrieser and wife, Helene Wirnsberger, Josef Kratzwald, Josef Weismann, Dr. Alfred Wallner, Josef Wegscheider, Marianne Wegscheider, and Anna Steinwender.

The daughter-in-law of Anna Steinwender was brought to me but was set free shortly after I examined her case. She did not have any connection with the agents. Still missing was the wood buyer George Haslitzer. According to Kinzian, Weismann told him that he, Weismann, was ready to give prisoners of war working for him to the agents. The truth of this report was strengthened through an apparently yet unsent cable requesting equipment for twenty men. Helene Wirnsberger was arrested because she cut the hair of one of the agents in her sister's apartment and most probably knew of the existence of the group. Except Josef Weismann, Josef Kratzwald and Helene Wirnsberger, all admitted that they knew about the agents, had fed them, given them shelter, and aided them in other ways possible. After all inquiries were made, Mrs. Bandrieser was released because of [her] advanced pregnancy. Mrs. Pichorner, because of ill health and seven children who were not provided for. Josef Kratzwald and Helene Wirnsberger were released because I found charges against them unfounded. After these people were sent home, I was ordered by my chief of section SS Lt. Col. Berger who demanded an explanation.

# APPENDIX E

## THE GERMAN VIEW OF THE DILLON MISSION, GESTAPO ANTI-PARACHUTE AGENT CHIEF IN KLAGENFURT, HELMUTH HELFRICHT

This especially because the Gauleiter, Dr. Reiner, wanted fast prosecutions of these persons and wished to publish the given sentence as a deterrent example. I argued that the police and not the party is responsible for matters concerning intelligence and that my actions are guided by the responsibility to my own conscience and not to the party. After this discussion, the case was closed, but I received the order not to release anyone again without first consulting my chief.

Julio Prester, during his questioning, concealed all information which would have given us further hints on the matter. He kept all names and identifications of involved persons secret. He also declared that most of Kinzian's statements were false. Ernst Fiechter's behavior was similar to Lt. Prester's. He admitted only such things as were already known to us through the questioning of Kinzian and others.

On or about March 1, shortwave radio contacts were started. I am not a radio operator; nor do I have any technical knowledge in this field. I, therefore, contacted the chief of the broadcast surveillance station in Klagenfurt, Plenitz. He took charge of all technical problems. Julio Prester was willing to operate for us. The aim of these contacts was getting in of new agents and to gain more knowledge of what countermeasure steps to take. Mostly Julio wrote the text and enciphered the message. Only once, after we were told of a probable drop of two new agents, I added three words to the text, which remained unknown to Julio and led to the eventual drop of Lt. and Otto Langer. During these radio contacts, which were held outside the city of Klagenfurt and to which I mostly led Julio myself, I learned more about him. Julio made many attempts to change my conviction. He argued that there was no more reason to kill any more people who had been arrested on account of his work now that the war is just about lost for us. "After all," he said, "they are all Austrians and acted as good patriots." Several times he also asked about his own fate, whether or not he would be shot. I promised that he would live as long as would the case be with me. I said this especially because men who stick to their cause impress me. We were both certain that we would become good friends once this war is finished. Julio and his men were always treated correctly by myself and received every favor possible under existing conditions, especially food out of my own supply. To make life under arrest easier, several men were put to work, which also gave them better rations. Pichorner and Bandrieser were working for some time without guard in the field of a known family. After the loss of the industrial area in Upper Silesia and the Ruhr Valley, there was no doubt in my mind that our war supplies could not hold out in order to offer continued resistance against the Allies. From this time on I could no longer believe in a German victory. I therefore gave way to Julio's urging not to add any more victims to the ones this war had already taken. It was clear to me that every available hand would be needed for reconstruction, once the war is finished. I therefore tried to delay the sentencing of persons arrested under these circumstances until the end of the war. This was made more difficult for me at times as my chief wanted a fast trial. Even though I was again ordered by my chief, at the suggestion of the Gauleiter, to hasten the condemnation, I did not react and let the case rest. Shortly before my department (*Referat*) was dissolved, I again went to my chief in order to get further instructions on what action to take in regard to my prisoners. First, it was their intention to shoot all main participants. I argued that there was no longer any ground for such an action in view of the imminent collapse of the German army and their probable unconditional surrender. I emphasized that after all we are only an interrogating authority (*ermittleungsbehorde*) and not a court. It was not my intention to dirty my fingers with blood at the last moment. One accepted my suggestion then but kept all persons under arrest. One required, however, that Lt. Hartley, Lt. Prester, and the three members of the German army be held responsible. As I had already destroyed all rules and regulations concerning treatment of parachute agents, it was easy for me to say that Lt. Hartley and Lt. Prester were in uniform and carried military documents. They had to be treated as prisoners of war. I also succeeded in convincing my superiors to give me permission to send them to a POW camp. However, I did not do so as their mission could be better accomplished from here than from an officers' POW camp. In order to prevent the action that was supposed to be taken against Fichter, Langer, and Kinzian, they had to be handed over to the army for trial, according to an order. The time gained was sufficient to keep all three alive. I have the following to say about the behavior of Lt. Hartley and Otto Langer. I picked up Lt. Hartley April 19, 1945, in Weissenstein. Like Otto Langer he was kept in the jail of the supreme court (*Landesgricht*) in Klagenfurt in solitary confinement. I visited Lt. Hartley several times in prison before the official interrogation in order to bring him additional food partly from Julio and partly from my own supply. Already, after my first encounter, he won my sympathy. We respected each other's convictions. Our attitude toward each other was that of chivalrous enemies. He verified partly what was known to me through the statements of already interrogated persons. The reason for his coming was clear to me, however, as his papers were found in one of the parachute containers. The name OSS which was found in these papers thus became known to me. This was the first time that this name was heard of in our office. All agents arrested so far had not mentioned OSS. Lt. Hartley just claimed that he came here to organize an American military mission in case Graz and Klagenfurt would be occupied by Russian troops. I believed this statement to be true. At least I believed that he would represent the interests of the American army in such a case. I realized, however, that this was his secondary mission as it was clear from his order that he had been made leader of the Dillon group. Otto Langer repeated mostly the statement Lt. Hartley made concerning the establishment of an American military mission. His further statements were not important and did not lead to new conclusions.

From Kinzian we heard that the mission of the Dillon group was to organize Austrian patriots and bandits. Information on military, economic matters, and industry, information on the political and military situation, to seize leading men of state and party and to reconnoiter on landing places for paratroops.

One British agent, a 1st Lt., who was also parachuted in, was handed over to our foreign dept. in Unterdrauburg. He was supposed to have jumped about a month ago. The mistake was made by above dept. As I had too much work to do, I could not ask to have him sent to us. I cannot recall his name, which has been in this particular dispatch. A bigger unit in the Sulzbach secured the broadcasts of an apparently English operator. As far as I know, these contacts were kept from the middle of October to the beginning of December. The contacts were made with Moscow. I only remember that the name Robert was mentioned. He was ordered to proceed to Villach or was already on his way. The messages also gave the result of bombing attacks with sources of information. Also, several target designations in Klagenfurt, including "Gestapo" HQ.

A Russian agent group of four men was also under arrest here. They were equipped with a shortwave radio set and had an assignment to give information about enemy troop movements to their HQ. I believe they were dropped March 31, 1945, in the Villach area. According to their statements their own working area was Krainburg. This might be true as the area in which they jumped was not marked on their maps. I cannot recall the names of these men, who are now free. They were sent in the direction of the Russian lines. During the jump, the whole group consisted of five men. The fifth man, also a Russian, Chruschtschov, is missing since the drop.

I have no knowledge about others captured. It is possible, though, that others were captured in the bandit area (*Bandengebiet*-partisan held territory), but they succeeded in keeping their real identity concealed and so were not handed over to us. They were then to be processed in another department and presumably sent as bandits into a camp.

My last week in Kärnten served mostly to help this land, which I learned to love during my stay here. This is the reason why I did all I could for Lt. Hartley and Lt. Prester. I had the idea that these two men would prevent demonstrations and unnecessary or unjustified bloodshed after the collapse with the help of other American and British prisoners of war. I had no fear for my person as I had a clear conscience and could calmly await further developments. I thought that the mistakes, which unfortunately were made by our previous government to arrest all persons who belonged to a certain organization without checking as to whether they only did their duty, would not be repeated.

# APPENDIX F

**FINAL REPORT ON GERMAN CIVILIANS WHO HELPED
THE DILLON TEAM BY JULES KONIG, CAPTAIN SIGNAL
CORPS (REPORT ACTS AS AN EPILOGUE FOR THE
CIVILIANS WHO HELPED THE DILLON TEAM)**

Arrived in Gmünd, Sunday May 20, and immediately had a conference with nearly all of the agents that had helped the Dillon team. First, I thanked them in the name of the U.S. government for their help and their sacrifices they have freely given for the common cause. Their response was enthusiastic. They were told that we do not forget. They are all very sincere peasants, some of them rather rich, half a dozen of them (the best) very poor, and one even was jailed for ten weeks while awaiting a child, which was born in jail.

Here are the names of the agents:

A.   Those condemned to death and rescued at the last moment (all people of Gmünd or Maltaberg):
    Haslitzer George
    Dr. Alfred Waliner
    Bertha Krabatt
    Maria Winkler
    Anna Sornik
    Gustav Filipcig

Finatzer, Josef
Finatzer, Luise, wife of the former
Finatzer, Elisabeth, daughter

B.    Other agents who were imprisoned but not sentenced to death:
Weissman, Josef
Pichorner, Johann
Pichorner, Maria
Sandrisser, Ferdinand
Sandrisser, Fanni
Aschbacher, Anna
Bfrerrer, Bertha
Martha Frais (killed in Miles's murder)
Maria Wernsberger
Leni Wernsberger
Maria Lagger
Dullnig Kunibert

When asked what I could do for them, they came with very little claims. For instance, they asked that their radios should be given back (something I arranged the next day with the British). I knew that in the crowd there were a number of very poor people (and those had helped the most). I could not publicly offer them monetary consideration, so I told everyone to see me in the hotel the next day individually, which they did.

## DEMANDS FROM AGENTS

Finatzer would like to buy his barrack where he lives and will need 1,800 reichsmarks for it.

Pichorner has a Volkswagen which he would like to take for himself. It was left there by German army units.

The family of Martha Frais demanded that permission should be granted to disinter her body and that it should be transferred to the family grave. We promised to do this and pay for it.

Julio will see Karl's mother (the agent liquidated for betrayal and general untrustworthiness) in EISENTRATTEN and will report to me.

## INFORMATION ON WAR CRIMINALS GIVEN TO US BY AGENTS AT THE CONFERENCE

A certain number of local Nazis were especially nasty against the arrested people. Incidentally it is symptomatic of the spirit of the present population of GMÜND that they consider our people (agents) as traitors of the fatherland and as scum because they helped the Americans. One man, GUSTAV FILIPZIC, who had a little vegetable store, cannot make a living any more because the people boycott him, and he wants to move out of GMÜND and make another living somewhere.

What can we do about this?

(And what can we do) about the local Nazi bigwigs who still run around and have been instrumental in the bad treatment of our agents:

1. There is first the gendarme that killed Captain Miles. His name is JOSEF HARTLIEB OF BERG DRAUTALE, quartered at the farm of the peasant Simon. His name will be handed over for arrest to the British.

2. The mayor of GMÜND, JOSEF OBERLECHNER, is responsible for the horrible neglect of the burial of Martha Frais. Did not permit the disinterment of Miles and Martha from the square hole dug in the cemetery. We will make arrangements for both tomorrow. Names will be turned over to the British (for arrest).

3. The local Gestapo man and SA leader insisted several times to the Gestapo in Spittal and Klagenfurt that all our agents should be hung. Information to be turned over to the British.

4. JOSEF KOIZIAN, general informer in GMÜND, is a cobbler and local big shot. Still terrorizes the people in GMÜND. He is the one who, when Miles was pushed in the square hole dug for him, pushed his head in with his boots so the body would fill the grave.

5. JOSEF WEGSCHEIDER, the peasant who betrayed all our people, is still at large. His brother, the local *Orstgruppenleiter*, has already been arrested. Name to be turned over to the British.

Photographs were taken of all the agents for the war diary.

The next day I inspected Miles's grave in the company of Julio Prester. Dr. Alfred Wallner accompanied us, and his opinion is that the body should by now be in a state of full decomposition. Miles was put in the grave without a cover or a coffin. So we have made arrangements to mark his grave with a cross, his name, and the U.S. flag. Incidentally the local population daily adorns his grave, and one woman religiously rakes and cleans the borders.

I have made photographs of Martha Frais's grave and will have her disinterred and transferred to the family grave. This had been previously refused by the mayor, but Mr. Prester, who will remain in GMÜND for another four or five days, will take care of it.

We saw Captain MORGAN of GSIB Eighth Army, attached for the operations to the Eighty-seventh Division Headquarters in Millstadt, and turned over the names and circumstances of the demeanors of the war criminals which I have mentioned before. He promised that the same day a security patrol with the necessary cars would proceed to Gmünd and arrest all the people indicated by us. Proper charges will be issued against them. Relations were very cordial, and I passed along a certain number of intelligence tidbits, which pleased him enormously. I told him also of the recurrence of the Nazis in Villach, something he likes very much. Captain Morgan promised to have all the radios belonging to the agents returned to them. We then proceeded to Spittal where we secured permission for Dr. Wallner to use his car and thus enable him to move around for his practice and also do some work for us eventually.

In the afternoon I saw all the people who are in need of money and who lived chiefly off pensions given to them by the town or by the government. Their needs follow:

1. Anna Aschbacher: Her husband is in the German army, received from the government RmK 135 per month. Would like to support her for at least six months and increase the amount ten times. Expenditure: RmK 4,050, or $405.
2. FRANZ WERNSBERGER: Father of the killed Martha Frais, received a pension of RmK 136 per month. We would like to multiply it by five and pay him for at least six months until arrangements be made for further payment of his pension. Cost to us: RmK 4,050 or $405.
3. Martha's sister would like a bicycle for her work. Walks 15 km to her work everyday. Prester will get her one.
4. MARIA WINKLER: These two women are the most deserving. They are extremely poor and have given shelter and all their food to the boys. Propose a reward of $500 each.

5. Anna Sornik: Same case. Husband in the army. No food, four
   children. Proposal: $500.


## USEFUL CONTACTS

Dr. Wallner, a medical doctor, works as chief surgeon of Railroad Company in Villach. I secured permission for his free circulation in this. Chief agent for Julio and
condemned to death. Wiry, resourceful, highly intelligent. Willing to do anything
he wants. Can be contacted through his father: Mr. Wallner at the Reichsbahndi-
rektion, Villach, telephone 5091, extension 379 or 491.

Mr. Sepp Weissman, now living at Krumpendorf (no further address necessary). Also one of Julio's agents. Condemned to death. A "procurist" of the
Osterrleichische-Amerikanische Magnesit Fabrik GMBH in Radentheil. Knows
the Gmünd, Spittal, Millstadt, Villach, and Klagenfurt areas perfectly.

Baroness Rodon, Gasthof Fellman, Gmünd. Her daughter is a good partisan
contact. Daughter lives on border of Woerther See in Klagenfurt.


## FURTHER DEVELOPMENTS

Julio Prester was left in Gmünd to arrange all small matters pertaining to reward-
ing of agents. Authorization for proposed payments will be demanded today by
me by cable. I will then proceed to Gmünd to pay out agents when approval arrives.

# NOTES

*They Dared Return* is the culmination of a journey that began over eight years ago when I first met Fred Mayer. It is written from thousands of documents that come from the National Archives, private collections, and scores of oral histories with the original participants. Below are the primary sources I used and their locations.

## GREENUP MISSION FILE (GREENUP)

The first large group of documents comes from the Greenup mission file, located at the National Archives and record administration in College Park, Maryland. The Greenup files include all the incoming and outgoing radio messages sent by the team, a very detailed report of the team's mission, and individual accounts written by the team members. The files include detailed packing slips for the mission's equipment, planning documents, and memos that memorialize what these men did behind the lines. Depositions from the Gestapo are also in the file. See National Archives, Record Group 226, Entry 124, Box 26, and Record Group 226, Entry 154, Box 42.

## DEADWOOD MISSION FILE (DEADWOOD)

The Deadwood file chronicles the extraordinary story of German deserter volunteer Hermann Matull. His amazing backstory is largely drawn from detailed OSS questionnaires located in the files. What happened to Deadwood behind the lines is compiled from his mission report, radio messages, and even from German officer Maj. August Schiffer's testimony located in War Crimes Case #36.

## WAR CRIMES CASE #36 (WC#36)

War crimes case #36 is located at the National Archives and was an extensive case file used to bring the Nazi war criminals who executed several Allied agents to justice. This section contains literally thousands of other documents. The testimony and depositions, which span hundreds of pages, provide us with the Germans' viewpoint in their own words. War Crimes Case #36 is located at the National Archives, Record Group 492, Entry 246, Box 2059.

## DANIA MISSION (DANIA)

The Dania mission report includes a detailed summary of the Dania mission and detailed analysis of the partisan movement and all incoming and outgoing radio messages. The report is located at the National Archives, Record Group 226, Entry 190, Box 138..

## DILLON MISSION (DILLON)

The Dillon mission report includes a detailed summary of the Dillon mission, detailed summaries and biographies of participants, and all incoming and outgoing radio messages. The report is located at the National Archives, Record Group 226, Entry 190, Box 138.

## PERSONNEL FILE (PERSONNEL)

The main characters in the book have what is known as a "personnel file" located at the National Archives. These files contain each agent's basic biographical details and were used extensively for individuals like Walter Haass and Dyno Lowenstein. They are located at the National Archives in various boxes located in Record Group 226, Entry 190.

## ORAL HISTORIES (OH)

Over the past eight years, I interviewed every surviving member of the "Jewish five." Of the more than two thousand World War II veterans I have interviewed, these men were among the most compelling. This journey began in 2001 when I interviewed Fred Mayer. Fred invited me to his mountainside home numerous times, and on every occasion his memory was crystal clear and never embellished. Always self-effacing, Fred sometimes downplayed his role and was humble. His memory also jived with the original Greenup mission report and all of the radio transmissions that accurately recorded to the smallest detail some of his most incredible exploits. I also spent many hours on the phone with Hans Wynberg and traded scores of e-histories with him. "E-history" is a term I coined in my fifteen-year-old e-history and oral history project called www.thedrop zone.org.

This book deals mainly with the Greenup mission since I felt the other missions required separate treatment. Nevertheless, this volume captures the essentials of the Dania and Dillon missions. I visited Bernd Steinitz and interviewed him extensively over the phone. George Gerbner and I spoke on many occasions in 2003 about the Dania mission. Sadly, I never had a chance to speak with Alfred Rosenthal, who passed away decades ago. The author also interviewed *Johnny B* pilot, John Billings, in 2003.

Through the intrepid Geoff Jones, the late and very generous former president of the OSS Society, I was able to interview Walter Haass and Dyno Lowenstein.

## PROLOGUE

The contents of the prologue come from the author's extensive interviews with Fred Mayer and from the Greenup mission file, which contains a postwar deposition from Güttner by OSS's Hart Perry (GREENUP, OH).

## 1. "GET ME OUT OF THE INFANTRY!"

3  The opening scene fleshing out Mayer's capture of the Eighty-first Division HQ comes from interviews with Mayer (OH).

5  "This was my military training" (OH)

5  "do your best at everything everyday, control what you can, and what you can't, don't worry about" (OH)

5  "Jew bastard"(OH)

6  "'a German officer, nothing [would] happen to [him and his family].' Mayer's mother was more pragmatic, stating bluntly, 'We are Jews and we are going'"(OH)

6  "the United States [had] provided [his family] a haven. I felt a need to give something back" (OH)

6  "enemy alien"(OH, GREENUP)

## 2. COUNTRY CLUB

9 "Chappell could pass for a Nazi officer" (OH). See also Patrick O'Donnell, *The Brenner Assignment: The Untold Story of the Most Daring Spy Mission of World War II* (Cambridge, MA: Da Capo Press, 2008), 21–24.

9 "aggressiveness of spirit and willingness to close with the enemy" Kermit Roosevelt, *War Report of the OSS*, vol. 1 (New York: Walker and Company, 1976), 224.

10 "espionage is by its very nature not to be considered as 'honorable' or 'clean' or 'fair' or 'decent'" Patrick O'Donnell, *Operatives, Spies and Saboteurs: The Unknown Story of the Men and Women of the OSS* (New York: Free Press, 2004), 12.

10 "The United States has always prided itself on the fact that no spies were used and its intelligence officers overseas have always kept their hands immaculately clean" Commander John Riheldaffer to Special Intelligence Section ONI, National Archives (hereafter NA), Record Group 38, Box 1.

10 "Gentleman do not read each other's mail" Norman Polmar and Thomas Allen, *Spy Book: The Encyclopedia of Espionage* (New York: Random House, 1997), 606.

12 "Donovan formulated an integrated 'combined arms' approach of shadow-war techniques: 'persuasion, penetration, and intimidation . . . are the modern counterparts of sapping and mining [used] in the siege warfare of former days,'" "Propaganda represented the 'arrow of initial penetration,'" "OSS organization and function" "June 1945," NA, Record Group 226, Entry 141, Box 4; "History," NA, Record Group 226, Entry 99, Box 75.

12 "play a bush league game, stealing the ball and killing the umpire" Richard Dunlop, *Donovan: America's Master Spy* (New York: Rand McNally, 1982).

12 "We looked for people with existing connections into Germany" (OH)

13 "The OSS undertook and carried out more different types of enterprises, calling for more varied skills than any other single organization of its size in the history of our country" OSS, *Assessment of Men: Selection of Personnel for the OSS* (New York: Rinehart & Company, 1948), 10.

14 "If you don't risk, you don't win" (OH)

14    "intelligent, resourceful, in splendid physical condition and known
      for his good judgment" (DANIA)
14    "quiet and conscientious" (GREENUP)
15    "Hans latched on to me and saw me as kind of an older brother"
      (OH)
15    "aggressive, husky, resourceful, and a natural leader who has a re-
      markable ability to improvise in special situations" (GREENUP)
15    "intelligent, cautious and completely loyal to Fred" (PERSONNEL)
15–16 "His father put $3,600 in a bank account, and the two boys lived with
      a diamond cutter, a business contact of their father's, in New York
      City. Hans enrolled in Brooklyn Technical High School and excelled
      in his studies, particularly chemistry," "'We understand you speak
      German, Dutch and English. Would you like to help your country?'
      Wynberg replied, 'Sure'" (OH, PERSONNEL)
16    "'good at it, [especially] the jujitsu.' The men learned their trade from
      a fifty-something, gray-haired combat instructor from Shanghai, British
      major Ewart Fairbairn, who developed one of the deadliest systems of
      street fighting known to man, called 'gutter fighting'" Gutter fighting
      quotes come from a script Fairbairn wrote for an OSS training film
      called *Gutter Fighting*, NA, Record Group 226, Entry 90, Box 11.
16    "Suppose I gotta ease up a bit" (OH)
17    "drunken fools driving [the tanks] and accidentally drove one of the
      vehicles into a ditch" (OH)
17    "I was a damn good tank driver" (OH)
17    "We had to wash our uniforms every night and put them on in the
      morning (dried or not, but at Fort Benning that spring it was warm
      enough for the clothes to dry). Boots had to be polished including
      the soles" (Wynberg e-history, OH)
17    "Punishment was frequent but fairly mild [twenty push-ups] for
      minor infractions" (OH)
18    "A crosswind caught us and we ended up in the Chattahoochee"
      (OH)

## 3. THE WAIT

19    "secret training ground" (OH)
19    "took the airport. [We] came in from the back. There were only a few
      guards [protecting the airport], and we took them too" (OH)

20   "The one time we got a few hours leave was a brief visit to the only
     port of Catalina Island, namely, Avalon. It was the first time in months
     that we had received a pass. All of us were of course far from home"
     (Wynberg e-history, OH)

21   "Lieutenant, the men are hungry and want more to eat" (OH)

21   "Wynberg, not another word. I do not want to hear such things"
     (OH)

21   "But, lieutenant, the men are hungry" (OH)

21   "Wynberg, I said 'not another word'" (OH)

21   "demoted to private for disobeying an order" (OH)

21   "snuck up on the cattle, much like Indians hunting buffalo," "picked
     out a calf at the edge of the herd and shot it," "worked in a New York
     butcher shop before the war," "did a masterful job converting part of
     our bounty into delicious steaks" (Chappell OH)

22   "'no one in Oran knew we were coming, and no one knew what to do
     with us,' recalled Wynberg" (Wynberg e-history, OH)

23   "'Sir, my name is Captain Howard Chappell of the OSS.' The gen-
     eral looked at him, sneering"

23   "Who the hell are you?" "OSS. Office of Strategic Services," "'We
     don't know anything about OSS,' responded the general, who then
     announced, 'You are to report as replacements for other units'"
     (Chappell OH)

23   "After almost getting court-martialed in Oran, I learned that the OSS
     had a secret base in Algiers" (Chappell OH)

23   "The train trip to Algiers was slow since the trains stopped in at least
     half a dozen villages" (Wynberg e-history, OH)

24   "In Algiers we had of course nothing to do, so our officers had to think
     of keeping us busy. Our captain, a bit of a cowboy, ordered us" (Wyn-
     berg e-history, OH)

25   "Having nothing to do in Algiers meant we did get evenings" (Wyn-
     berg e-history, OH)

25   "After two months in Algiers we received orders to embark on a
     British troopship" (Wynberg e-history, OH)


## 4. A ROLL OF THE DICE

27   "I lost my blood" (OH)

27   "I don't want anyone to know how fucked up the situation is" (OH)

28  "We are going to sit here until doomsday unless we do something about it" (OH)

28  "We're going to go to Allied Intelligence in Caserta and try to change our fate" (OH)

28  "We essentially mutinied" (OH)

28  "Chapin was an advertising executive for General Foods" (PERSONNEL)

29  "I told him I was Jewish and that I wanted to jump behind the lines to help end the war" (OH)

29  "You will hear from me" (OH)

29  "Lt. Alfred C. Ulmer Jr., a sales and advertising executive before the war, known for his quick wit and boyish demeanor" (PERSONNEL)

29  "Mayer responded yes without hesitation, but Hans Wynberg allegedly said no" (PERSONNEL, OH)

29–30  "'Do you appreciate what can happen to you?' Mayer stared directly into Ulmer's eyes: 'This is more our war than yours'" (OH)

30  "All terror and sabotage troops of the British and their accomplices, who do not act like soldiers but like 'bandits,' are to be treated as such by the German troops" Directive 46, more widely known as the infamous "Commando Order," Fuhrer Order, October 18, 1942 (NARA)

30  "The order arose from Hitler's excitement about two kinds of intensified warfare which made their appearance about the same time in the autumn of 1942. One was the fatal efficacy of excellently equipped sabotage detachments, which landed by sea or were dropped from the air. The other, special agents running wild in the fighting methods of enemies [Russian partisans] who acted singularly or in small groups" Philip Blood, *Hitler's Bandit Hunters: The SS and Nazi Occupation of Europe* (Washington, DC: Potomac Books, 2006), 115, 183.

31  "They compiled complete data on the 'southeast wall,' including the exact location of fortified hills, anti-tank ditches, pillboxes, artillery sites, machine gun emplacements, etc. . . . They also located some excellent targets for Allied bombing raids, including a locomotive factory and a secret airfield" Dupont mission report, NA, Record Group 226, Entry 110, Box 4, hereafter called (DUPONT).

31  "bought his girl a diamond ring" (DUPONT)

32  "On October 25, the men, with a band of Yugoslavian partisan guides, crossed the Reich border and the 'New German Boundary'" Orchid

mission report, NA, Record Group, Entry 110, Box 5, hereafter referred to as (ORCHID).

33    "'refused to move any further north without a large supply drop from
the OSS.' They 'politely declined permission for the team to move
north of the Drava River without them'" (ORCHID)

34    "The intelligence forwarded by the team contained some items of extreme value to the Air Forces: information about bomb damage"
(ORCHID)

34    "Hans [one of the deserted-volunteers] agreed to lead the police to
Lt. Pavlovich's hideout" (DILLON)

34    "The police made no effort to enter the house until morning" (DIL-
LON)

35    "'He was resolute and had a thorough knowledge of the European
underground and the German order of battle.' Soft-spoken yet decisive, he had recently graduated from the army's intelligence program
at Camp Ritchie, located in the bucolic Blue Ridge foothills of western Maryland" (PERSONNEL)

36    "[His] analytic mind, keen intelligence, complete dependability and
discretion and a highly activist temperament, in my opinion, makes
him ideal for field work" (PERSONNEL)

36    "'border secretary.' In this capacity, he 'performed extremely valuable work in maintaining underground contacts [with German and
Belgian Jews]'" (PERSONNEL)

37    "only possible chance to penetrate Germany and Austria" Kermit
Roosevelt, *War Report of the OSS*, vol. 2, *The Overseas Targets* (New
York: Walker and Company, 1976), 294, 315–23.

37–38    "Shortly after the pair settled in, Lowenstein introduced them to their
new teammate, Paul Kröck. With a round baby face and doe eyes"
(DILLON, PERSONNEL)

38    "Dyno was a damned good teacher" (OH)

39    "When we got up in the morning and before we sat down for break-
fast he made the [very small group] of OSS members stand up and
take out our .45 caliber pistols" (Wynberg e-history, OH)

39    "One evening, Hans and Freddie crept into the motor pool of a
nearby army unit and 'procured' a half-track. Freddie recalled, 'We
would use the vehicle all over the place and then park it in the back of
the villa'" (OH)

39  "Thank you and Merry Christmas" (OH)
40  "Luke [my brother] had participated in the Normandy landings and his outfit [with the First Army] remained in Normandy for a while" (Wynberg e-history, OH)
41  "With very strong German accents and no papers, we looked for maps that showed the location of all Allied minefields in the Brindisi and Bari harbors" (OH)

## 5. INTO THE CAGE

43  "Aversa, Italy, January 1945: A compliment of OSS MPs pushed through the front gate of the stockade" (OH and various documents)
43  "get me up-to-date on my German" (OH)
44  "If you see a British or Amis [American] officer, it is still 'Heil Hitler' around here, got it?" (OH)
44  "Confidant and cool, Franz Weber was no ordinary soldier" (GREENUP, PERSONNEL)
44  "a *Himmelfahrtskommando* team, whose members had essentially been given a 'one way ticket to heaven'" (PERSONNEL, GREENUP, OH)
45  "terrible" (OH)
45  "I am glad that the war is over for the two of us" (OH)
45  "I trust him" (OH)
45  "surprise" (OH)
45  "'Are you willing to parachute behind enemy lines with us?' 'Yes'" (OH)
46  "risk my life going in with him" (OH)
46  "The team's mission, soon to be code-named Greenup, involved gathering intelligence in the Innsbruck area on everything from the rumored *Alpenfestung* to German jet production" (GREENUP)

## 6. THE HUSTLER

47  "Three months earlier, on October 1, 1944, Haass and Lowenstein had stridden confidently through the POW camp's alleys of canvas tents" (DEADWOOD)
48  "You're a German spy" (OH)
48  "Do you know what your people did to my people?" (OH)

48    "Born in Hamburg, Germany, on December 21, 1918, to middle-class
      parents with Communist sympathies, Matull joined the Communist
      Youth Organization at an early age" (DEADWOOD)

49    "Being a sailor and having been abroad, he [did] not like a system of
      dictatorship," "known to help underground people in difficulties with
      the police" (DEADWOOD)

49    "'In December of 1940,' he later recalled, 'I was accused of a self-
      inflicted wound, a bullet accidentally shot me in the leg'" (DEAD-
      WOOD)

49    "lack of proof" (DEADWOOD)

49    "lowering the morale of troops" (DEADWOOD)

49    "accidentally" (DEADWOOD)

49    "When released from the hospital, he lived on false papers for three
      months in Germany, one month in Hamburg, and two months in
      southern Germany" (DEADWOOD)

50    "probationary battalion Z.B.V. #7" (DEADWOOD)

50    "[giving] him furlough papers twice a month' to travel back to Ham-
      burg to treat his 'wound,'" "applied on his arm [would] make it swell
      considerably for about a month" (DEADWOOD)

50    "He's a hustler. If he wants to do a mission, let him hustle for the OSS"
      (OH)

## 7. ALPENFESTUNG

51–52   "Hofer seized upon the idea of creating what the American's feared,
        an Alpine fortress, and coined the term *Alpenfestung*, or 'Alpine re-
        doubt.' In the fall of 1944, he sent a proposal to Martin Bormann,
        Hitler's secretary, for approval" Donald Detwiler, ed. *WWII German
        Military Studies*, vol. 23 (New York: Garland, 1979).

53      "The *New York Times* ran a an article with the ominous headline 'Last
        Fortress of the Nazis'" *New York Times*, April 8, 1945.

54      "The information we get here locally seems to tend more and more
        towards a withdrawal toward the Austrian Alps with the idea of mak-
        ing a last stand there" OSS cables found at NA in Record Group 226,
        Entry 90, Box 7.

54      "When organized German resistance collapses, there will probably
        be more than one Reduit [*sic*] or fortress of Nazi resistance" OSS ca-
        bles found at NA in Record Group 226, Entry 90, Box 7. Also see the

excellent account on the Redoubt debate in Mauch and Christof, *The Shadow War Against Hitler* (New York: Columbia University Press, 2003), 192–196.

54      "'Substantial amounts of foodstuffs being collected here and . . . some underground factories are being prepared to supply arms for mountain warfare.' Food was considered 'the main economic deficiency (of the Redoubt)'" "The Alpine Reduit [*sic*] Survey of Available Intelligence," NA, Record Group 226, Entry 90, Box 7.

55      "'no opportunity' to establish the 'redoubt'" Gen. Dwight Eisenhower to Gen. George Marshall, March 31, 1945, 1698, WWII collection, Marshall Library, Lexington VA.

55      "[I spent] seven months in jail for an extended furlough which I took to Bad Schaller, as well as several minor incidents which probably caused me to lose the respect of the SS and Gestapo" (GREENUP)

55–56   "the evil genius," "This headquarters did not accomplish anything to defeat the enemy, and that must be changed!" (WC#36)

56      "In several instances where Schiffer's instructions were not executed properly, he threatened his men at the point of a gun to carry out his orders immediately. . . . Without hesitation . . . [he] would have liquidated us" (WC#36)

56      "far more tightly controlled than any other part of Europe [including the rest of Germany previously attacked by OSS]" Kermit Roosevelt, *War Report of the OSS*, vol. 2, *The Overseas Targets* (New York: Walker and Company, 1976), 285.

56      "parachuted [fake Allied agents] into Austria [with the knowledge of Franz Hofer] complete with agent equipment to seek safe houses and friendly contacts in the area" Roosevelt, *War Report of the OSS*, vol. 2, 294–295.

56      "Locals discovered offering help and support 'were liquidated.' As a result, Austrians were too terrified to offer much assistance to real Allied agents" Roosevelt, *War Report of the OSS*, vol. 2, 294–295.

56      "never cooperated extensively with the OSS" Roosevelt, *War Report of the OSS*, vol. 2, 295.

## 8. OPERATION GREENUP

58      "drop a pickle in a barrel" Telephone OH with *Johnny B* pilot John Billings, 2002.

58    "'If they're crazy enough to jump, we're crazy enough to fly 'em,' quipped Lieutenant Billings" Telephone OH with *Johnny B* pilot John Billings, 2002.

59    "Oberleutenant Erich Schmitzer of the Hochgebirgsjäger Battalion Four and the other as an Italian railroad worker by the name of Niccolò Palmezano" (GREENUP)

59    "usually notify [them] of a drop scheduled for late that night or the following day." The Austrian BBC coded message for Greenup was "Achtung Alice Moll. Florence Nightinggale geht Krankenhäuser" (GREENUP)

60    "Turn, turn, turn, damn it!"(GREENUP, OH)

## 9. OPERATION DEADWOOD

61    "'Irritant Ointment' above the word 'POISON'" stamped in black letters (DEADWOOD)

61    "most promising candidate" (DEADWOOD)

62    "Mason [a.k.a. Matull] has a high degree of intelligence and was always able to quickly grasp the idea involved in every step of instruction" (DEADWOOD)

62    "He was also able to apply his knowledge to the successful completion of all of the training exercises" (DEADWOOD)

62    "Easily aroused, and in order to prove his points [he] would often relate revealing experiences from his past" (DEADWOOD)

62    "the OSS furnished Matull with papers identifying him with the German Fourth or First Parachute Division" (DEADWOOD)

62    "It depends on the swelling of the arm, whether Mason [Matull] has to be on emergency furlough or can be an individual transferred from a field hospital to a home hospital. If he gets an emergency furlough, I would suggest his paper reflect that his home was 'totally bombed out with loss of next of kin'" (DEADWOOD)

63    "The dollar is worth a hundred marks and opens every door" (DEADWOOD)

63    "completely unfit" (DEADWOOD)

63    "[His] intentions were not completely altruistic; he was also motivated by money. He hoped to open a restaurant when the Allies occupied Germany after the war.... We told Mason [Matull] we would do what we could for any families who would help him" (DEADWOOD)

63   "great butchery store, who was at the same time a meat control official. He was working for the black market in a very clever way using
his official capacity as a cover," "'a big lawyer's firm in Hamburg,' as
well as with several noncommissioned officers in the German navy
with whom Matull had gone through service schools and who were
permanently stationed at German manufacturing plants in Hamburg.
They would be able to furnish information on German shipbuilding
and Navy experiments" (DEADWOOD)

64   "In Hamburg he would contact Charley and send him down to Munich to accept the job as waiter in a restaurant in which he was working previously. Charley would provide for quarters for Mason to follow
him. . . . With the help of the black market Mason will be able to travel
to almost any town that we would want him to go" (DEADWOOD)

64   "SUBJECT: scar on Mason's left-hand: There's a scar on the back of
Mason's left hand between the base of the first and second fingers.
The scar was caused by a bullet and has left a permanent swelling.
SIGNED ACU" (DEADWOOD)

65   "'How frequently can preparation be reapplied without permanent
or serious injury to the member?' Carpenter responded, 'It should be
only dermal in character and the worst effect should be scarring'"
(DEADWOOD)

66   "Menthol 0.5, Phenol 3.0, Salicylic Acid 1.5, Petroleum 9330: Will
burn skin—poison" (DEADWOOD)

## 10. THE JUMP

67   "150 miles an hour" (GREENUP, OH)

67   "Two minutes to drop zone" (Billings OH)

68   "125 knots" (GREENUP)

68   "two or three seconds" (GREENUP: most of this scene is captured in
a memo from Walter Haass in the Greenup mission file)

69   "'As I looked around, the jump was beautiful, floating down over
those Alpine peaks,' recalled Mayer. In seconds his feet and legs
plunged into the deep powder, which absorbed the impact of his landing. Ice and rocky crags could break limbs like dry timber. For Mayer,
the flakes also served another purpose: 'It was so cold in the plane
that I was happy to get out, and the snow felt warm'" (OH)

69   "all okay" (OH)

69 "Hopefully we were unobserved" (OH)

70 "Ten steps in snow up to our hips, the air that high up was hard to breathe, so we had to rest because we became exhausted quickly" (OH)

70 "virtually had to crawl the whole distance" (OH)

71 "hard tack" (OH)

71 "The forty-four-pound shortwave radio had an operational range of three hundred to a thousand miles" Kermit Roosevelt, *War Report of the OSS*, vol. 2, *The Overseas Targets* (New York: Walker and Company, 1976).

71 "succeeded in contriving a makeshift pair of snowshoes out of a metal floor mat" (GREENUP)

71–72 "buried their Eureka (a top-secret signaling device), one battery, and rations behind" (GREENUP)

72 "I am Lieutenant Erich Schmitzer, and I was accidentally detached from my Alpine Corps unit. I need your assistance to get to the bottom of the glacier" (GREENUP, OH)

72 "This looks like Santa Clause's sled" (OH)

73 "It was the ride of my life. It was the scariest part of the entire mission" (OH)

73 "'I acted as the break man,' Mayer remembered. 'The tip of the pole glowed red and sparked as we went down the side of the cliff, which was very steep at several points'" (OH)

73 "routine" (GREENUP, OH)

73 "Come inside. You, of course, can't be partisans" (GREENUP, OH)

73 "To Mayer's horror, Wynberg gave them a rare delicacy—a chocolate bar from their American rations" (GREENUP)

## 11. THE COUNTERFEIT GAMBIT

74 "Hermann Böckmann, 2nd Battalion Fallschirmjäger Regiment 3" (DEADWOOD)

74 "Wilhelm von Donovan" Joseph E. Persico, *Piercing the Reich: The Penetration of Nazi Germany by American Secret Agents During World War II* (New York: Viking, 1979).

75 "Sir, you know what we do here"

75 "RR control Munich, 2nd Battalion Fallschirmjäger Regiment 3"

75 "the unbreakable one-time [code] pads" (DEADWOOD)

75 "Talked to Colonel Sloan on Mason [Matull] this afternoon, prospects look dim" (DEADWOOD)

76 "Please do not jolly us anymore. As Col. Chapin pointed out in his memo one month ago, we want unequivocal answer with someone taking full responsibility therefore" (DEADWOOD)

76 "'Operation Deadwood has been unconditionally approved by (OSS) Caserta including One-Time-Pads and finances. We are instructed to mount it at soonest.' Approval had come 'reluctantly and begrudgingly'" (DEADWOOD)

76 "Luftwaffe officer uniform, overcoat Luftwaffe, rucksack, one sweater, three pairs of German army socks, leather belt Luftwaffe" (DEAD-WOOD)

76 "Hermann Matull would go behind the lines a rich man" (DEAD-WOOD)

76 "'suitcase radio,' which became the 'standard sender-receiver for all branches in the field.' The model operated on 220 to 110 ac or dc commercial power and had a range of several hundred miles. It relied on the dots and dashes of Morse code, which were enciphered in a one-time pad" Kermit Roosevelt, *War Report of the OSS*, vol. 1 (New York: Walker and Company, 1976), 139–40. The original OSS war report was completed by OSS agent and son of Teddy Roosevelt, Kermit, after the war and remained classified for decades.

## 12. TICKET TO RIDE

78 "The smell of fresh-burning embers assaulted the men's nostrils as they looked at the bucolic scenery around them" (OH, GREENUP)

79 "'These damned Americans are bombing our cities!' Mayer recalled, 'She probably had lost a house to a bombing raid'" (OH, GREENUP)

80 "Your papers" (GREENUP)

80 "'Show me your papers!' With nerves of steel and the confidence of a movie star, Weber looked the agent squarely in the eyes and stated, 'We've just been checked.' 'It was pure luck at [that] point. We were in American uniforms, had our radio and codebooks. If they would have searched our papers, they would have picked us up and it would have been the end of the mission. Franz was a deserter. They would have shot him on the spot. It was all luck'" (Wynberg OH, GREENUP)

## 13. THE GAME

81–82  "He figured that the best person to introduce him and the team to his family was the former mayor of the town, Koecheles Luis" (GREENUP)

82  "I've never heard of him" (GREENUP, OH)

82  "But aren't you Koecheles Luis?" (OH)

82  "You need to go back and tell him my name is Tomasson Franz and that I'm a friend of yours" (OH, GREENUP)

82  "Luis had been forced to take in several refugees, including a Russian girl, a Yugoslav worker, and a family from Berlin whose house had been destroyed" (OH, GREENUP)

83  "'typical farmer's daughter,' 'very sweet and helpful' with long brown hair" (OH, GREENUP)

83  "'Mother Niederkircher,' was a 'very determined' woman who 'made no bones about how much she hated the Nazis,'" "those two went on their own way" (OH)

84  "Roosevelt, Hitler, and the American Way of Life" (GREENUP)

84  "All well. Patience until March 13. Hans" (All of Greenup's radio messages are found in the Greenup mission file, GREENUP)

84  "he had lost all his credentials in a bandit action while on the road from northern Italy" (GREENUP)

84  "saying he had been admitted for treatment" (OH)

85  "typical city crowd" (OH)

85  "Old Dolomite frontier of 1917 is being rebuilt and occupied by *Volkssturm*, already called up in south Tyrol. Source *Volkssturm* leader" (GREENUP)

85  "self-proclaimed leader of a resistance movement of five hundred men" (GREENUP)

85  "no further dealings with this man" (GREENUP)

86  "becoming good friends" (OH)

86  "Fritz had been appointed finance representative for a group of Wehrmacht deserters (about fifty) hiding out in a remote Alpine chalet" (OH)

86  "electrical technicians among foreign workers" (GREENUP, OH)

## 14. IN THE BELLY OF THE BEAST

87    "Come over. Join us" (OH)

87    "I think they felt sorry for me; my head was bandaged and they saw
      me alone, so they asked me to join them" (OH)

87–88  "The German staff had brought the engineer to Berlin to make im-
      provements to Hitler's *Führerbunker* twelve days earlier. The thirty-
      something captain boastfully painted an amazing scene: He had
      witnessed a gaunt and haggard Hitler gazing from the balcony of the
      *Führerbunker* as Allied planes mercilessly pounded the capital of his
      thousand-year Reich. In his drunken tirade, the Austrian engineer in-
      credulously spouted out technical details regarding the thickness of
      the bunker's walls, its depth, and its exact location in the heart of
      Berlin" (GREENUP)

88    "Hitler is tired of living" (GREENUP)

88    "I blended right in and felt like I was one of them" (OH)

89    "Mussolini reportedly lives in Zurlsarlberg Hotel, Zueushof [*sic*] Zür-
      shof" (GREENUP)

89    "Daladier, Schlossitter near Brixlegg, guarded by a company of SS
      men: source, local teacher" (GREENUP)

90    "I blended right in" (OH)

90    "Oh boy, there's a lot of trains" (OH)

90    "Wait til tomorrow morning. Assembled at Hall, we have over twenty-
      six trains, each with thirty to forty cars, loaded with ammo and tanks,
      that will be leaving April 3 and going straight through the Brenner"
      (OH)

90–91  "26 Trains, 30 to 40 cars each loaded with tractors, ammo, gasoline,
      ack-ack guns, light equipment, assembled at Hall and Innsbruck Main
      and West. Leaving for Italy April 3 after 2100 GMT via Brenner.
      Trains are guarded. Loadmaster of *Hauptbahnof* is source."

91    "Delighted by the quality of the intelligence, headquarters responded,
      '15th (Air Force) delighted your 21 [a reference to 26 trains] veri-
      fied by photos. Heavy op against your target cancelled last minute by
      weather'" (GREENUP, OH)

91  "After the war a source in Eisenhower's headquarters revealed that Mayer's intelligence leading to the destruction of the trains shortened the war in Italy by six months" (OH, GREENUP)

91  "All mobile targets in the Innsbruck are dispersed daily between 0900 and 1300 GMT" (GREENUP)

## 15. THE ELECTRICIAN

92  "How am I gonna pull this one off?" (OH)

93  "Frederick Mayer" (GREENUP)

93  "I definitely looked French" (OH)

94  "Production zero in Messerschmidt-Kematen because of lack of resupply for the past three months. Made parts formerly for assembly plant in Jenbach. Trustworthy worker is source" (GREENUP)

## 16. WHERE THERE WERE NO BORDERS

95  "A familiar name: Paul Kröck" (GREENUP)

96  "You go out and it seems like an eternity before the parachute opens. The wind from the slip stream hits you like a hammer. As I was parachuting down, I landed in a tree. And instead of an open field, I landed in a steep valley between two snow-capped mountains" (OH)

96  "Shortly afterwards, Gerbner heard whistles. Descending the mountain, he eventually found Rosenthal in one of the gullies" (DANIA)

97  "Salmhofer, who was prepared to release him because his papers were in 'good shape'" (DANIA)

97  "a circular stamp rather than a square one" (DANIA)

98  "'on more intimate terms with SS and Vlasov Cossack troops in the neighborhood than mere political sympathy would seem to indicate was necessary.' The two girls were constantly inviting these soldiers into their home, a practice that Kröck wisely understood was 'endangering his life'" (DANIA)

98  "He boldly wrote a 'vague letter' to the rector of the school Weber once attended 'inquiring about Weber's address'" (DANIA)

99  "George Mitchell alive and working. Letter contact established" (DANIA, GREENUP)

99   "George [Gerbner] and Al [Rosenthal] ok too. Will Mitchell join you? We can drop Henry Hague and Cole to him with radio if you send us necessary info" (DANIA)

99   "the group decided to affect a crossing of the main road, on which German guards were stationed at 200-meter intervals and number of units were encamped. Three of the party were able to make a successful dash across the highway, but heavy machine gun fire prevented the Dania team members and an English flight officer from following them. Accordingly, the trio turned back into the hills" (DANIA)

## 17. FLY IN THE OINTMENT

100   "'Hey, Lieutenant Dyno,' Matull said, 'I want to get to the airfield, not the hospital'" (DEADWOOD)

100   "'Have you forgotten anything?' the lieutenant asked. Matull grinned. 'Yes, a handkerchief'" (DEADWOOD)

101   "At 7:40 p.m. the pilot pulled back the throttle of the B-24, and the twin-row, fourteen-cylinder Pratt & Whitney Wasp engines roared into action. The plane shot down the runway" (DEADWOOD)

101–102   "Tell everyone that they are all a nice bunch. . . . In the beginning, I thought you just wanted me to do a job, but now I consider you friends" (DEADWOOD)

102   "I know you bastards don't trust me, but I am going to prove you wrong" (OH)

102   "Quick 'dits' signaled 'all okay'; long flashes signaled that something had gone wrong" (DEADWOOD)

102–104   The remaining quotes are contained in the Deadwood mission report (DEADWOOD)

102   "reports from the area indicated a German garrison in the vicinity likely witnessed the drop" (DEADWOOD)

103   "'to hide his radio set which he was carrying on his chest.' The operative continued heading south in order 'to come back to Italy and then try again'" (DEADWOOD)

## 18. *ALPENFESTUNG?*

105 "If desired, can take Innsbruck and area ahead of airborne landings. Political prisoners would need five hundred M-3 pistols. Details await answer" (GREENUP)

106 "someone who saw the handwriting on the wall" (OH)

106 "'[These fanatical troops] will have to be taken by the application of or the threat of force. This would lead into a form of Guerilla Warfare, which would require for its suppression, a very large number of troops,' wrote Eisenhower." Christof Mauch, *The Shadow War against Hitler* (New York: Columbia University Press, 2005), 189.

106–107 "'It now seems generally accepted that a delayed defense fortress will lie in the Bavarian and Austrian Alps.' Later, on March 3, he stated correctly, 'A critical analysis of data received so far it does not appear that the preparations have as yet progressed very far'" Mauch, *The Shadow War*, 189.

107 "No airborne landing currently scheduled. If you have top-notch plan, give complete outline to AFHQ, otherwise continue YR [*sic*] intelligence program which G-2 likes" (GREENUP)

107 "1,000 partisans and all other parties under my command. A full planeload of explosives for bridges and sabotage and a quantity of propaganda materiel should be sent to me at once, white and green lights reception will be used in Stubaier Mountains" (GREENUP)

108 "I don't remember his name, but he was willing to make a deal" (OH)

108 "The whole area was alerted and searched [by the SS and Gestapo] the following day" (OH, GREENUP)

109 "After the sixth pass over the drop zone, the B-24's second engine burst into flames, and the bomber ominously nosed downward toward the formidable crags below" (GREENUP)

109 "On Greenup resupply, one engine of B-24 burned out" (GREENUP)

109–110 "Dillon mission body and supply drop a success to reception last night" (DILLON, GREENUP)

110 "On April 16, Bernd Steinitz, the fifth member of the Jewish five, was the 'body' referred to in Ulmer's memo" The author extensively interviewed Steinitz in 2006 in his apartment in Los Angeles and over the phone.

110    "Two special trains with Fuehrungstab (der) Oberst Reichsbehoerden [High-Ranking Operation Staff] left Berlin April 14, members
now in off-limits area, Imsterberg. Eighteen members of Ministry of
Interior in hotel post. Undersecretary of State, Von Bergsdorf in
Garmisch Partenkirchen. Source, copy of secret order" (GREENUP)

110    "[Heinrich] Himmler arrived with staff, night of 17th in Ingalls near
Innsbruck in hotel, Gruberhof. Three SS divisions expected, but so
far, only one regiment, of which Company A is rounding up all politicals [*sic*] possibly dangerous, source Kripo" (GREENUP)

## 19. CAPTURED

112    "A gleaming Mercedes command car pulled up along the side of the
road in Franzensfeste, Italy" (WC#36)

113    "female without feelings . . . [who had] attached herself to Schiffer
just . . . so that she could enjoy the trappings that came to her through
her boss" (WC#36)

113    "Are you also coming from Bari?" (WC#36)

113    "Do you want to play ball with us?" (WC#36)

114    "Do you know Lieutenant Jewels and what his functions are in school
[the OSS spy school]. Teacher?" "If you do not talk, they will be
killed," "loosen control and became very interested in doubling Matull" (WC#36)

## 20. THE *KRIMINALRAT*

116    "Not knowing under which charge he had been apprehended and after
a slight beating [Moser] gave away several addresses" (GREENUP)

## 21. DOWNFALL

117    "Are you Frederic Mayer?" (OH, GREENUP)

117    "Oui" (OH)

117    "At this time I thought they were picking me up because I was not
working at the foreign worker's camp," "I didn't think they suspected
I was an American agent. I decided to play it cool" (OH)

118    "He's just a little rat" (OH)

118    "Put on your shoes" (OH)
119    "quite jubilant" (GREENUP)
119    "Nationality, landing site, persons who accompanied him, radio operator, place where the sender [radio] was located, and contacts with the OWB" (GREENUP, OH)
119    "They know everything. Tell them everything, or they are going to hurt you more" (GREENUP)
119    "I don't know the man" (OH)
119    "In his belt, they discovered $600 in gold coins—damning evidence," "'I was very tired,' Güttner later explained, 'having not slept for several days'" (GREENUP)
119    "Use extreme measures in your questioning" (GREENUP)
119–120    "'hit Mayer in the face several times and quite strongly.' Mayer remembered Beringer as 'the tall one'" (GREENUP)
120    "The abuse continued. And now they believed Mayer to be a Jew" (GREENUP)
120    "The more they hit me the less inclined I was to talk" (OH)
120    "Where is the radio operator?" (GREENUP)
120    "Where is the radio operator?" (GREENUP)
120    "Put him down! He is unconscious" (GREENUP, OH)
121    "It was probably the coldest I had ever been in my life" (OH)

## 22. *FUNKSPIEL*

122    "It was agreed with Matull that he would organize in Innsbruck a few resistance cells, which, however, I would infiltrate with my own confidants" (WC#36)
123    "We are proud of you old boy. Bad penny always turns up. Go to Munich fastest, if this is absolutely impossible, proceed immediately to other strategic southern Germany" (DEADWOOD)
123    "Believing they would eventually catch on, Matull persisted in inserting extra words into his radio messages" (DEADWOOD)
123    "Brudder," "Leone" (WC#36)

## 23. GENERAL FRED MAYER

125    "Do you know an American agent by the name of Fred Mayer?" (WC#36)

125  "I know a Fred from Bari" (WC#36)
125  "'He's probably the one that I know,' Matull stated flatly. 'I need some more information, but [you] have made a good catch'" (WC#36)
126  "Do you know this man?" (WC#36, GREENUP)
126  "Yes, [I] have been together with him in Italy" (WC#36, GREENUP)
126  "'a "Big Shot" with the Americans, with a rank of colonel or even general. And, Matull ominously warned Güttner, he and all of them 'would all be killed by the Americans if they shot Freddie.' Furthermore, he insisted, 'Freddie [should] only be interrogated by the Gauleiter personally'" (WC#36)

## 24. INTO THE HILLS

128  "they found the spare parts for the radio, extra equipment, gold pieces, a chemistry book and three chemistry theses" (OH, GREENUP)
128  "lost his nerve and said that he knew Fred, that Hans and Franz had left the night before accompanied by Thomas Marie" (OH, GREENUP)
128  "Lead us to the radio operator or you will be shot!" (GREENUP)
128  "the time that he wasted in telling his lies, [Mayer] was able to warn his comrades and make it possible for them to escape" (GREENUP)
128  "'while Mayer was fed by villagers,' he and his patrols 'were not fed at all'" (GREENUP)
129  "We don't have much time. Pack everything" (OH)
130  "'There were only a few moments when I became mildly religious,' recalled Wynberg about that night. 'One of those moments was when there was a knock on the door and four uniformed German firemen entered. [They were] firemen, merely checking on the facilities [which were] very vulnerable to fires'" (OH)
130  "They were merely part of the German forest service on a routine patrol" (OH)

## 25. THE TABLES ARE TURNED

132  "This is Frederick Mayer. He's an American agent" (OH)
133  "It's okay" (OH)
133  "I'm going back to Zurich, and I plan on contacting your people and letting them know that you're alive" (GREENUP, OH)

134    "Fred Mayer reports he is in Gestapo hands but cabled 'Don't worry about me, I'm really not bad off.'"

135    "He is in my custody now" (OH)

135    "Ja?" (OH)

135    "Should we open up the doors of our warehouses so that civilians can help themselves?" (OH)

135    "Under no circumstances, we are going to need them later," "Who were you speaking to on the phone?" (OH)

135    "That's exactly what I would have said" (OH)

136    "Go talk some sense into him. Make him declare Innsbruck an open city" (OH, GREENUP)

136    "Hard times need hard people. Our age is the hardest that mortal men have ever had to face. We have faced setback after setback, but that is no reason to resign and let things take their course. They will not give up if we give up" One of Joseph Goebbels's final lead articles titled "Kämpfer für das ewige Reich," *Das Reich,* April 8, 1945.

137    "Once armored troops break through the mountain passes, Innsbruck will be destroyed. It is insane to order a last-ditch effort. If you love Innsbruck and its people, why destroy it? You haven't got a chance (against American forces)" (OH)

137    "I need fair treatment" (OH)

137    "I will make you and your staff my prisoners and guarantee your lives" (OH)

137    "You're right," "I had no authority to take anyone prisoner or guarantee their safety, I just thought it was a good idea" (OH)

## 26. TO THE END

138    "something much more" (OH)

139    "There was high tension. I had trouble putting the spoon up to my lips without shaking. I was twenty-one years old, in front of some of the most powerful Nazis of the Third Reich," "Wynberg was not too overawed to recall, 'They were fat slobs, all trying to save their own necks'" (OH)

139    "'Why did America have to mix herself up in a completely European affair?' the Germans bizarrely demanded. '[The] word of Hitler meant nothing and *no country* was safe from the aggression of the Nazis'" (GREENUP)

139 "How can you say that we invaded neutral countries?" (GREENUP)
140 "The remarkable thing about [their] answers is that [they] believed what they said. [Their] faith in Hitler seemed something more than fanatic and was also very noticeable in Hofer and all of his helpers" (GREENUP)
140 "friction between the Russians and Western Powers," "They kept on warning us of the menace of Russian domination of Europe" (GREENUP)
140 "they wanted to know if we had decided to split Greater Germany again to its [pre-1938 components]," "expected this [independent Austrian] state to act as a buffer against the Russians" (GREENUP)
141 "the Gauleiter's capitulation of Germany's Army Group C" (GREENUP)
141 "order of unconditional surrender and his declaration that Innsbruck an open city" (GREENUP)

## 27. MATULL'S PLIGHT

142 "[Schiffer] pass[ed] over to Matull's side. . . . Matull was to be convinced that Schiffer had completely changed his mind and that he wanted nothing to do with the SS, the police or the entire Nazi clique" (WC#36)
143 "The final nail in the coffin came when Matull received the following the radio message from Bari: 'Stop all further activities and await the occupation by American troops'" (WC#36)
143 "How much U.S. money and gold do you have?" (WC#36)
143 "'small sum.' Ever the micromanager with a high attention to detail, Schiffer then said, 'You should tell the Americans that you used [the money] up'" (WC#36)
143 "small, closed package containing money and some personal items" (WC#36, DEADWOOD)
143 "I drove April 30, 1945, with Andergassen and Storz, to Innsbruck and also wanted Hans Butz to join us there the following day. . . . I had in my possession documents made out in the name of Emil Brudder and . . . for the time being I was using this name" (WC#36)
143 "'I had the feeling that Matull did not agree with my plans anymore and that he wanted to follow his own plans,' he recalled."

## 28. THE SURRENDER OF INNSBRUCK

145 "How'd you get your face smashed in?" (OH)

145 "Hit by Gestapo, truck, I think" (OH)

145 "The 'Forest Brothers' continued the fight into the '50s, causing thousands of casualties among the occupying Russian forces" (ID source)

146 "given orders for them to pull back beyond the city of Innsbruck" (GREENUP)

146–147 "They had their BARs trained upon me; it was a tense moment. Luckily the lieutenant in charge of the outfit believed me," "Innsbruck has been declared an open city" (OH)

147 "Innsbruck has been declared an open city" (OH)

147–148 "At approximately 1630 3 May 1945, advance elements of the Division were moving East from ZIRL to launch an attack on INNSBRUCK. German troops had withdrawn and taken up positions on the western edge of the city. At this time, Lt. MAYER crossed the INN River in a civilian sedan and contacted Major Bland WEST, AC of S, G-2, and Lt. Peter RANDON, MII, and offered to lead them to a farm South of HALL where he was holding Gauleiter Franz HOFER and his staff in custody awaiting the arrival of the American troops. LT. MAYER led a small party to the Gauleiter and through this contact it was possible (1) to order the German troops on the western edge of the city to cease all resistance and admit the American troops in the city of INNSBRUCK without opposition, (2) to obtain a statement from the Gauleiter HOFER for a radio broadcast exhorting the Standschutzen [sic] of the TYROL-VORARLBERG Area to lay down their arms. In addition, the Gauleiter gave much valuable information on the disposition of troops and non-existence of defenses throughout the area" (GREENUP)

148 "the war was absolutely lost, not to participate in Werewolf activities, and to cooperate with the Americans" (GREENUP, OH)

## 29. TURNABOUT

150 "RM 15,000 and other personal items of value" (GREENUP)

150 "he died in 1975" (GREENUP)

## 30. THE DOUBLE AGENT

151 "I'm willing to stay anywhere in central Europe. I'll stay with the OSS until you throw me out" (DEADWOOD)

152 "Mason [Matull] watches Schiffer and [informs OSS] as soon as Schiffer is strong enough to talk again. Then OSS should interrogate him and get confirmation of [Matull's story] told to me" (DEAD-WOOD)

152 "'cleared of any suspicion and brought to Salzberg for discharge from the organization.' Despite all the blatant snubs and obvious distrust, Matull accompanied the CIC group to Vipetno and through 'his close association with the Gestapo, helped track down many more of its members who had gone [underground] in the area'" (DEAD-WOOD)

## 31. "WHO DO YOU THINK WE ARE, NAZIS?"

153 "Our second night [at the villa], soldiers burst in while we were on the couch and told us to get out" (GREENUP)

154 "We've got Güttner. Do you want to see him?" (GREENUP)

154 "'CIC had already roughed him up,' Mayer recalled. '[I was] upset because he was already beat up. I wanted to beat him myself'" (GREENUP, OH)

154 "Do anything you want with me, but don't hurt my family" (GREENUP, OH)

154 "'Who do you think we are, Nazis?' Then he turned his back on Walter Güttner for the last time" (GREENUP, OH)

## EPILOGUE

155 "Gadsen to base; close my circuit net, taking over this morning. Many thanks for three months cooperation. Best Regards from Fred and Hans" (GREENUP)

156 "Miraculously, he survived and was able to attend the reunion" (GREENUP)

156 "From Hope we went to [our] target . . . and no signals were seen," "four bodies had been found in the wreckage of a plane" (GREENUP, PERSONNEL)

# INDEX